HUMAN
RELATIONS:

Law Enforcement
in a Changing Community

HUMAN
RELATIONS:

Law Enforcement

in a Changing Community

Alan Coffey
Edward Eldefonso
Walter Hartinger

PRENTICE-HALL, INC., Englewood Cliffs, N. J.

James D. Stinchcomb, *Consulting Editor*

13-526442-1

Library of Congress Catalog Card Number: 70–132173

Printed in the United States of America

Current printing (last number):
10 9 8 7 6 5 4 3

PRENTICE-HALL INTERNATIONAL, INC., LONDON
PRENTICE-HALL OF AUSTRALIA, PTY. LTD., SYDNEY
PRENTICE-HALL OF CANADA, LTD., TORONTO
PRENTICE-HALL OF INDIA PRIVATE LIMITED, NEW DELHI
PRENTICE-HALL OF JAPAN, INC., TOKYO

PREFACE

According to police executives, physical assaults on officers, vilification of policemen, snarling, spitting rioters defying police orders, and the lawbreaking activities of campus anarchists are all symptoms of a lack of respect for law and order and for the policeman ... a symptom of community ignorance and indifference to the problems of the lawman. A task force of the *National Commission on the Causes and Prevention of Violence* directed by Jerome H. Skolnick, a noted author and member of the Center for the Study of Law and Society at the University of California, Berkeley, viewed the police situation with particular alarm (in a 262-page report entitled Task Force on Demonstrations, Protests, and Group Violence). The report stated, "We find that the policeman in America is overworked, undertrained, underpaid, and undereducated."

The authors of the report, released June 10, 1969, further stated: "The policeman's difficulties are compounded by a view expounded at all law enforcement levels—from the director of the Federal Bureau of Investigation to the patrolman on the beat. This view gives little consideration to the effects of such social factors as poverty and discrimination and virtually ignores the possibility of legitimate social discontent."

The California Commission on Peace Officers Standards and Training (POST) conceived in the California legislation in 1959 to upgrade the training of peace officers, put it this way: "In some urban areas, the police and the community seem to stand in conflict which interferes seriously with public confidence in the police, and consequently, with the ability of the police to deal effectively with the crime problem." Without doubt, the hostility of the community to police, or lack of confidence on the part of the public, interferes with police recruiting, morale, day-to-day police operations, safety of the individual officer and, in general, has an adverse effect on the "total community stability." In short, the police department's capacity to deal with crime depends to a large extent on its relationship with the citizenry. Indeed, no lasting improvement in law enforcement is likely unless police-community relations are substantially improved.

There is nothing new about the field of law enforcement seeking to anticipate and prevent violation of law or the disturbance of peace. Nor is there anything new about deliberate efforts to keep the public informed about law enforcement. What *is* new, however, is an emerging law enforcement concept of *active* involvement in programs designed to reduce community tensions in general.

Government officials, criminologists, political scientists, police officials, and many other competent citizens are of the opinion that with a steady increasing emphasis on constitutional rights, the law enforcement methods used to anticipate and prevent disturbance has shifted toward community relations and human relations programs. The relatively uncomplicated function of dealing with traditional crime may well prove one of the policeman's lesser responsibilities as the tensions mount between various segments of the population.

Though addressed to a complex subject, the philosophy of this volume is quite simple: Describe the development of contributing community social forces and the problems presented to the development of effective law enforcement. And because this philosophy is cast in the broadest possible definition of law enforcement, this volume also seeks to suggest and define appropriate avenues of solution.

Acknowledgments

Many obligations have been incurred during the preparation of *Human Relations: Law Enforcement in a Changing Community*, some of them as impossible to identify as they are to repay.

A special word of gratitude, however, must be expressed to the Santa Clara County Juvenile Probation Department, San Jose, California, for the unfailing spirit of cooperation shown by its staff. We are especially grateful for the thoughtfulness, understanding, and cooperation of the administrators of the aforementioned agency: Robert E. Nino, Chief Juvenile Probation Officer; Richard Bothman, Assistant Chief Probation Officer; and Michael Kuzirian, Director of Probation Services. We are also indebted to B. Earl Lewis, Director of the Department of Law

Enforcement Education, De Anza College, for his thorough and candid criticism of the original manuscript.

We are particularly grateful to the law enforcement agencies—specifically the City of San Francisco Police Department, Ben W. Lashkoff, Inspector, intelligence unit, and the City of Berkeley Police Department—for their assistance in the gathering of photos and other illustrations. We are once again appreciative of the help and cooperation extended by the International Association of Chiefs of Police. The IACP have been extremely helpful in other projects we have completed (*Law Enforcement and the Youthful Offender: Juvenile Procedures* and *Principles of Law Enforcement*) ; specifically Nelson A. Watson.

Finally, we offer our deepest gratitude to Beverly May Coffey, Mildred Ann Eldefonso (particularly for compiling the index), and Patricia Hartinger for reading and criticising the manuscript. Furthermore, their enthusiasm and support during the initial and final stages of refining the manuscript was an inspiration.

Alan Coffey
Edward Eldefonso
Walter Hartinger

CONTENTS

PART ONE

POLICE
AND
THE
COMMUNITY
IN
TRANSITION

CHAPTER ONE

AN
INTRODUCTION
TO
THE
PROBLEM

Figure 1.1 *Police officers attempt to control sniper fire during a riot. Photo courtesy of the San Francisco Police Department, San Francisco, California.*

Figure 1.2 *Police officers protecting private property after a riot. Photo courtesy of the San Francisco Police Department, San Francisco, California.*

LAW ENFORCEMENT AND THE EQUAL ADMINISTRATION OF JUSTICE HAVE BECOME MAJOR NATIONAL CONCERNS IN RECENT YEARS. The rapid growth of our cities, with attendant problems in housing, education, employment, and social welfare services, has accentuated these concerns and has been highlighted by the increasing urban concentration of minority groups.

Crime rates have generally been higher in those areas where poverty, family disintegration, unemployment, lack of education, and minority group frustration and resentment in the face of social and economic discrimination—the ghetto syndrome—are manifest. The expectations, excitement, and additional frustrations engendered by the civil rights movement have compounded the difficulties inherent in the entire process of law enforcement and the administration of justice.

Foremost among these difficulties are the relationships between police and minority groups and the general community. Deterioration in these relationships, particularly between police and Negroes, is increasingly evident. There are widespread charges of police brutality and demands for greater assertion of civilian control over police actions. Many police officials, on the other hand, decry the growing disrespect for law, the apathy of the public, mollycoddling of criminals by the courts, and political influence on the law enforcement process. Some policemen continue to view civil rights groups as troublemakers who disrupt the law and order the police have sworn to uphold. At the same time, a stereotyped image of the policeman beclouds minority group attitudes, severly hampering potentially beneficial cooperative relationships.

The National Advisory Commission on Civil Disorders, named to investigate the 1967 street riots, issued a 200,000-word report to President Johnson. In harsh, vivid detail, it etched the horrors of that year's long, hot summer. The report stated that many Negroes may "come to support not only riots but ... rebellion," unless multibillion dollar measures are quickly taken to heal racial bitterness and riot-caused ravages in city slums. Regarding police-Negro relationships, it contained some quite startling information:

> The police are not merely a "spark" factor. To some Negros, police have come to symbolize white power, white racism and white repression. And, the fact is that many police do reflect and express these white attitudes. The atmosphere of hostility and cynicism is reinforced by a widespread belief among Negroes in the existence of police brutality and a "double standard" of justice and protection—one for Negroes and one for whites.
>
> The plight of the policemen assigned to the Negro slum is a sorry one.
>
> The policeman has become a symbol of all those social forces the Negro believes are pinning him down.
>
> He is a symbol of not only law but of the system of law enforcement and criminal justice.

The situation confronting the law enforcement officer in the United States is undoubtedly far from ideal, but he is still responsible for the maintenance of an orderly society through law. The laws of the United States, of course, continue to include the minimum obligations imposed on any free society: to provide in an *impartial manner* both *personal safety* and *property security*.

In a fundamental context, all regulated behavior from some family activities to vehicle speed are law enforcement functions. And as the complexities of maintaining order throughout law enforcement multiply, an ever-increasing responsibility must shift to those who enforce the law. This responsibility is to learn to *anticipate* and *prevent* the disruption (of any kind) of an orderly society.

*The Perplexing Problems
of Police-Community
Relations*[1]

Racial tension and riots are not new phenomena in the United States. Considerable difficulties for law enforcement accompanied the growth of American cities. A series of riots reflecting the economic unrest of the country took place several years before the riots of 1844. (The 1844 riots pitted native-born Americans against recent immigrants.)

Daniel P. Moynihan of the M.I.T.-Harvard Joint Center for Urban Studies (selected by President Nixon for an important government post involved with alleviating the problems of the cities), states, however, that "the violence of this age is different: It is greater, more real, more personal, throughout the society, and associated with not one but a dozen issues and causes. It is invoked by the most rational public and respected of our institutions, as well as the most obscure and piteous lunatic."

Also, the American law enforcement tradition appears to be influenced by the major differences in the background of those comprising the population of the cities; i.e., Negro, Italian, Mexican, and white culture, Oriental influences, et cetera. What these various peoples sought in terms of law and order no doubt varied, as did the methods of those providing the enforcement. Some idea of the variation might be had by considering a mythical western sheriff attempting to bring his anti-cow-rustling skills to bear on the violence of San Francisco's early Chinatown or New York's 1844 immigration riots or interstate prostitution.

The frustrations of this imaginary sheriff would probably be no greater than those experienced by many contemporary police officers confronted with civil disobedience, sit-ins, protest demonstrations, riots, and unfounded charges of brutality—all occurring in the most affluent society the world has ever known. Indeed, on a comparative basis, the mythical

---

[1] Portions of this section were adopted with permission of John Wiley & Sons, Inc., from *Principles of Law Enforcement*, E. Eldefonso, A. Coffey, and R.C. Grace (New York: John Wiley & Sons, Inc., 1968), pp. 163–75.

sheriff might well be envied for his firm and uncomplicated belief that people were either good or bad—with the bad ones placed in jail, where they learned to be good. Uncomplicated beliefs of this nature would permit the ever-increasing forces of social change to be interpreted simply. But they are not simple; neither is the tremendous task of understanding and programming effective community relations.

Through evolution, society's enforcing of behavior regulations has moved beyond the point of simple, uncomplicated answers for law enforcement agencies. Now police teams, chemicals, and noise generators are steadily replacing individuals in the control of violent demonstrations. And the causes of these demonstrations—the various community tensions —have become a legitimate law enforcement concern.

In our grossly complicated, urbanized society the philosophy of enforcing law must continue to expand. In the matter of *personal safety* and *property security* (refer to Table 1.1) law enforcement must include

TABLE 1.1

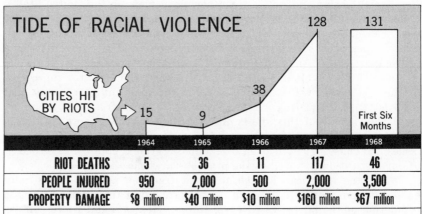

TIDE OF RACIAL VIOLENCE			128	131
CITIES HIT BY RIOTS ⇨ 15	9	38		First Six Months
1964	1965	1966	1967	1968
RIOT DEATHS 5	36	11	117	46
PEOPLE INJURED 950	2,000	500	2,000	3,500
PROPERTY DAMAGE $8 million	$40 million	$10 million	$160 million	$67 million

NOTE: In addition to 160 million dollars' property damage in 1967, a Senate committee estimated economic losses at 504 million. 1968 property damage includes only insured losses as reported by the American Insurance Association. On top of that were uncounted millions in business losses, tax losses and governmental costs for troops and police required to deal with riots.

U. S. NEWS & WORLD REPORT, July 15, 1968   Copyright © 1968, U.S. News & World Report, Inc.

positive efforts to anticipate and endeavor to redirect those social forces which jeopardize the personal safety and property security of individuals. Discharge of this particular police responsibility must necessarily become a matter of community relations.

COMMUNITY AND HUMAN RELATIONS[2]

If society is to survive, or at least to survive in a civilized manner, it is imperative that laws be enforced. Since the observance of law is so

[2] From Eldefonso, Coffey, and Grace, *Principles of Law Enforcement*, pp. 35–49. Adapted with permission of John Wiley & Sons, Inc.

vital, society cannot depend on simple persuasion for its accomplishment; rather it must rely in part on force. The term *enforcement*—and indeed, the very nature of man—implies a possible use of force. This potential to wield force then is necessarily part of the police image. The manner in which the potential is viewed by the public often determines whether the police image is good or bad. And, because a good police image tends to affect favorably an individual's willingness to observe the law voluntarily, police retain a rightful interest in having a good image. The police officer embodies the law so visibly and directly that neither he nor the public find it easy to differentiate between the law and the enforcement of such law. The public is confused and unable to recognize the broad concept of the police officer. As B. Smith pointed out:

> Relatively few citizens recall ever having seen a judge; fewer still, a prosecutor, coroner, sheriff, probation officer or prison warden. The patrolman is thoroughly familiar to all. His uniform picks him out from the crowd so distinctly that he becomes a living symbol of the law—not always of its majesty, but certainly of its power. Whether the police like it or not, they are forever marked men.[3]

Any officer of the law is partly a symbol, and law enforcement work consists to some extent in creating impressions based on symbolic attributes. Thus, an unoccupied police vehicle can slow down turnpike traffic or motivate drivers to stop at designated intersections, and the presence of half a dozen officers can control a large crowd.[4]

The uniform of the police officer is viewed as a symbolic license to judge and punish. It does so not only by representing the right to arrest but also by connoting the role of a disciplinarian. Unfortunately, it is for this reason, for instance, that parents may make small children behave through repeated pointed references to policemen. Needless to say, this "punishing role" does not lend itself to the promotion of any social role other than as an "enforcer."[5]

Police interest in a good image is vital for a number of reasons, one that is singularly practical is that the greater the voluntary law observance, the less the need for forceful enforcement. So the question becomes, What can be done to promote the standing of the police officer and of social influences to encourage voluntary law observance?

The various theories presented in numerous books make clear the lack of agreement concerning the causes of crime among biologists, anthropologists, criminologists, sociologists, and psychologists and psychiatrists. Yet these behavioral scientists generally agree that societal influences both encourage and discourage crime. As it relates to criminal behavior, influence is merely a power to affect human willingness to con-

---

[3] B. Smith, "Municipal Police Administration," *Annals of the American Academy of Police and Social Science*, Vol. 40, No. 5, p. 22.
[4] H. H. Toch, "Psychological Consequences of the Police Role," *Police*, Vol. 10, No. 1 (September-October 1965), p. 22.
[5] *Ibid.*

form to law. And so the question of influence becomes a consideration of those forces having enough power to encourage voluntary law observance.

The manner in which the public views a police method of enforcement is considered as one such force. Another perhaps more fundamental force relates to the manner in which children are raised. The old saying, "As the twig is bent, so grows the tree," has particular significance in every society. The citizen who holds little respect for law enforcement goals may merely reflect the values he learned as a child. Racial tensions, economic conditions, and various physical and emotional deprivations have probably helped shape his attitude. But it is likely that the major contributing factor might have been early and unfortunate experiences with police. The detrimental and sometimes lasting effects of such unfortunate encounters will be discussed in later chapters. For now, mention of experiences of this nature will serve merely to introduce the subject of *human relations*—a subject of increasing concern to police as evidenced, for example, by the great number of courses devoted to this subject at the New York Police Academy. You might wish to read the article on this in the *New York Times*, April 6, 1967.

HUMAN RELATIONS DEFINED[6]

More and more the literature reflects an implied definition of human relations in terms of "avoiding police brutality."[7] A further definition includes police discretion or decision in terms of "police attitudes."[8] Going beyond these rather narrow considerations, a definition of law enforcement human relations might be: *police participation in any activity that seeks law observance through respect rather than enforcement.* This definition will be further elaborated and clarified as this chapter and other chapters progress.

Regardless of how the term *human relations* is defined, however, police interest in the subject should be related in some way to the "causes" of crime. It has been noted already that behavioral scientists fail to agree on these. A cause or a group of causes can be isolated—such as alcoholism, poverty, broken homes, and parental neglect—which seem to turn one individual to crime but not another, although both may be subjected to precisely the same influences. Even such an extensive catalog of human characteristics as the Yale University Human Relations File (originally the Cross-cultural Survey) fails to clarify how cultural causes affect different people in different ways.

---

[6] Eldefonso, Coffey, and Grace, *Principles of Law Enforcement*, p. 36.

[7] See, for example, L. E. Berson, *Case Study of a Riot: The Philadelphia Story* (New York: Institute of Human Relations Press, 1966); C. Westley, "Violence and the Police," *American Journal of Sociology*, Vol. 59, No. 34 (1953); *The Economist*, December 31, 1955, p. 1159; E. H. Sutherland and D. R. Cressy, *Principles of Criminology*, 6th ed. (Philadelphia: J. B. Lippincott Co., 1960), p. 341; D. R. Ralph, "Police Violence," *New Statesman*, Vol. 66, No. 102 (1963).

[8] J. H. Skolnick, *Justice Without Trial: Law Enforcement in Democratic Society* (New York: John Wiley & Sons, Inc., 1966).

Regardless of the behavioral scientists' lack of agreement on crime causes, law enforcement practitioners tend to agree that there appears to be a relationship between at least some kinds of crime and certain community influences. These influences, more often than not, relate to combinations of problems such as poverty, racial tensions, and parental inadequacies. An additional influence that has already been indicated is the police image—which will be thoroughly discussed in another chapter —held by the community.

Because the community's attitude toward police (or the police image) is one of the primary influences with enough force to encourage voluntary law observance, it is of primary concern to law enforcement. For the individual citizen who is convinced that police are brutal will probably find it difficult to respect police goals, particularly if the brutality is believed to be directed only toward certain minorities. And, as a practical matter, the *validity* of the belief matters less than the *strength* of the belief. An individual usually functions on the basis of what he believes, regardless of the validity of the beliefs.

Law Enforcement— a Period of Unusual Uncertainty

Currently—specifically since 1964—law enforcement agencies are finding themselves caught in a period of unusual uncertainty. Primarily, this state can be attributed to two separate but relatively interdependent developments. The *first*, elaborated upon in Chapter 3, is directly related to the United States Supreme Court. The Court has made a series of decisions relative to the protection of personal liberties of those accused of crimes. In 1963, the Supreme Court ruled on the appeal case of *Gideon versus Wainwright*. The effect of the ruling was that new trials could be demanded by anyone convicted of crime who did not have legal counsel. Moving closer to the field of law enforcement, a 1964 decision was handed down in the case of *Escobedo versus Illinois*. This decision, based on a 5-2-4 majority, protected the Constitutional right of an indigent to be provided with legal counsel at the time of interrogation. Then, in June, 1966, a ruling was handed down in *Miranda versus Arizona* (again by 5-2-4 majority), with the effect of providing legal counsel as soon as the interrogated person is considered a specific suspect in an investigation.

These decisions have elicited a great deal of debate—"hot debate"— and have been attacked as "placing a great deal of restraint on the police by 'coddling' the law violator." Furthermore, according to the dissenters, the police are placed in a position where they must fight by "Marquis of Queensberry Rules," while criminals are not bound by such rules. On the other hand, these decisions have been received as evidence that the Supreme Court has finally become more concerned with human liberty than with the protection of property rights.

The *second* development, which is just as important, is that law enforcement is experiencing a series of civil disturbances associated with a wide range of efforts to upgrade minority groups to the full citizenship and socioeconomic privileges guaranteed by the U.S. Constitution. The strategies and nonviolent techniques of civil rights groups are creating unusual problems for law enforcement agencies because exploiting excessive use of police coercion is one of their major weapons. *This nonviolent method is the explicit and knowing violation of a particular law by persons who are quite ready to accept, without resistance, the retribution attached to that specific law violation.* By utilizing the nonviolent resistance method, minority groups dramatize certain laws as unjust. Furthermore, the use of police coercion is invited (and welcomed) as an opportunity to identify peace officers as "the intimidators or aggressors" against "peaceful demonstrators." It is not unusual to use children, women, and ministers and other responsible persons who have a favorable public image as "victims" for police "aggression." Needless to say, the resulting arrests play havoc with the judiciary machinery. Nonviolent resistance has its ideological genesis in the values of Christian morality and humanitarianism through the premise that minority groups (specifically Negroes) have a moral obligation *not* to cooperate with the forces of "evil."

> In essence, the non-violent resistance is a form of passive aggression, in that it frustrates its opponents by enveloping them in a cloud of "Christian love" for one's enemies." The established power structure of the community is to be forced into the role of "bad guys," whereas the Negroes assume the mantle of Christian heroes. Non-compliance with carefully selected laws creates a community crisis, but, by refraining from violent resistance, the law violators make application of police coercion an opportunity to present social protest as consistent with the highly prized values of humanitarianism and concern for the underdog.[9]

As has been so explicitly pointed out by noted authors in the fields of criminology and law enforcement—specifically, Elmer Johnson:

> Every community has dominant and subordinate groups. Whites first dominated Negroes in the United States through slavery. When slavery was abolished as a social institution, the value system of racism became embedded in folk beliefs of the southern states as an informal control system, supplanting the formal controls expressed in laws of segregation and disenfranchisement. Among southern whites, the race attitudes became part of morality and religion. In the North, the value system of racism is also present, but it is deluded by humanitarian ideals and adherence to values of equal rights under the Constitution. But in both regions, the informal system exists as a latent barrier to racial equality. The current disturbances in the North demonstrate thoroughly the stress of this informal control system in spite of the lack of legalized segrega-

9 E. H. Johnson, "A Sociological Interpretation of Police Reaction and Responsibility to Civil Disobedience," *The Journal of Criminal Law, Criminology, and Police Science*, Vol. 58, No. 3 (September 1967), p. 407.

tion and disenfranchisement. These disturbances occur because the civil rights movement, as directed in the North, has succeeded in forcing the hidden informal control system to the overt level of expression.[10]

Racial Disorders—
Why Now?

Although racial disorders will be thoroughly covered in Chapter 2, "Nature and Scope of the Problem," the authors feel that it would be appropriate at this time to briefly discuss a few factors within society at large that have created a mood of violence among many urban Negroes.

Why has the Negro revolted *now*? The late 1950's and the early 1960's have been favorable years, relatively speaking, for Negroes, and even white liberals are extremely hard-pressed to comprehend why more positive conditions have served only to develop a new Negro militancy. This militancy appears to be completely out of line with the "favorable impression" of Negro life in this country. One can view Negroes in well-furnished homes in the suburban area of the city, or appearing to be quite happy in their idleness along the streets of the Negro ghetto, or hustling in the commercial centers of our great cities, and conclude that, although deprived, these people are quite content and certainly not very angry at all. Furthermore, if one journeys to the South to visit a member of the Negro middle class and there sees the black masses that support the black bourgeosie in their comfort, it is more than easy to believe that although Negroes desire civil rights, they are not going to work up a real sweat about it.

In addressing ourselves to the question "Why did it happen?" we shall shift our focus from the local to the national scene, from the particular events of the summer of 1967 to the factors, previously stated, that have created such a hostile demeanor among many Negroes.

The most important fact about the relationship of the Negro to American society is his subordinate social status. In the South, social position is so rigidly defined as to constitute a caste system, and even in the North and the West, in spite of a certain amount of equality with respect to civil rights, the Negro is generally subjected to social ostracism and economic discrimination.

> Of all the ethnic groups to have come to this country, the Negro is the only one to experience the degradation of slavery and a persistent status of subordination. Slavery in a sense dehumanized the Negro. It disrupted his native culture and taught him the rudiments of white civilization, but it did not permit him to develop as a whole man. It prevented the development of three things which are generally considered essential for normal group life: stable family relationships, stable economic organization, and stable community life. Furthermore, slavery nurtured a set of

[10] *Ibid.*, See also by E. H. Johnson, *Crime, Correction and Society* (Homewood, Ill.: Dorsey Press, 1968).

habits and attitudes which still aflict many thousands of Negroes. Among these are lack of self-respect, lack of self-confidence, a distaste for hard work, a habit of dependence upon white friends, lack of regard for the property of others, a feeling that "the white folks owe us a living," a distrust of the white man's law and a tendency to "let tomorrow take care of itself."[11]

Opportunity for Negroes was not given impetus by emancipation: the Negro is still unable to compete on even terms with other citizens in his attempts to obtain a moderate existence. His heritage—reinforced by a continuing vicious circle of caste barriers—has, to a large degree, caused cultural retardation and economic disabilities. The answer to the question "Why is it that other minority groups have managed to move *ahead?*" can only be, then:

> The difference between the experience of the Negro and the experience of other ethnic groups in American society is not merely one of degree but actually a difference in kind—a fact which certainly has some connection with the incidence of social conditions which are associated with crime.[12]

THE BASIC CAUSES

Because of the nature of this chapter, it is appropriate at this time to introduce the rudimentary rationale pertaining to "The *Negro Revolt.*"[13] These factors will be elaborated upon in Chapter 2, which has been specifically designed to investigate this area. The factors are complex and interacting; they vary significantly in their effect from city to city and from year to year; and the consequences of one disorder that generates new grievances and demands become the causes of the next. Thus was created the "thicket of tension, conflicting evidence and extreme opinions" cited by the President of the United States.

Despite these complexities, however, certain matters are clear. Of these, the most fundamental is the racial attitude and behavior of white Americans toward black Americans. Racial prejudice has shaped our history decisively; it now, according to the *Report of the National Advisory Commission on Civil Disorders*, threatens to affect our future.

White racism is essentially responsible for the explosive mixture which has been accumulating in our cities since the end of World War II. The government report states that among the ingredients of this mixture are:

> *Pervasive discrimination and segregation* in employment, education and housing, which have resulted in the continuing exclusion of great numbers of Negroes from the benefits of economic progress.

[11] G. B. Johnson, "The Negro and Crime," *The Annals of the American Academy of Political and Social Science* (September 1941), pp. 93–104.

[12] *Ibid.*

[13] For a competent analysis of the reasons racial protest is sweeping America today, as well as the history behind Freedom riders, sit-ins, prayer marches, refer to: L. E. Lomax, *The Negro Revolt* (New York: Harper & Row, Publishers, 1964).

Black in-migration and white exodus [this area will be thoroughly covered in Chapter 2], which have produced the massive and growing concentrations of impoverished Negroes in our major cities, creating a growing crisis of deteriorating facilities and services and un-met human needs.

The black ghettos where segregation and poverty converge on the young to destroy opportunity and enforce failure. Crime, drug addiction, dependency on welfare and bitterness and resentment against society in general, and white society in particular, are the results.[14]   ‡

At the same time, most whites and some Negroes outside the ghetto have prospered to a degree unparalleled in the history of civilization. Unfortunately, through television and other media this affluence has been flaunted before the eyes of the Negro poor and jobless ghetto youth.

Yet these facts alone cannot be said to have caused the disorders. Recently, according to the Commission, other powerful ingredients have begun to catalyze the mixture:

Frustrated hopes are the residue of the unfulfilled expectations aroused by the great judicial and legislative victories of the Civil Rights Movement and the dramatic struggle for equal rights in the South.

A climate that tends toward approval and encouragement of violence as a form of protest has been created by white terrorism directed against non-violent protest; by the open defiance of law and federal authority, by state and local officials resisting desegregation; and by some protest groups engaging in civil disobedience who turn their backs on non-violence, go beyond the constitutionally protected rights of petition and free assembly, and resort to violence to attempt to compel alteration of laws and policies with which they disagree.

The frustrations of powerlessness have led some Negroes to the conviction that there is no effective alternative to violence as a means of achieving redress, of grievances and of "moving the system." These frustrations are reflected in alienation and hostility toward the institutions of law and government and the white society which controls them, and the reach toward racial consciousness and solidarity reflected in the slogan, "Black Power."

A new mood has sprung up among Negroes, particularly among the young, in which self-esteem and enhanced racial pride are replacing apathy and submission to "the system."

The points mentioned have attempted to identify the prime components of the "explosive mixture." In the chapters that follow, we seek to analyze them in the perspective of history and in a manner through which law enforcement personnel may find possible solutions applicable for use in their chosen profession. Their meaning, however, is clear: *The "holding down" of the Negro in American society—with all that this means in terms of subordination, frustration, economic insecurity, and incomplete participation—enters significantly into almost every possible aspect of racial strife and tension.* Indeed, it is so important as to con-

[14] *Report of the National Advisory Commission on Civil Disorders* (Washington, D. C.: Government Printing Office, 1968), "The Basic Causes," pp. 9–11.

stitute virtually a special, and major, set of sociological and psychological factors which can "explain" Negro protest, insofar as it needs special explanation. The *administration of justice* itself is from beginning to end so much a part of the whole system of Negro-white social relations that it must be viewed as a process which discriminates against Negroes and thus acts as a direct and indirect causative factor in producing poor relations between Negroes and police. The administration of justice is beyond the scope of this chapter and will be analyzed in Chapter 6, "Equal Justice and Minority Groups."

Dissent and Civil Disobedience

In the United States, the question is *not* "May I dissent?" because that *right* is guaranteed by both the Constitution and the courts; however, there is a question as to *how* the dissent shall be carried out. The First Amendment confers: "the right of the people peaceably to assemble and to petition the Government for a redress of grievances"—but there are limitations to the right. And contrary to popular belief, freedom of speech does not guarantee the individual's right to offer a false statement about an individual (there is a possibility of a civil suit, or tort)[15] nor does it permit him to state what is on his mind anytime, anywhere. No one, according to Justice Oliver Wendell Holmes, may shout "Fire!" in a crowded theater when he is fully aware that such a warning is untrue. Regardless of how positive one's motive may be, e.g., dissatisfaction with inadequate fire regulations, actions that will injure others cannot be excused.

Policemen are being called pigs to their faces by both whites and blacks who resent them. Freedom of speech entitles these individuals to their own opinions and to the selection of their own descriptions, but it does not entitle them to insult people to their faces. Should the community allow its law enforcement officers to be insulted with impunity? Should a policeman be required to permit others to call him a pig in public? The intent is certainly provocative, the purpose to reduce the authority of and respect for the law. Policemen, unlike judges, cannot punish people directly. Insults to an officer of the law in the performance of his duties are, however, every bit as detrimental to public order as insults to a judge, and they should be treated as misdemeanors and be legally punished.

Abe Fortas, former justice of the Supreme Court, stated that the term *civil disobedience*, which has been utilized to apply to an individual's refusal to obey a law—a law believed to be immoral or uncon-

---

[15] For a concise definition of *tort*, refer to W. L. Marshall and W. L. Clark, *A Treatise on the Law of Crimes* (Chicago: Callaghan, Callaghan and Co., 1952), pp. 102–5.

stitutional—has in recent years been misapplied. Civil disobedience does not apply to attempts to overthrow or seize control of the government by force; nor does the term apply to the use of violence in order to force mediation or to compel the government to grant a measure of autonomy to a segment of its population. Such programs advocate revolution and the term *civil disobedience* is not appropriately used in this context.[16]

> Some propagandists seem to think that people who violate the laws of public order ought not to be punished if their violation has protest as its purpose. By calling criminal acts "civil disobedience," they seek to persuade us that offenses against public and private security should be immune from punishment and even commended. They seek to excuse physical attacks upon police; assaults upon recruiters for munitions firms and for the armed services; breaking windows in the Pentagon and in homes; robbing stores; trespassing on private premises; occupying academic offices, and even looting, burning and promiscuous violence.[17]

The First Amendment freedoms are not a sanction for riotous behavior; freedom of speech, freedom of the press and of assembly do not correlate with looting, burning, assault, and physical abuse. The United States Supreme Court has stated explicitly that the First Amendment protects the right to *assemble* and to *petition*, but it requires that the rights be peacefully executed.[18]

THE FUTURE

In the final analysis, effective law enforcement depends upon the full participation of all members of our society in the legislative and administrative process. In this period of dynamic social change and the movement toward full integration of hitherto excluded minorities into the decision-making structure, there will continue to be difficulties, tensions, and crises that spring from the dissatisfaction and despair fostered by social, economic, and political patterns of discrimination against minority groups.

The recent series of race riots offer perhaps the most poignant evidence of the growing alienation between police and Negroes. Much of the hostility of the violent crowds in Watts, Harlem, Philadelphia, Rochester, and Chicago was directed toward the most visible symbol of community restrictiveness, the police force. As civil rights organizations continue to use nonviolent demonstrations to dramatize and revoke the inequities of racial discrimination, inevitably there will be increasing confrontation of police and minority groups, requiring special insights and attitudes on the part of both law enforcement officials and civil rights leaders.

[16] A. Fortas, *Concerning Dissent and Disobedience,* (New York: The New American Library, Inc., 1968) p. 10.

[17] A. Fortas, *Concerning Dissent and Disobedience.*

[18] *Ibid.*

Summary

Racial tension is not a new phenomenon in the United States. The growth of the cities has resulted in the emergence of considerable difficulties for law enforcement agencies. American law enforcement tradition appears to have been influenced by major differences in the ethnic background of those comprising the cities' population; i.e., Negro, Italian, Mexican, Oriental, white, et cetera. Therefore, society's enforcement of behavior regulations has moved beyond the point of simple, uncomplicated answers, and law enforcement in the grossly complicated urbanized society increasingly demands that positive efforts to anticipate and endeavor to redirect those social forces tending to jeopardize the personal safety and property security of individuals. Discharge of this particular police responsibility therefore must necessarily become a matter of community relations.

Law enforcement human relations is defined as: police participation in any activity that seeks law observance through respect rather than enforcement.

Law enforcement agencies have found themselves caught in a period of unusual uncertainty. This is due primarily to two developments:
(1) Recent decisions made by the United States Supreme Court;
(2) The series of civil disturbances associated with a wide range of efforts to upgrade the status of minority groups.

As to the basic reasons for the increase in civil strife, research conducted by the National Advisory Commission on Civil Disorders reveals that the following factors were conducive to the racial disorders of 1967: pervasive discrimination and segregation in employment, education, and housing; black in-migration and white exodus in major cities; and the black ghettos, where segregation and poverty converge on the young to destroy opportunity and enforce failure.

Civil disobedience does not apply to violent and destructive behavior, but instead the term applies to peaceful demonstration against a law believed to be unjust or immoral. Recently, the term has been misapplied and under the guise of "civil disobedience," anarchy has appeared on the scene.

QUESTIONS

1. Discuss the perplexing problem of police-community relations.
2. Define human relations.
3. Why is law enforcement undergoing a period of uncertainty?
4. What are the basic causes of racial strife?
5. Discuss the misapplication of the term *civil disobedience*.

ANNOTATED REFERENCES

Barrett, E. L., "Personal Rights, Property Rights and the Fourth Amendment," *1960 Supreme Court Review.* Chicago: University of Chicago Press, 1960. A fine discussion of the subject with emphasis on the individual in constitutional government.

Berson, L. E., *Case Study of a Riot: The Philadelphia Story.* New York: Institute of Human Relations Press, 1966. A particularly good discussion of human dynamics involved in community tension.

Fortas, A., *Concerning Dissent and Civil Disobedience.* New York: The New American Library, Inc., 1968. A fine discussion of civil disobedience and the "right to dissent."

Johnson, E. H., "A Sociological Interpretation of Police Reaction and Responsibility to Civil Disobedience," *The Journal of Criminal Law, Criminology, and Police Science,* Vol. 58, No. 3 (September 1967), 407–11. An excellent overview of the dimensions of human dynamics in police problems.

Lomax, L. E., *The Negro Revolt.* New York: Harper & Row, Publishers, 1964. Explains the history behind freedom riders, sit-ins, prayer marches and the development and meaning of the racial protest sweeping America today.

Report of the National Advisory Commission on Civil Disorders (a United States Riot Commission Report). New York: E. P. Dutton & Co., Inc., 1968. A thorough discussion on "What happened?" "Why did it happen?" and "What can be done?"

Rose, A., *The Negro in America.* Boston: Beacon Press, 1960. A comprehensive study of the entitled minority group in the United States.

Sowle, C. R., ed., *Police Power and Individual Freedom.* Springfield, Ill.: Charles C. Thomas, Publisher, 1962. A discussion of the title subject, with emphasis on the potential impact of authority.

CHAPTER TWO

THE NATURE AND SCOPE OF THE PROBLEM

Figure 2.1 *There is hardly a single American city that has not been confronted with mob violence. The events which touch off riots are* not *the real causes of such riots. The causes are rooted more deeply in the* neighborhood, *the* community, *the* family, *and the* times *in which we live.*

THERE CAN COME A SUDDEN AND SEARING CRISIS IN THE LIFE OF ANY MAN WHICH BETRAYS THE WORST WITHIN HIM. It may be a brutish time of depravity or cowardice or greed or hypocrisy or violence. A like time can befall a whole nation. And with clarity almost ghastly, this has come to pass in America with the savage urban revels of the summers of 1967 and 1968.

The shame is singular and stunning. For it rarely happens in man's society that a grievous crisis neither rouses nor reveals a single hero, real or fancied. Yet the crises of American urban life bears this chilling distinction, as the drama has seemed overwhelmingly dominated by manic agitators, pathetic pilferers and craven politicians.

There is no doubt that both the black and white citizenry are guilty of lack of sound judgment. There has been overreaction on both sides. It appears that the nation's Negro leaders have not been forceful enough in condemning violent revolt as a definite threat to civil liberties. It would appear that their voices have been barely audible above the call "to arms" by the black militants. In Newark, the National Conference on Black Power degenerated into a cry for black racism, as its leaders threatened a separate Black nation. In Detroit the worst riot in the nation's modern history exploded in the face of a progressive city leadership that had wrested from Washington more than 200 million dollars in federal aid. And nowhere was the base nature of the upheaval more sharply etched than along Detroit's Grand River Avenue, where Negro and white looters roved and thieved in integrated bands.

These are extremely difficult times for police, especially in the cities. Race riots have forced them into the middle of personal peril and public controversy. And court decisions limiting the use of confessions and otherwise restricting their procedures, have greatly hampered the police in making cases against suspects.

During riots, the duty of the police is to try to keep order. In many disturbances, they have been under orders for long periods to endure snipers and fire bombers without retaliating. When they do shoot back, some denounce them as murderers. When they use force to subdue people, the cry of police brutality is frequently raised. In the dangerous confusion of riots, some police conduct has, no doubt, been excessive; there definitely has been overreaction, but it is clear that the police draw criticism from one side or another no matter what they do. Of course, the conduct of policemen in these dreadful moments is terribly important, and the dilemma of precisely how they should behave is troubling indeed. It is very doubtful that there is any real consensus in our society about the right way and the wrong way to put down a huge riot, and surely this general uncertainty is reflected in many police departments. Some policemen have shot down looters; others have chased and arrested them by the hundreds; others have *ignored* them. In New York, police agreed to demands that several patrolmen be removed from rooftops above unruly crowds; in Cleveland the mayor withdrew most of the police from troubled areas in hopes that community leaders could settle the problem; and in Newark, police (with national guardsmen and state troopers) were restricted from using all possible force at their disposal. In all these instances such approaches did not alleviate the problem in the respective communities. Needless to say, then, in the midst of fierce action the balance of discretion is awfully delicate, and police officers, as any member of society might, can easily tip it the wrong way.

Inevitably a season of riot must lead into a spell of frustration and disgust, for a dormant answer to a national need must rank as a kind of spiritual treason. Meanwhile the urban Negro ghettos of the North keep growing by another half million people a year. The cities thus affected hold 70 percent of America's population, and they account for 90 percent of the gross national product. Sadly it appears to be much more than a crisis of the American city; rather, it signals a crisis of the American conscience.

A realistic appraisal of civil disturbances in our society necessarily results in an awareness that the operation, and struggle, of a democratic society contains inherent violence-producing factors. Identifying and labeling these factors should not be misconstrued as implying criticism of either the society or its philosophical basis but rather as an attempt to reasonably define the *nature* of the problem. Society must endeavor to become cognizant of the attainable goals of law enforcement *before* programs are devised that seek either total elimination of destructive riots and civil disobedience—or, conversely, a feeling of total inability to increase the protection of our society. Therefore, it is important to point out that the *degree* of police power required to provide a society free from chaotic racial disorders would be such that it would destroy all pretense of individual liberty. Similarly, *rejecting* the concept that such disorders can be reduced and better controlled would result in *anarchy*, or the complete absence of government and law. Law enforcement must continue to strive between these two alternatives. The use of police power in civil disturbances must find a delicate balance if it is not to be a barrier against long-term changes of the community's social structure and to the sociological forces pressing the community to change.

The events which touch off riots are not their real causes; the causes are deeply rooted in the neighborhood, the community, the family, and the times in which we live. But once this type of disturbance begins, it snowballs at a fantastic rate; and soon thousands of citizens are in the streets, fires are started, windows are smashed, looting is widespread, and the police are physically attacked by the mobs.

The attacks upon both persons and property are ageless manifestations of man's inhumanity to man. Almost from the very beginning, civil disobedience and mob violence have been part of our society and of the societies of other countries. From the time of the enactment of the first riot law, they have constituted a violation of the legal codes of the city, state, and federal government.

The standard accepted definition in American law has remained unchanged since September 12, 1849, when it was stated by Judge Charles P. Daly in the New York City Court of General Sessions. He was presiding at the trial of ten persons charged with riot or conspiracy to riot during the Astor Place riot. In his charge to the jury, Judge Daly first defined unlawful assembly, saying, "Any tumultuous assemblage of three or more persons brought together for no legal or constitutional object, deporting themselves in such manner as to endanger the public peace and incite terror and alarm irrational and firm-minded persons, is unlawful."

Then he added the following to complete the definition of riot: ". . . and whenever three or more persons, in a tumultuous manner, use force or violence in the execution of any design wherein the law does not allow the use of force, they are guilty of riot." This legal definition, then, includes all the elements which make a riot—three or more persons, a gathering for the purpose of enforcing a demand or expressing a protest instead of using due process of law, the use of violence, and the endangering of public peace through terror.[1]

Crime and violence in the life of citydwellers have long evoked complaints which have quite a comtemporary tone. For example, people in eighteenth-century London daily confronted a level of danger to which they and their spokesmen reacted indignantly. A letter was dictated by these irate citizens to their spokesman, who proceeded to dictate a pamphlet on crime to the lord mayor.

"We are living in climates of violence," a *New York Herald Tribune* editorial stated after the Los Angeles (Watts) riot in August, 1965. Turmoil is everywhere, in many countries throughout the world, as well as in our own nation. Ever since the end of World War II, a serious discontent has seized the world's people, erupting constantly into protests.

Riots and Civil Disobedience Are Not New Problems

As previously indicated, mob violence has been part of the history of the United States and other countries for many centuries (specifically, in the United States since the Stamp Act disturbances of 1763). Civil disobedience has existed as a law enforcement problem in one form or another down through the centuries, and has undoubtedly existed as a police problem in our country for as long a period as we have had police. Perhaps, civil disobedience is indigenous to a society largely founded by dissenters, which was from the beginning dedicated to freedom of expression and liberty of conscience.

Thus, the contemporary literature, eloquently professing a great deal of concern about crime and violence, draws on established elements of both past and contemporary social problems; an indignant sense

[1] W. A. Heaps, *Riots, U.S.A. 1765–1965* (New York: The Seabury Press, Inc., 1966), pp. 3–4.

of pervasive insecurity; a mounting current of crime and violence as a result of unaccustomed prosperity along with prolonged poverty; the bad example of the self-indulgent wealthy; the violent proclivities of immigrants and other newcomers; and the ironic contrast between the greatness of the metropolis and the continued spread of crime.[2]

J. E. Curry and G. D. King, authorities in the field of interracial relations, in their book *Race Tension and the Police* state that violence has changed very little in recent years. Many of the contemporary disturbances in the United States are quite similar in many respects to the disturbances in America throughout its history.

HISTORICAL ASPECTS

Few men had more insight into America than John Quincy Adams, son of a president, himself a president, close enough to Thomas Jefferson to be called his adopted son. Adams visualized clearly the intricate balance between good and evil on which the United States as a nation rests. In referring to the country's democratic system, he once stated, "The American Government is an experiment upon the heart."

Most men were of the belief that human nature could not be trusted with freedom. They were certain that if the right to protest, to resist injustice, and to criticize the government itself were accorded to the citizen, the inevitable result would be revolt, violence, and anarchy.

During the last few years, there has been a great deal of anxiety on the part of a significant number of Americans who have expressed concern over whether the pessimists were correct after all. Riots have left their marks on our cities and have disrupted our colleges; the tragic assassinations of John Kennedy, Martin Luther King, Jr., and Robert Kennedy have, without doubt, taken their toll on the confidence of many citizens in the ability of America to survive and continue as a free society. However, the problems confronted by the American people throughout their history serve as a reminder that contemporary violence is not a new problem.

The following are brief summaries of major riots that have occurred in the history of the United States. Selected from Thomas J. Fleming's article, "Revolt in America,"[3] they represent the varied types of problems, prejudices, and emotions which have led to violence over a broad period of time and in different geographical areas.

> *SHAYS' REBELLION*: In 1786, Daniel Shays—captain of a regiment during the War of Independence—along with 1,500 farmers prevented the State's Court from convening for the purpose of foreclosure proceedings for debts resulting from a depression in the State of Massa-

---

[2] D. J. Bordua, ed., *The Police: Six Sociological Essays* (New York: John Wiley & Sons, Inc., 1967), p. 3.

[3] Adapted with permission of T. J. Fleming from, "Revolt in America," *This Week*, United Newspapers Magazine Corp., New York, N.Y., September 1, 1968 ©, pp. 2–8.

chusetts. They blocked all attempts on foreclosures of property for debt. The mob soon got out of control and proceeded to physically abuse officials, loot homes, and make serious threats to burn government buildings.

Shays' "army" soon disintegrated into a handful of fugitives, with Shays himself fleeing to Vermont when the Governor of Massachusetts declared the state "in a period of rebellion" and ordered the militia into active status.

NAT TURNER'S REVOLT: This significant rebellion on the part of some of the state of Virginia's 400,000 slaves has been covered by numerous books; one, *The Confessions of Nat Turner*, written by William Styron, received an excellent response.

Nat Turner launched an insurrection in Southampton County, Virginia, in 1831. On the night of August 21, he and a few companions murdered several farmers and their families throughout the countryside. Twenty farms were attacked, and before the rampage was brought to an end by the country militia, at least 40 Negroes died in the fighting and 12 were executed. The death toll of the whites totalled approximately 57.

Figure 2.2 *Nat Turner (1800–1831). American slave leader. From a 19th century American wood engraving. Reproduced with permission from The Granger Collection.*

Nat Turner was subsequently hanged, and although his insurrection was neither the first nor the last Negro revolt, its mindless violence was "so appalling, he [Turner] silenced all hope of emancipating the Negro by peaceful vote, as Thomas Jefferson and James Madison had for decades pleaded."

THE DRAFT RIOTS: In 1863, President Abraham Lincoln's Administration had decided that the war was going badly, and the North was in
need of a considerable increase in manpower. Therefore, the draft was
initiated as a desperate measure. Unfortunately, Congress, in its efforts
to "push through the Bill," constructed a rather unfair—that is, unfair
to the poor—draft law (a substitute could be hired for $300 to take the
place of the person who was initially drafted), which precipitated the
infamous draft riots in New York City on July 13, 1863.

Figure 2.3 *The New York City Draft Riots of July 13–16, 1863. Wood engraving from a contemporary German-language American newspaper. Reproduced
with permission from The Granger Collection.*

Approximately 800,000 draft-eligibles resided in New York City, and
about 10,000 people protested the drawing of names for the city's first
draft on July 11, 1863. With the assistance, in the opinion of some
historians, of Confederate soldiers who had infiltrated the city, the mob
surged down Broadway to 29th Street, where the Federal Provost
Marshal was scheduled to draw more names of those eligible for the
draft out of a revolving drum. Police officers, attempting to control the
situation, were severely beaten—some critically. The "demonstrators"
forced the Provost Marshal and his staff to withdraw and devastated
the building, eventually setting it on fire.

The riot continued for four days and on several occasions, troops
(Federal authorities eventually dispatched troops to the embattled city)
were forced to use point-blank artillery fire to disperse howling charges.
On the fourth day, battle-tired regiments from the Army of the Potomac
poured into the city, and the draft riot was brought to a halt.

THE GREAT STRIKE: In 1877, America was in its fourth year of a
terrible depression. At this particular period, the four largest railroads
in the country announced that wages were going to be decreased by at
least 10 percent. Since the non-unionized employees were being paid very
poor wages (approximately $1.75 per day) and a single railroad, the
Pennsylvania, reported showed net profits of $25,000,000 a year, the
attempt to slash the workers' pay touched off a national crisis.

Figure 2.4 *The Great Railroad Strike of 1877. Wood engraving from a contemporary American newspaper. Reproduced with permission from The Granger Collection.*

Employees on the Baltimore and Ohio, the Pennsylvania, the New York Central, and the Erie refused to work—in essence, they struck. The strikers seized the railroad yards in Baltimore and did not permit any trains to move. Freight and buildings were destroyed. And the rioters numbers grew to an estimated 15,000. The President of the United States, Rutherford B. Hayes, responded to the plea from the governor of the state and dispatched 500 Federal troops to Baltimore. The disturbance subsided almost immediately upon the show of force.

In Pittsburgh, the strikers followed the same pattern, but there they were far better organized, and their leaders were men with wilder ideas. It was necessary, therefore, to rush 650 state militiamen from Philadelphia. Upon their arrival, they fought a battle with the strikers, killing approximately 25. The rioters forced the Philadelphia militia into the Pennsylvania roundhouse and bombarded them with bricks; in fact, in several instances, the dissenters utilized firearms. Freight cars were burned, and the Philadelphia militia was forced to "fight their way out from the roundhouse and retreat."

Like a contagious disease, the strike moved from city to city; Omaha, San Francisco, and St. Louis felt the sting of the reactionary mob. In New York and Buffalo, the Central yards were seized. Rioters stormed through the streets of Chicago, forcing workers to quit their jobs, shutting down factories, stores, and construction projects and intimidating officials into signing papers promising to raise wages.

Acting on advice from a Civil War general, President Hayes actually ordered a proclamation prepared declaring that the unruly rioters were "levying war" against the United States. However, before the proclamation was made, the great strike had begun to be brought into control by state militias, local policemen, and on several occasions, Federal troops.

JACOB COXEY'S "INDUSTRIAL ARMY": In 1894, Jacob Coxey, a reformer, led a group of unemployed in a march on Washington. In order to sustain themselves, his followers stole food as they advanced. However, Coxey soon ascertained that a majority of the people of the United States were extremely hostile to his "industrial army." He gathered only 1,200 protestors in Washington instead of the 100,000 he had so confidently predicted prior to the march.

The riots, mob disturbances, and *all-out rebellion* described above certainly do not represent the entire scope of disturbances that have taken place in the United States. There have been other times when Americans were extremely concerned, fearing that the nation was on the fringe of anarchism. Situations such as the Industrial Workers of the World issuing a cry for removal of the system utilized to set wages and calling for strikes that sabotaged the war effort during World War I also caused Americans to be apprehensive. At this time, the federal government struck back quickly by taking the union leaders into custody and filing charges of sedition. Such violent tactics by the Industrial Workers of the World eliminated them as a force in American labor. The IWW was nicknamed "Imperial Wilhelm's Warriors" by the American public. Then, in 1932, World War I veterans, 15,000 strong, were involved in the "Bonus March." The veterans assembled in Washington to demand from Congress immediate payment on certificates that had been issued for their war service, and which were not legally due until 1945. The majority returned home peacefully when Congress declined to pass the bill they wanted. The President reluctantly ordered the army to expel the 300 who refused to leave the Capitol grounds.

Today the United States is confronted with a problem that is as old as this nation's experiment in freedom; questions are being asked, such as: Where does legitimate protest end and revolt begin? Up to now, mass uprisings, however justified, have failed to produce the desired effect. Will history repeat itself? Can Americans continue to rely on the lessons of history?

The Changing American Scene

The problems of crime control, in general, and law enforcement, in particular, are always related to changes in the social scene. The dimensions and substance of community life are undergoing such wholesale and radical transformation in our time that it behooves us to pause and reflect upon the influences that are sharply modifying the conditions of contemporary community life and posing new problems for the agencies of law enforcement.[4]

There are basic changes going forward in the community, and these are transforming the problems which confront law enforcement officials. Cities are becoming the residence of lower-class Negro groups, while whites are moving to the hinterland. This wholesale settlement has coincided with problems of housing, of income, etc. The specific features of the discontent and deprivation are separately and together an expression of radical changes in population and population distribution. The central features of the times, which are commonplace to our society, make up the context in which we must identify all the problems. And if we so identify them, it may be possible that we will see them quite differently than as the "lion hunter and the lion." In any event, if there are those in America who expect groups in our society to act differently than they currently do, they should realize that this will happen only if the necessary conditions come about. The view law enforcement has of minority groups is a necessary condition of the attitude these groups take toward law enforcement. And, if law enforcement sees them only as persons who are troublesome and difficult and have shortcomings, without reference to the conditions which have their formed their behavior, then police officers will not be disposed to act in such ways as to invite any kind of response other than hostility, anger, and, indeed, outright violence.

BLACK INNER CITIES

Between 1950 and 1960, the 12 largest cities of the United States lost over two million white residents. In that same period, when white

---

[4] Much of the information in this section was adapted with the permission of N. A. Watson, from D. J. Lohman, "Race Tension and Conflict" in N. A. Watson, ed., *Police and the Changing Community* (Washington, D. C.: International Association of Chiefs of Police, 1965), pp. 42–47.

residents were moving beyond the formal municipal limits into the bordering metropolitan region, the cities gained almost exactly the same number of nonwhite residents. *Two million Negroes moved into the places evacuated by the two million white residents.*[5] It was not until very recently in our society that the fact that, as cities grow, people have economic and social success was generally understood. People came as foreigners from other hands, to move into the great cities. Residents of the older portions of these cities had social and economic success, and the young people moved on, in the widening circle of residential resettlement, to the middle-class suburbs. Everyone who has lived in America has noted—particularly the police—that many of the problems of law and order are concentrated in particular neighborhoods in the trials and tribulations of those groups in transition. But the neighborhoods have now burgeoned into veritable cities in transition. They are *no longer* pinpointed, in terms of few areas of those great urban centers, in the places where immigrant groups are first accommodated and then move on. Vast sections of the cities have been occupied by the new immigrant group. In cities like Baltimore, Detroit, Cleveland, Chicago, Washington, D.C., and St. Louis, as much as a third of the city is made up of these new immigrant groups. And so, the transition is a transition of cities rather than a transition of neighborhoods.[6]

The consequence of this trend is a new way of life for many people. Diverse groups with conflicting customs and interests suddenly find themselves side by side. And there have been changes in the relative wealth and power of various groups. From these many changes have come special problems, such as housing, which throw groups into competition with one another and thereby may become police problems.[7]

The National Commission on Urban Problems recently released a study which reports that if present trends continue, "America by 1985 would be well on a road toward a society characterized by race stratification along racial and economic lines as well as geographic separation."[8]

A projection of population figures by a team of demographers shows that by 1985 central cities will have gained ten million more nonwhites, a 94 percent increase. This would be an acceleration of the trend begun in 1960 of increasingly black inner cities, ringed by burgeoning white suburbs.

Unhappily, the projection vividly portrays the geographic fulfilment of the fears expressed by the President's Commission on Civil Disorders —that American society is becoming an apartheid society, that it is becoming divided into two societies—black and white, separate and unequal.

[5] Watson, *Police and the Changing Community,* p. 46.
[6] *Ibid.,* p. 47.
[7] *Ibid.*
[8] *The National Commission Report on Urban Problems* (Washington, D. C.: Government Printing Office, 1968), p. 8.

At a news conference former Senator Paul Douglas of Illinois, chairman of the commission appointed by President Johnson in 1967, cited a study by Patricia Leavuy Hodge and Philip Hauser of the University of Chicago which stated that although nonwhites are expected to increase numerically in the suburbs to 6.8 million in 1985 (from 2.8 million in 1960), they "will still be all but lost in a sea of whites, with the nonwhite suburban population increasing from only 5 to 6 percent of the total." Hodge and Hauser also pointed out that, because of their high fertility rates, nonwhites will increase at a greater rate throughout the nation than whites, their proportion of the total population rising from 11 percent in 1960 to 14 percent in 1985.

However, in the central cities the increase of nonwhites is expected to be greater by 1985; according to projections, the white population will have dropped to 69 percent (82 percent in 1960), and the nonwhite population will have increased to 31 percent (18 percent nonwhite in 1960), with many major cities having nonwhite majorities.

Louis Danzig, head of the Newark (New Jersey) Housing Authority, estimated that since 1950 some 200,000 whites have moved out of Newark, while 85,000 Negroes have moved in. More than half the residents of the city of Oakland, California, will be Negroes by 1983 if present trends continue, the President's Commission on Civil Disorders stated in its recent report. Washington, D.C., and Newark, New Jersey, are already at that point, the commission noted. It listed these other cities where Negroes will be a majority by 1984:

> New Orleans, and Richmond, Virginia, 1971; Baltimore, and Jacksonville, Florida, 1972; Gary, Indiana, 1973; Cleveland, 1975; St. Louis, 1978; Detroit, 1979; Philadelphia, 1981, and Chicago, 1984.
>
> In addition in 1985, Dallas, Pittsburgh, Buffalo, Cincinnati, Harrisburg, Louisville, Indianapolis, Kansas City, Hartford, and New Haven will probably have Negro majorities.

The majority of Negroes now are immigrants. Often they are deficient in education and job skills. Some of them must be supported by public welfare, and many do not know how to live in cities. Obviously, with such persons, dialogue and communications are difficult.

Racial Violence: a Problem or a Product?

The general view of antisocial behavior relating to mob violence holds that such actions are not in and of themselves the *problem* but instead are *product* of various social conditions. (Mob behavior will be covered extensively in a later chapter.) Indeed, the fact is that some individuals in all societies and in all classes of society respond to economic, social, and psychological pressures by violent acting-out behavior.

Although violence is to be expected when social change is rapid, the Commission on Civil Disorders reported in 1967 that the "typical" violence or disorders did not take place. The disorders of 1967 were unusual, irregular, complex, and unpredictable social processes. Like most human events, they did not unfold in an orderly sequence. However, an analysis by the commission leads to some conclusions about the process in these riots:

> The civil disorders of 1967 involved Negroes acting against local symbols of white American society, authority, and property in Negro neighborhoods—rather than against white persons.
>
> Of 164 disorders reported during the first nine months of 1967, eight (5 percent) were major in terms of violence and damage; 33 (20 percent) were serious but not major; 123 (75 percent) were minor and undoubtedly would not have received national attention as "riots" had the nation not been sensitized by the more serious outbreaks.
>
> In the 75 disorders studied by a Senate subcommittee, 83 deaths were reported. Eighty-two percent of the deaths and more than half the injuries occurred in Newark and Detroit. About 10 percent of the dead and 38 percent of the injured were public employees, primarily the law officers and firemen. The overwhelming majority of the persons killed or injured in all the disorders were Negro civilians.
>
> Initial damage estimates were greatly exaggerated. In Detroit, newspaper damage estimates at first ranged from $20,000,000 to $500,000,000; the highest recent estimate is $45,000,000. In Newark, early estimates ranged from $15,000,000 to $25,000,000. A month later, damage was estimated at $10.2 million, over 80 percent in inventory losses.[9]

The white population of the United States often comforts itself with the thought that the black rage which pours out of the ghetto each summer in paroxysms of rioting and looting is the work of the "misfits" and "riffraff." Only a few Negroes, mainly recent immigrants from the South or teen-agers without jobs and with criminal records, cause the disturbances which most ghetto residents oppose, or so the thinking goes. However, a special study made for the Kerner Commission by Robert M. Fogelson, professor of history at MIT, and Robert B. Hill of the Bureau of Applied Social Research at Columbia University disapproves the "misfit-riffraff theory." In the Newark, Detroit, Dayton, Cincinnati, Grand Rapids, and New Haven riots, commission study groups ascertained that three-fourths of the rioters had jobs and more than two-thirds were over eighteen years of age. Many were women. While 44 to 90 percent of the men arrested did have criminal records, Hill and Fogelson point out that it is very easy to get a record in a ghetto, and as for the immigrant theory, Kerner Commission researchers found that lifetime residents of the ghetto are the ones most likely to riot.

[9] *Report of the National Advisory Commission on Civil Disorders* (Washington, D. C.: Government Printing Office), p. 3.

Social and economic conditions in the riot cities constituted a clear pattern of severe disadvantage for Negroes, whether the Negroes lived in the area where the riot took place or outside it. Compared with whites, Negroes had fewer years of education and fewer had attended high school. Negroes were twice as likely to be unemployed and three times as likely to be in unskilled and service jobs. Their income averaged 70 percent of that of the whites, and Negroes were more than twice as likely to be living in poverty. Although housing costs Negroes relatively more than it costs whites, they had worse housing—three times as likely to be overcrowded and substandard. And when it is compared with the white suburbs, the relative disadvantage is even more pronounced.[10]

It is easy to understand the "why" of the Negro rebellion in America. It is even easy to suggest what ought to be done about it. What is not easy is to make the break with the past, which must be made before the obvious solutions can be undertaken.

When the Constitution was adopted, we were a rural people numbering fewer than 4 million. Today, we number more than 200 million, and 32 years hence our population, according to the experts, will be about 300 million. In the 1800s 95 percent of all Americans lived on farms, by 1960, 70 percent lived in the cities. In a process of our almost instant organization, we have jammed millions of people of different backgrounds and cultures together in our cities.

But our governmental system has changed little. It was created to deal with a mainly farming population. It now has to deal—but cannot—with a totally different condition. According to Dr. Philip M. Hauser, director of the Population Reference Bureau, "This outmoded system is exacerbating virtually every problem that afflicts our contemporary American scene."

The tragic violence in American cities—the eruption of the ghettos, the bloodshed in the streets, the agonized cries for jobs and justice—cannot be understood apart from the historical conditions that brought them about. They cannot be understood simply as a consequence of white racism or black rebellion. They cannot be controlled or eliminated by slum clearance projects or social welfare or crash programs to find jobs for the unemployed. The problem can only be understood and managed, in its historic context, as the consequence of profound disruption of traditional relationships between men and the land around them.

A process has taken place in the United States that has afflicted many great civilizations in the past and has usually been a prelude to their disintegration. It is that people who have traditionally made a living from agriculture were driven from the land by technological changes

[10] *Report of the National Advisory Commission on Civil Disorders* (Washington, D. C.: Government Printing Office, 1968).

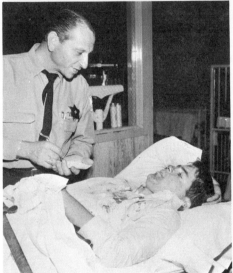

Figures 2.5, 2.6, 2.7 *Although the police always try to eliminate bloodshed in the streets, it is difficult and, during riots, injuries and death unfortunately do occur. Photos courtesy of the San Francisco Police Department, San Francisco, California.*

and poured into metropolitan cities that were not able to absorb them.

In the third century A.D., for example, there were drastic changes in the agriculture of the Roman world. Small farms gave way to the latifundia—hugh holdings engaged in mass production based on slave labor. The productivity of the land was increased by the new technology, but when free farmers were no longer able to till the soil, their migration caused chaos in the cities. "The social consequence," wrote Arnold Toynbee in *A Study of History*, "was the depopulation of the countryside and the creation of a parasitic urban proletariat in the cities...."

The parallel with the American dilemma is striking. Technological changes in agriculture—primarily the replacement of men by machines—have uprooted masses of farm workers and driven them to the cities to seek precarious refuge in the slums and ghettos. Thus far, American leaders seem as helpless before the problem as were the Romans. Welfare programs are little more effective than bread and circuses.

State legislatures and the United States House of Representatives have refused to reapportion themselves sufficiently as the population has moved from farm to town, and have become "a barrier to progress." As pointed out by Philip Hauser, "all cities are paralyzed. As creatures of state legislatures which have not yet entered the 20th Century, they have neither the authority nor the resources to solve their problem. So mayors, with hats in their hands, have to ask Washington for help. To most, the urban problem means the Negro problem. Commissions, federal and local, have investigated it, but it does not take all that research to understand why it exists." It is common knowledge that the American Negro has been in this country for three and one-half centuries. He spent two and one-half in slavery and half a century in the rural slum South with the unfulfilled promises of the Emancipation Proclamation. He spent another half century in the slums and ghettos of metropolitan areas, both North and South. Furthermore, in recent decades, rising Negro expectations have not been matched with anything real. Federal civil rights actions have not been followed through on the state and local level, and stark reality has remained the same.

Race Relations:
Major Forces Causing
Rapid Change

Any analysis inevitably involves a selection of what is most significant from the standpoint of the complexity of current reality. However, the necessity to make this presentation brief prevents the authors from offering a detailed exposition of the basis of selection and a statement of all assumptions. Most authorities[11] in the field of race relations

[11] A. Rose, *The Negro in America* (Boston: Beacon Press, 1956). See also G. Myrdal, *The American Dilemma* (New York: Harper & Row, Publishers, 1962 ed.); G. W. Allport, *The Nature of Prejudice* (Boston: Beacon Press, 1954); and J. Greenberg, *Race Relations and American Law* (New York: Columbia University Press, 1959).

accord significant weight to dynamic forces involving *social power* (both political and economic) and secondary weight to changes in *ideologies*; we have done this also.

There are many major forces in race relations which have given great impetus to rapid change in America. Since the early 1940s and 1950s, these forces appear to have been: *economic prosperity; continuous industrialization* and *technological advance; the high level of mobility among the American people*; and *the increased American awareness of world opinion*, e.g., the threat of an Olympic boycott by Negro athletes in 1968 focused world attention on racial problems in the United States; *the organization and political education of minority groups; a thoroughly consistent support for civil rights on the part of the Supreme Court and legislators*; and *the educational effort for more equal civil rights*.[12] One must not presume that these forces are not susceptible to change. If the more conservative elements fail to produce results, new forces such as militant student groups and advocators of black power are likely to have an increase in influence.

ECONOMIC PROSPERITY

To predict continued economic prosperity would be impossible if not extremely hazardous; however, it appears that the present state of world affairs does not dictate extensive unemployment in the United States. Needless to say, minority groups are in many cases most affected by unemployment. Because of their relatively marginal role in the economy, and because of discriminatory practices on the part of individual employers the United States Civil Rights Commission concludes:

> Although their occupational levels have risen considerably during the past 20 years, Negro workers continue to be concentrated in the less-skilled jobs. And it is largely because of this concentration in the ranks of the unskilled and semiskilled, the groups most severely affected by both economic layoffs and technological changes, that Negroes are disproportionately represented among the unemployed. ... Negroes continue to swell the ranks of the unemployed as technological changes eliminate the unskilled or semiskilled tasks they once performed. Many will be permanently or chronically unemployed unless some provision is made for retraining them in the skills required by today's economy. The oppressed economic status of Negroes is the product of many forces, including the following: discrimination against Negroes in vocational as well as in academic training; discrimination against Negroes in apprenticeship training programs; discrimination against Negroes by labor organizations—particularly in the construction and machinist's crafts; discrimination against Negroes in referral services rendered by State Employment offices; discrimination against Negroes in the training and "employment" opportunities offered by the armed services, including the

---

[12] *Ibid.*, p. xviii (in the foreword by G. Myrdal).

"civilian components;" and discrimination by employers, including Government contractors and even the Federal Government.[13]

Furthermore, the unemployment rate of Negroes is such that if it were experienced by the white population, it would be viewed as part of a depression worse than that of the 1930s. According to information from the United States Bureau of Labor Statistics:

> Only 3.5 percent of the Nation's workers were unemployed in April, matching a 15-year low, but the jobless rate was double in big city slums. The number of jobless workers in the Nation dipped under 2.5 million for the first time since 1953. Total employment rose by 600,000 to 75.1 million. But a new study showed the poorest ghettoes in the 100 largest United States' cities were islands of poverty and hardships surrounded by expanding jobs and income for most other Americans.
>
> In the slum districts covering 11.5 million persons of working age, the jobless rate was 8.7 percent for the Negroes and 5.7 percent for the whites.
>
> For those in the slums who were employed, jobs were more likely to be menial and low-paying. The concentration at the lowest end of the occupation scale was especially marked for Negroes in poverty neighborhoods. About half the slum residents covered in the survey were Negroes. The overall unemployment for the slum neighborhoods was 7 percent.[14]

Arthur M. Ross, commissioner of the Statistics Bureau, stated that the 1966 study was designed to spotlight the problems of poverty, low employment, and hardship in the slums at a time when most Americans were enjoying the fruits of economic growth. Ross said that, in the nation as a whole, Negroes appeared to be benefiting from growing job opportunities at the same rate as white workers, but the national Negro unemployment rate of 6.7 percent remained more than double the white rate of 3.1 percent. He stated further that although Negroes were moving ahead at the same pace as other workers and gaining more and better jobs, it was a case of "running pretty fast to stand still."

INDUSTRIALIZATION

The use of nuclear energy and the prospects for widespread automation are such as to promise a *new* industrial revolution. Needless to say, *industrialization* is moving at a more rapid pace than ever before. There are some evils as well as positive aspects to such a revolution. Although automation certainly results in higher productivity—and thereby a higher standard of living—it also involves some disruption for manual workers. Therefore, the need for occupational training and retraining has never before been so crucial. The new technology has also been invading the

---

[13] U. S. Civil Rights Commission, *Employment*, Report No. 3 (Washington, D. C.: Government Printing Office, 1961).

[14] U. S. Department of Labor, Bureau of Labor Statistics, *The Negroes in the United States : Their Economic and Social Situation*. Bulletin No. 1511, June 1966, p. 10.

farm, reducing the number of farms and sending minority workers to the cities at a rapid rate. With increased productivity in farming and manufacturing, sales and service personnel will be relatively more in demand, and minority groups concentrated in those occupations (such as Jews and Orientals) will be relatively well off.

TECHNOLOGICAL CHANGE

Residential and occupational mobility among the American people will increase as there is a broadening of *technological change*. The position of minorities has improved in at least two ways owing to their mobility.

> *First*, it has provided a measure of flexibility and impersonality to the whole social structure, and reduced the number of communities in which there was cohesive and fixed sentiment against minorities. *Second*, for Negroes, particularly, it has involved their moving to areas where they have considerable civil rights. Only a little over half of the Negroes still live in the South, whereas, 50 years ago, nine-tenths lived there.[15]

With reference to the change in technology, as previously indicated there is still a lack of opportunity. Automation has produced results very different from those generally assumed to be the case. It is a popular belief that Negroes have achieved new occupational opportunities and status. The truth, however, is that the Negro unemployment ranges from 12 to 20 percent in many communities; in some up to 40 percent of the nonwhite youths are unemployed. These figures are in sharp contrast to the national unemployment rate of 4 to 5 percent. In certain respects since the end of World War II, the position of the Negro with regard to employment has deteriorated rather than advanced. Often during the war Negroes were employed in upgraded positions, and they held jobs which they had never previously held. The end of the war and the subsequent development of automation (which has special implications for blue-collar workers) resulted in pushing Negroes out of jobs and into the ranks of the unemployed. The Negro, therefore, is deeply concerned about employment, but suburban whites who see Negroes picket grocery stores and factories do not understand the reason for the concern. Negroes picket because they know that things are not as good as they are declared to be, but whites do not understand this, and their failure to understand means that they will communicate a gross misconception to their children —to a whole generation.

MINORITY GROUPS—RAISING LEVELS OF EDUCATION

Academically, minority groups are raising their average levels of education. The educational system has shown drastic improvement, and

[15] From the Foreword by G. Myrdal in A. Rose, *The Negro in America.* Reprinted with permission of Harper & Row, Publishers.

as better schools are opened to the minority groups, there will be an increase in political and organizational sophistication. Membership in minority defense and improvement associations has been rising rapidly; this can be attributed at least in part to the better educational system.

UNITED STATES SUPREME COURT

The liberalism displayed by the United States Supreme Court has clearly paved the way for a de-emphasis on *discrimination*. Whether the Court's unanimous decisions that the Fifth, Fourteenth, and Fifteenth Amendments specify that no branch of government may show discrimination to any citizen have been able to eliminate *prejudice* (prejudice is an attitude; discrimination is an attitude acted upon) is a moot question. However, the last shred of doubt on the subject of discrimination was removed by the decision of May 17, 1954, in which even segregation— because it is forced and invidious—was held to be discrimination, and, hence, illegal. Therefore, in ruling on the appeal of Joseph Lee Jones, a Negro, who with his white wife had been refused a house in a St. Louis suburb, the Supreme Court revived an obscure statute that had nestled in the United States Code for more than 100 years. Passed by Congress in 1866 as a supplement to the Thirteenth Amendment prohibiting slavery, the act provided simply that "all citizens of the United States shall have the same right in every State and Territory, as is enjoyed by white citizens thereof to inherit, purchase, lease, sell, hold, and convey real and personal property." Almost everyone who knew about this law, including past Supreme Courts, had assumed that it applied only to racial discrimination in the public, not the private, domain.

In some respects, the 1866 statute is a trifle less vigorous than its 1968 counterpart. It provides no penalties for those who violate the law until they are specifically ordered to stop by court injunction, while the 1968 law allows the injured party to collect any actual damages plus punitive damages up to $1,000. Yet the older law casts a far broader net. It exempts no type of property, whereas the 1968 act is limited to residences and contains a "Mrs. Murphy" clause, exempting operators of small rooming houses. What is more, the Jones decision appeared to open the way for further extensions of the concept of civil rights into the realm of private behavior.

Riots:
Implications and Effect
on Law Enforcement

Police work is a phrase that conjures up in some minds a dramatic contest between a policeman and a criminal in which the party with the stronger arm or the craftier wit prevails. To be sure, when a particularly desperate or guileful criminal must be hunted down and brought to justice, there are heroic moments in the police work. The situations that the majority of policemen deal with most of the time are of quite another order, however. Much of American crime, delinquency, and disorder is associated with a complexity of social conditions: poverty, racial antagonism, family breakdown, or restlessness of young people. During the last 20 years, these conditions have been aggravated by such profound social changes as the technological and civil rights revolutions, and the rapid decay of inner cities into densely packed turbulent slums and ghettos.

It is in the cities that conditions of life are worst, social tensions are most acute, riots occur, crime rates are highest, and fear of crime and the demand for effective action against it are strongest. This, however, is not to say that crime rates have increased only in the big cities; actually crime has shown a drastic increase in the entire United States. According to a police statistics gathered by the Federal Bureau of Investigation in 1967, serious crimes soared throughout the nation. Over 3.8 million serious crimes were reported—a 16 percent rise over 1966 figures. There was also a jump in crimes against property (refer to Tables 2.1 and 2.2). Accompanying this sharp increase in crime rates was the revelation that 123 policemen had been killed and 26,755 injured in the line of duty.

More than 494,500 *violent crimes* in 1967, a 16 percent rise over 1966. *Serious crimes* were up 17 percent in the large cities but also increased by 12 percent in the rural areas. Suburbia likewise continued to show an upswing, with a 16 percent increase. Following is a capsule summary of the 1967 report on crime in the United States by the Federal Bureau of Investigation.

> Over 3.8 million serious crimes reported during 1967, a 16 percent rise over 1966.
>
> Risk of becoming a victim of serious crime increased 16 percent in 1967; there were 2 victims per each 100 inhabitants.
>
> Firearms used to commit over 7,600 murders, 52,000 aggravated assaults, and 73,000 robberies in 1967.
>
> Since 1964, use of firearms in murder up 47 percent; in aggravated assault up 76 percent. Armed robbery during the same period up 58 percent.
>
> Daytime burglaries of residences rose 187 percent from 1960 to 1967.
>
> Property worth more than $1.4 billion stolen as a result of 202,050 robberies, 1,605,700 burglaries, 3,078,700 larcenies, and 654,900 auto thefts.
>
> *In 1967, the rate of 2 police employees per 1,000 population was unchanged from 1966.*
>
> Arrests of juveniles for serious crimes increased 59 percent from 1960 to 1967, while the number of persons in the 10–17 age group increased 22 percent.

The authors are able to present further statistical information which would support the contention that the national scene has indirectly con-

TABLE 2.1

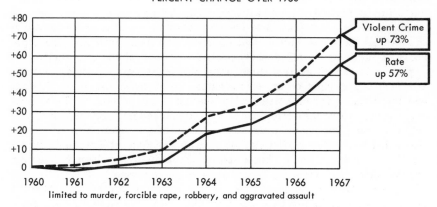

CRIMES OF VIOLENCE

1960 - 1967

PERCENT CHANGE OVER 1960

Violent Crime
up 73%

Rate
up 57%

limited to murder, forcible rape, robbery, and aggravated assault

TABLE 2.2

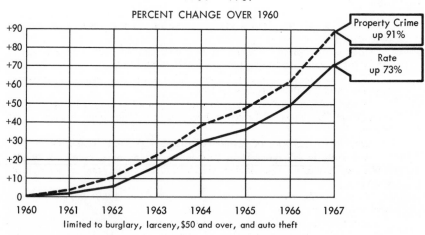

CRIMES AGAINST PROPERTY

1960 - 1967

PERCENT CHANGE OVER 1960

Property Crime
up 91%

Rate
up 73%

limited to burglary, larceny,$50 and over, and auto theft

tributed to the upsurge in criminal activity in the United States, but they feel that at this stage, it is unnecessary to do so. The situation has deteriorated to a point where *seven serious crimes are committed each minute.* Table 2.3 shows this; it also shows a breakdown of such crimes, along with their rate of occurrence.

TABLE 2.3

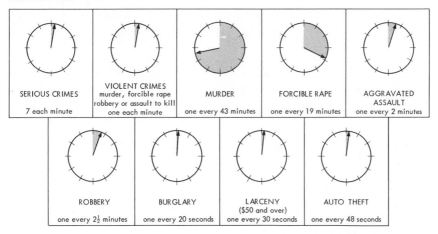

Urban Crime and Conditions Associated with High Crime Rates

One of the best-documented facts about crime is that the "common" serious crimes that worry people the most, such as forcible rape, robbery, aggravated assault, and burglary, usually take place in the slums of large cities. Study after study, in city after city, in all regions of the country, has traced variations in the rates for these crimes. With monotonous regularity, the results show that the offenses, the victims, and the offenders are found most frequently in the poorest, most deteriorated, and socially disorganized areas of cities.

Studies of the distribution of crime rates in cities and of the conditions most commonly associated with high crime rates have been conducted for well over a century in Europe and for many years in the United States. The findings have been remarkably consistent. Burglary, robbery, and serious assaults occur in areas characterized by low income, physical deterioration, dependency, racial and ethnic concentrations, broken homes, working mothers, low levels of education and vocational skills, high unemployment, high proportions of unmarried males, overcrowded and substandard housing, high rates of tuberculosis and infant mortality, low rates of home ownership or single-family dwellings, and high population density. Studies that have mapped the relationship of these factors and crime have found them following the same pattern from one city to another.

Crime rates in American cities tend to be highest in the city center and decrease in relationship to distance from the center. This pattern has been found to hold fairly well for both offenses and offenders, although it is sometimes broken by unusual features of geography, enclaves of socially well-integrated ethnic groups, irregularities in the distribution of opportunities to commit crime, and unusual concentrations of commercial and industrial establishments in outlying areas. The major irregularity found in the clustering of offenses and offenders beyond city boundaries occurs in satellite areas that are developing some characteristics of the central city such as high population mobility, commercial and industrial concentrations, low economic status, broken families, and other social problems.

The big-city slum has always exacted its toll on its inhabitants, except where those inhabitants are bound together by an intensive social and cultural solidarity that provides a collective defense against the pressures of slum living. Several slum settlements inhabited by people of Oriental ancestry have shown a unique capacity to do this. However, the common experience of the great successive waves of immigrants of different racial and ethnic backgrounds that have poured into the poorest areas of our large cities has been quite different.

A historic series of studies by Clifford R. Shaw and Henry D. McKay of the Institute of Juvenile Research in Chicago has documented the disorganizing impact of slum life on different groups of immigrants as they struggled to gain a foothold in the economic and social life of the city. Throughout the period of immigration, areas with high delinquency and crime rates maintained such rates, even though members of new nationality groups successfully moved in to displace the older residents. Each nationality group showed delinquency greatest among its members who were living near the center of the city and lower for those living in the better outlying residential areas. Also, for each nationality group, those living in the poor areas had more of all the other social problems commonly associated with life in the slums.

This same pattern of high crime rates in slum neighborhoods and low crime rates in the better districts holds for Negroes and members of other minority groups (refer to Table 2.4) who have made up the most recent waves of migration to the big cities. (Minority groups and crime will be discussed in another chapter.) As other groups before them, they have had to crowd into areas where they can afford to live, while they search for ways to live better. The disorganizing personal and social experiences of life in the slums are producing the same problems for the new minority group residents, including high rates of crime and delinquency. As they acquire a stake in urban society and move into better areas in the city, crime rates and incidence of other social problems drop to lower levels.

TABLE 2.4   BREAKDOWN OF ARREST BY RACES
(Source: Federal Bureau of Investigation)

Two and one-half times more whites than Negroes were arrested in 1967 for all crimes. During the same year, 5402 whites were arrested for criminal homicide compared to 5512 Negroes for the same crime.

Last year 34,713 Negroes were arrested for possession of weapons compared to 31,977 whites.

In 1967, approximately 30 percent of all arrests of whites and Negroes were for drunkenness. However, 70 percent of the arrests of Indians were for drunkenness. Incidentally, the Indians referred to in the report are American Indians.

ARRESTS BY RACE FOR 1967

RACE	Under 18 Years	Over 18 Years	Total by Race
White	929,204	2,701,583	3,630,787
Negro	322,127	1,140,429	1,462,556
Indian	10,086	111,312	121,398
Chinese	434	1,292	1,726
Japanese	1,177	2,313	3,490
All Others	13,586	31,759	45,345
TOTAL	1,276,614	3,988,583	5,265,302

However, there are a number of reasons to expect more crime and related problems among the newcomers to the city than among the more established immigrants. Major changes in the job market (previously discussed) have greatly reduced the demand for unskilled labor, and most new immigrants have no job skills to offer. At the same time, educational requirements for jobs has been rising. Also discrimination in employment, education, and housing, based on such a visible criterion as color, is harder to break than discrimination based on language or ethnic background.

What these changes add up to is that slums are becoming ghettos from which escape is increasingly difficult. It could be predicted that the frustration of aspirations that originally led Negroes and other minority groups to seek out the city would ultimately lead to more crime. Such evidence as exists suggests that this is true.

Riots:
Conditions of Slum Living?

One hypothesis about everyday crime in the slums is that much of it is a blind reaction to the *conditions of slum living*. The ghetto riots of 1964, 1965, 1966, 1967, and 1968 were crime in its most aggravated form. In the 1965 riot in the Watts section of Los Angeles alone, 34 persons were killed, 1,032 injured, and 3,952 arrested. Some 600 buildings were damaged and some $40 million in property was destroyed. In Newark, New Jersey, in less than a week, approximately 38 people were dead, more than 1,000 injured, and another 1,600 arrested. Property damage was estimated in the millions. Plainclothes Patrolman Frederick Toto, age 34, who in 1964 was cited for heroism for saving a drowning child, was shot through the chest by a sniper and died a short while later; a fireman was also shot in the back and killed. Among the Negro dead were innocent children and women, as well as looters and snipers. The fifth largest city in the United States, Detroit, was turned into a holocaust only a few days after the Newark "fire storm." Although federal troops were employed throughout the city as quickly as possible under the circumstances, death and destruction surpassed that of Newark and Watts. At least 38 persons died, including a policeman and a fireman. Two thousand, two hundred and fifty suffered injuries and 4,000 arrests were made. Those taken into custody had to be incarcerated in buses converted into temporary jails. Considering property alone, the destruction was unprecedented (again, much higher than Watts or Newark) and estimated as high as $1 billion.

The size of the threat that riots impose on a community cannot be reckoned as merely the sum of the individual acts of murder, assault, arson, theft, and vandalism that occur during them, of course. Riots are a mass repudiation of the standards of conduct which citizens must adhere to if society is to remain not only safe but also civilized and free. They give a sort of moral license to compulsive or habitual criminal offenders of the ghetto community to engage in their criminal activities, and to citizens who are ordinarily law abiding to gratify some submerged tendencies toward violence and theft they may have.

Riots, however, are every bit as complicated as any other form of crime, and another way of looking at them is as direct and deliberate attacks on ghetto conditions. This is what all the studies show—particularly those of the Watts riots by the McCone Commission, an independent nonpolitical body; by the Attorney General of California; and by members of the faculty of the University of California at Los Angeles. Although once underway, some riots were exploited by agitators, the riots were not deliberate in the sense that they were planned at the outset; the best evidence is that they were spontaneous outbursts, set off more often than not by some quite ordinary and proper action by a policeman. They were deliberate in the sense that they were directed— to an extent that varied from city to city—against specific targets.

The principal objects of attack were most often those people or institutions—insofar as they were within reach—that the rioters regarded as their major oppressors: policemen, white passers-by, or white-owned commercial establishments, especially those that charged high prices, dealt in inferior merchandise or employed harsh credit policies. Loan offices were a favorite target. Homes, schools, churches, and libraries were, by and large, left alone.

The studies also show that the rioters were not preponderantly wild adolescents, hoodlums, racial extremists, and radical agitators, as is sometimes asserted, although such people undoubtedly took part. They were a more or less representative cross section of the Negro community, particularly of its young men, many of whom had lived in the neighborhood for many years and were steadily employed. According to the *Report of the National Advisory Commission on Civil Disorders* ("The Profile of a Rioter") :

> The typical rioter in the year of 1967 was a Negro, unmarried male, between the ages of 15 and 24, in many ways very different from the stereotypes. He was not a migrant, he was born in the state and was a life-long resident of the city in which the riot took place. Economically, his position was about the same as his Negro neighbors who did not actively participate in the riot.

> Although he had not, usually, graduated from high school, he was somewhat better educated than the average inner-city Negro, having at least attended high school for a time.

> He feels strongly that he deserves a better job, that he is barred from achieving it, not because of lack of training, ability, or ambition, but because of discrimination by employers.

> He rejects the white bigot's stereotype of the Negro as ignorant and shiftless. He takes great pride in his race and believes that in some respects Negroes are superior to the whites. He is extremely hostile to whites, but his hostility is more apt to be a product of social and economic clash than of race; he is almost equally hostile toward middle-class Negroes.

> He is substantially better informed about politics than Negroes who were not involved in the riots. He is more likely to be actively engaged in civil right efforts, but he is extremely distrustful of the political system and of the political leaders.

The aforementioned studies, furthermore, showed that many of those who participated in the riots, when questioned subsequently about their motives, stated quite explicitly that they had been protesting against, indeed trying to call the attention of the white community to police misconduct, commercial exploitation and economic deprivation, and racial discrimination. (See Table 2.5.)

It is ironic that after the passage of the antisegregation laws, segregation in the United States is far more widespread than when it had a legal basis. One reason, of course, is that greater numbers of people are involved. The second and more important reason is that a subtle *de facto* system of discrimination has come into existence. The practice of subtle discrimination is pervasive, and it often serves as a more accurate measure of the attitudes of individuals than an expressed declaration to members of minority groups.

At the present time, many people are inclined to question the propriety of the civil rights movement. Why, they ask, do Negroes feel it necessary to mount a civil rights program when they have already been

TABLE 2.5 WEIGHTED COMPARISON OF GRIEVANCE CATEGORIES*

	1st Place (4 Points)		2nd Place (3 Points)		3rd Place (2 Points)		4th Place (1 Point)		Total	
	Cities	Points	Cities	Points	Cities	Points	Cities	Points	Cities	Points
Police Practices	8	31½	4	12	0	0	2	2	14	45½
Unemployment & Under-employment	3	11	7	21	4	7	3	3	17	42
Inadequate Housing	5	18½	2	6	5	9½	2	2	14	36
Inadequate education	2	8	2	6	2	4	3	3	9	21
Poor Recreation Facilities	3	11	1	2½	4	7½	0	0	8	21
Political Structure and Grievance Mechanism	2	8	1	3	1	2	1	1	5	14
White Attitudes	0	0	1	3	1	1½	2	2	4	6½
Administration of Justice	0	0	0	0	2	3½	1	1	3	4½
Federal Programs	0	0	1	2½	0	0	0	0	1	2½
Municipal services	0	0	0	0	1	2	0	0	1	2
Consumer and Credit Practices	0	0	0	0	0	0	2	2	2	2
Welfare	0	0	0	0	0	0	0	0	0	0

* The total of points for each category is the product of the number of cities times the number of points indicated at the top of each double column except where two grievances were judged equally serious. In these cases the total points for the two rankings involved were divided equally (e.g., in case two were judged equally suitable for the first priority, the total points for first and second were divided, and each received 3½ points).

(Source) *Report of The National Advisory Commission on Civil Disorders* (Washington, D.C.: Government Printing Office, 1967), p. 83.

emancipated from the traditional system? It is easy to reply that Negroes do this because they have tasted the fruit of freedom and want more, but this answer is not the whole of the matter. White Americans believe that nonwhite Americans have achieved their victory and established their positions as free, independent, and equal citizens. This simply is not so; it is untrue and a few examples will suffice to prove its falseness.

Consider the Negroes' position in large cities of the North in terms of residence. More Negroes live under conditions of residential segregation today than 20 years ago. This is true of every northern city—Chicago, Detroit, San Francisco, New York, to name only a few. Negroes have moved into all the northern cities, but as they have moved in, the whites have moved out to the peripheral suburban areas. This has created a new pattern of social relations whose distinguishing feature is greater segregation of whites from Negroes and Negroes from whites than ever before in our history. A generation ago in Chicago, 50 percent of the nonwhites lived in communities in the city in which half the population was white. Today there are almost a million Negroes in Chicago, and in the areas where they live 85 percent of the population is nonwhite. *A whole generation is living under more highly segregated conditions than their forebears.* This is illustrative of conditions throughout the country, and it refutes the widely held idea that progress in residential desegregation has been made in which Negroes should take satisfaction.

Summary

Civil disobedience and mob violence have been a part of our society and of the societies of other countries almost from time immemorial. From the enactment of the first antiriot law on September 12, 1849, they have been a violation of the legal codes of the city, state, or federal government. Therefore, although riots and civil disobedience have been much more pronounced during the last few years, the problem of riots and civil disorders are *not new problems.* Brief summaries of major riots that have occurred in the United States are presented in this chapter in an effort to point out that contemporary disturbances are often quite similar in many respects to disturbances throughout America's history.

The general view of antisocial behavior relating to mob violence holds that such actions are not in themselves the *problem* but, instead, a *product* of various social conditions. In fact, individuals in all societies and in all classes of society respond to economic, social, and psychological pressures by violent acting-out behavior.

Social and economic conditions in cities where riots have taken place constitute a clear pattern of disadvantage for Negroes, when compared with whites, for Negroes living either in the area where the riot took place or outside it. Although special grievances varied from one city to another, at least 12 deeply held grievances can be identified and ranked into three levels of relative intensity. Table 2.5 shows these to be: *First Level*—Police practices, unemployment, and inadequate housing; *Second Level*—inadequate education, poor recreational facilities and programs, and ineffectiveness of the political structure and grievance mechanisms, and the *Third Level*—disrespectful white attitudes, discriminatory administration of justice, inadequacy of federal programs and municipal services, discriminatory consumer and credit practices, and inadequate welfare programs.

Although American society has undergone a rapid transition from rural to urban, the governmental system has changed very little. Technological changes in agriculture—primarily the replacement of men by machines—have uprooted masses of farm workers and driven them to the cities to seek precarious refuge in the slums and ghettos. Thus far, American leaders seemed helpless before the problem.

Statistical information in the area of employment, population, and crime brings into focus the effect of the aforementioned problems on racial strife in American cities. To cite but one problem—that of *Negro unemployment*—information from Department of Labor Statistics points out that the national Negro unemployment rate of 6.7 percent remained more than double the white rate of 3.1 percent.

QUESTIONS

1.   Discuss the major riots in the United States throughout its history.

2.   This chapter lists the levels of "relative intensity" as to special grievances. Catalog the grievances and assign them to their respective levels.

3.   List and briefly discuss the many major forces in race relations which have given great impetus to racial change in America.

4.   Describe the typical rioter as revealed by the study of the National Advisory Commission on Civil Disorders.

5.   Discuss the problem of the black inner cities.

ANNOTATED REFERENCES

Bordua, D. J., *The Police*. New York: John Wiley & Sons, Inc., 1967. A collection of six essays touching on some of the multifarious problems confronting today's police. This book attempts to view the problem of law enforcement in a society faced with a rise in the demand for civil liberties, as well as an increase in the crime rate.

Brown, C., *Manchild in the Promised Land.* New York: The Macmillan Company, 1965. An excellent work by an author who displays much empathy in discussing the Negro's psychological problems in American society.

Cohen, J., and W. S. Murphy, *Burn, Baby, Burn!* New York: E. P. Dutton & Company, Inc., 1966. A fascinating book delving into the "why's" of the Negro revolt in the ghettos and focuses its attention particularly on the Watts riot of 1965.

Heaps, W. A., *Riots, U.S.A. 1765–1965.* New York: The Seabury Press, Inc., 1966. Covers in depth the thirteen major riots that have occurred in the history of the United States. More contemporary disturbances are treated in the last two chapters, along with new ways of protest.

U.S. Department of Labor, Bureau of Labor Statistics, *The Negroes in the United States: Their Economic and Social Situation.* Bulletin No. 1511, June 1966. What is the economic and social situation of the Negroes in the United States? This given manual provides most of the answers. The statistical information is invaluable.

Watson, N. A., ed., *Police and the Changing Community: Selected Readings.* Washington, D.C.: International Association of Chiefs of Police, 1965. A book of selected readings covering every aspect of human and community relations by authorities in the field. Very useful as a supplement to a text in police-community relations.

CHAPTER THREE

SOCIAL PROBLEMS AND CONSTITUTIONAL GOVERNMENT:

Impact

On

Law

Enforcement

Figure 3.1 *Social problems in the United States—not the least of which are wars and student revolt—have a tremendous impact upon law enforcement. Photo courtesy of the San Francisco Police Department, San Francisco, California.*

CHAPTERS 1 AND 2 DISCUSSED THE NATURE AND SCOPE OF CERTAIN SOCIAL PROBLEMS THAT HAVE IMPACT ON LAW ENFORCEMENT. The very nature of these problems suggests the further discussion of a number of significant influences, not the least of which are wars, student revolt, crime, and the *rate* of social change. Before considering these, however, let us first examine the specific restrictions imposed on law enforcement by government in general and *constitutional government* in particular. For it will be seen throughout this volume that the complexity of enforcing law has increased steadily throughout history with the Magna Charta, Bill of Rights, Fourth Amendment, and other rulings and events molding the foundation of modern constitutional government. However, one function of law enforcement has remained consistent in all governments over the centuries—the promotion of an orderly environment.

Evolving an Orderly Environment Through Government

Many years ago a student of nature expressed a belief that a small child isolated from human society would likely grow into an adult *homo ferus*—a hairy man who walks on all fours and lacks an intelligible language. Linnaeus, the Swedish naturalist was the scholar who held this belief, and there has since been occasional corroboration.[1] But insofar as government is concerned, the individual human must be thought of as a talking member of society who walks upright like his fellowman. More importantly, the individual must be thought of as depending on government to provide a safe or at least an orderly environment.

Entire volumes have elaborated on the many ways in which the individual depends on society for a safe or orderly environment. One of the more obvious has to do with regulating human behavior. When primitive man had advanced sufficiently to acquire the rudiments of a language, the necessity of regulating behavior was not long in developing, at least not long by historical standards. This is not to say that with language came the civilized philosophy *Cogito, ergo sum* ("I think, therefore I am"). Indeed, primitive man tended to assign as much entity to stones or animals as he assigned to himself. But primitive man, nevertheless, soon contrived methods of regulating the behavior of humans—particularly, when it became apparent that doing so was necessary for survival.

The Biblical Cain's assault on his brother, Abel, posed (at least from Abel's viewpoint) the continuing need for society to regulate behavior. The absence of such regulation proved grossly unfortunate to Abel. For in the absence of deliberate and concrete efforts at such regulation,

---

[1] K. Davis, *Human Society* (New York : The Macmillan Company, 1949), p. 204.

man has historically demonstrated an inclination to foster his own survival and well-being at the expense of his fellowman.

An individual's relationship to his society is one of dependence, with government the system of providing a safe or at least orderly environment. In exchange for permitting his own behavior to be regulated, the individual depends on his society to provide *personal safety* for him. In this context, society is, or should be, an enforcer. And because human beings present such great variety in their willingness to be regulated, this enforcement function becomes necessary for society's very existence.

Still another consideration in evolving an orderly environment has to do with the freedom extended to the individual by his society. All societies provide for the personal safety of individuals who permit their own behavior to be regulated (although some regulations at times appear virtually impossible to either observe or enforce). But in societies that permit great personal freedom, as is the case with modern constitutional governments, the individual can acquire property, or at least property rights. Societies permitting individual property rights obviously differ from those in which the state attempts to retain the rights to all property. The question of property rights relates to government enforcement of rules, and the retaining of an orderly environment when there are as many potential property violations as there are property owners becomes far more complicated than when the state is the only potential victim of property rights violation. The rules regulating human behavior, along with the standards of enforcing these rules, obviously increase in complexity accordingly.

Early societal rules that ultimately became criminal law might then be thought of philosophically as being society's formal effort to promote an orderly environment. If the individual is to remain willing to permit his behavior to be regulated, he must believe that enforcement will be impartial, predictable, and consistent; being provided with an orderly environment will not serve as an inducement to him.

In seeking to promote an orderly environment, government restricts human behavior to protect the freedom of others, or it restricts behavior for the sake of controlling the individual. In either case, impartiality is necessary to convince the individual that there exists a definite relationship between conformity and personal safety (as well as property security "in free societies"). But in either case, the main function of government is to maintain an orderly society.

With the goal of an orderly society, government, particularly constitutional government, must take into consideration the relationship between the society's power and the power of man's *will*. Much of what is called the wisdom of the ages probably deals with this very relationship in one way or in another. So also does this very relationship define most of what are called social problems. For in the final analysis, the individual power of the person is equally potent whether in support of, or in dissent from the societal system of providing personal safety and property security.

FOR EXISTING GOVERNMENT OR AGAINST

War is frequently discussed as one of many major influences on social conditions defined as problems—particularly when defined as problems involving societal power and the power of an individual's *will*. Examples such as the social implications of the Korean and Vietnamese conflicts

Fgures 3.2 and 3.3 *The impact of the Vietnamese conflict has resulted in demonstrations by organized and unorganized groups. Some of these demonstrations have not been peaceful. Thus they created problems for police. Photo courtesy of the Elizabeth Police Department, Elizabeth, New Jersey.*

are appropriate to such discussions, but perhaps even more fundamental is the gross impact of World War II on American society. The following summary by Francis Merrill will serve to clarify this.

During World War II:

1. The rate of social change was increased.
2. Certain technological changes were accelerated.
3. Corresponding changes in the adaptive culture lagged further behind than ever before.
4. The rate of social mobility was intensified, with 15 million civilians and 12 million soldiers and sailors on the move.
5. Social congestion was intensified in certain industrial and military centers.
6. The gradual decline of the traditional functions of the family was accelerated.
7. The trend toward the employment of women was intensified by the war-time shortage of labor.
8. Many of the tensions which led to the peace-time disorganization of the family were increased.
9. Desertion probably increased.
10. The long-term trend toward a higher divorce rate and a greater yearly number of divorces was accelerated.
11. The emotional deprivation of children caused by the employment of mothers was increased.
12. Adolescent adjustment was complicated by the accelerated differences between the generations.
13. The trend toward increased sexual freedom was intensified by war-time decline in the mores.
14. The number of illegitimate births increased but not as fast as legitimate births.
15. Juvenile delinquency increased sharply, especially among girls.
16. Certain crimes against the person showed a considerable increase.
17. Various minor crimes and offenses against the public morality increased.
18. First admissions to mental hospitals for all psychoses increased.
19. First admissions to mental hospitals for certain organic psychoses of old age increased.
20. First admissions to mental hospitals for the functional psychoses showed a mixed trend, with manic-depressive psychoses decreasing slightly, and dementia praecox increasing substantially.[2]

Regardless of whether the individual is *for* existing (established) government or against it, problems such as these would appear likely to

---

[2] J. Nordskog, E. McDonagh, and M. J. Vincent, eds., *Analyzing Social Problems*, (New York: The Dryden Press, Inc., 1950), p. 689.

influence *against* government. This would seem likely if for no other reason than the jeopardy in which the government's existing system of providing an orderly environment is placed by changes inherent in solving such problems. For in attempting to solve problems such as these, existing government, or *the Establishment*, as it is known to many, often finds itself choosing between two rather restrictive alternatives: *suppress change* or *make change*. And to whatever degree the position of suppression of change is taken, to *at least* that degree, can there be certainty of opposition—surely from those seeking solutions through changes in the governmental system of providing an orderly environment.

Law enforcement obviously retains a crucial interest in governmental reaction to social problems. Suppression of change has conspicuous implications in this context but so have governmental decisions to make changes. Determining precisely *what* changes are being sought and *by whom* frequently becomes a concern of law enforcement, *whether law enforcement desires to become involved or not*. Student revolt, while only one of myriad signs of unrest, might serve as an example of how law enforcement becomes caught up in social problems and governmental efforts to retain an orderly environment.

CONSTITUTIONAL GOVERNMENT AND UNREST

Of course, the notion of student nonconformity is by no means new. Even before panty raids and goldfish swallowing, most college campuses had accumulated a history of incidents in which segments of the student body had drawn attention to themselves via nonconformity. But insofar as the Establishment was concerned, there was little reason to believe that questions were being raised regarding the very system of providing an orderly environment.

A somewhat different pattern of dissent began to emerge on college campuses at approximately the time of enrollment by students whose parents had been directly involved in World War II. By the early 1960s this new pattern of dissent had drawn mass attention through student demonstrations supporting demands ranging from free speech to preventing campus recruitment by the military forces or defense industry. The deluge of publicity given to draft card burning dramatized the increasing inclusion of the Establishment as the source of considerable student unrest.

In the spring of 1968 a survey by the National Student Association noted 221 demonstrations on 101 campuses across the nation—in 59 cases, involving the virtual take-over of an administration building. At the October, 1968 convention held at the University of Colorado by the Students for a Democratic Society (SDS), a call was made for a national student strike to disrupt the pending presidential election. The eruptions at the political conventions (as reviewed in Chapter 4) are profound comments on the magnitude of the unrest. So also are the violent out-

Figure 3.4 *From November, 1968 through May, 1969, the San Francisco Police Department was confronted with daily student unrest at San Francisco State College. Professional police action was one of the major factors in settling the unrest. Photo courtesy of the San Francisco Police Department, San Francisco, California.*

breaks on many campuses since—Columbia University and San Francisco State College serving as particularly salient examples in 1968.

Of course, student revolt is merely *one* sign of unrest, and only *one* social problem. Many other problems, perhaps of greater immediate concern to law enforcement, are dealt with throughout this volume. But student revolt, as it functions under a constitutional government that guarantees the right of dissent, may provide many clues to the process of interpreting social tension—a process of vital importance to the police in a changing community.

INTERPRETING THE DEGREE OF EXTREMISM

If there was a time when panty raids were thought to be the behavior of extremists, the nature of current student nonconformity certainly modifies this view. However, an analytic method of identifying the most extreme philosophy—racial philosophy—is possible by examining the relative militancy in the beliefs of Black Muslims, Black Panthers, and the Third World in relation to the position of the National Association for the Advancement of Colored People (NAACP) and the views espoused by the late Reverend Doctor Martin Luther King. Of course, depending on the orientation of the observer, the views of any or all of the foregoing could be called extreme. Their *degree* of demand for change might therefore, prove a more effective way of assessing the potential impact on law enforcement. For with the tremendous social changes occurring, today's "extremist" or "activitist" may (by comparison) be tomorrow's "conservative." This knowledge becomes important because interpreting social tension requires a distinction between consequential and inconsequential patterns of change.

Student unrest in itself may or may not be of consequence to law enforcement. Whether or not a student feels satisfied with his grades is of little concern to police, whereas large groups of students violently demonstrating to deny local draft boards access to grade records is clearly a police problem. Again, this is a matter of degree.

As a model of how law enforcement might interpret social problems well enough to anticipate direct involvement, student grades might be thought of in a context similar to complaints about public assistance and ghettos. The point becomes, of course, what is (or is not) being done to relieve this stress before the problem erupts into violent demand for law enforcement intervention.

Returning to the example of student unrest, a number of matters are of concern, among which is the virtual certainty that bureaucracies, colleges included, treat individuals as abstractions or statistics rather than as persons. This being the case, a student's concern about grades may often be merely a symptom of the problem rather than the problem itself. But the student concerned enough about grades or other scholastic problems usually raises another meaningful issue—the issue of relevance.[3] It might also be noted that, with equal uniformity, the inhabitants of ghettos expressed dissatisfaction with a number of public assistance programs prior to the violent outbursts reviewed in Chapter 2. *Relevance* may then be viewed by the student as crucially significant in much the same way as a ghetto inhabitant desires sufficient power to influence his own destiny; the student's *relevance* deals with college education in relation to the student's needs in a changing society and the ghetto inhabitant's desire with sufficient political and economic power to modify a system of continuing relegation.

A college student's grades per se would seem to remain outside the scope of police concern. But when students collectively decide that they are receiving grades for subjects that fail to meet the needs of either the students or society, police intervention may ultimately be required, particularly if these very same grades influence standing with a selective service system for a war effort opposed by large numbers of the students. *The increase in police concern is based on the recognition that dissent and protest are not likely to be viewed a success unless and until they*

---

[3] Western Interstate Commission for Higher Education, *WICHE*, XV, No. 1 (November 1968), pp. 3-7.

bring about a system that is deemed to be relevant. The frustration resulting from a lack of success makes predictable greater demands for significant changes, and with the increased demands comes the increased jeopardy of violence. For law enforcement, the question becomes one of overall governmental response to mounting demands—frequently a difficult question in constitutional forms of government. Police interest in the developmental stages of social unrest, whether on the campus or in a ghetto, can no longer be denied.

Other Social Change Influences in Constitutional Government

In a rather profound manner, Warren Freedman commented on social change as follows:

> In the chaotic growth of modern society the individual is being coerced, conformed, and threatened in new and unique ways by social changes. At the same time, "society is on trial," for we must determine whether or not the dynamics of society are equal to the task of coping with the slow-to-change law and legal processes which measure the social values of the individual's right amid disturbing social, political, and economic conditions.[4]

Mr. Freedman's comments cast the judicial process inherent in constitutional government in a significant role insofar as social change is concerned. For it is the judicial process, particularly Supreme Court decisions, that more often than not influences government response to the mounting social demands previously discussed.

Of equal or even of greater importance in the response of constitutional government is the legislative process. Indeed, the judicial process, including Supreme Court decisions, necessarily flows almost entirely from the legislative process. However, notwithstanding the power of the legislative process, it remains abundantly clear that the judicial process through Supreme Court decisions has had far more direct effects and dramatic impact on law enforcement than any other single aspect of governmental response to social change.

SUPREME COURT DECISIONS

It has been said that American courts function as social controls of values and attitudes toward law, while at the same time reconciling grievances—grievances between either the state and the individual or between individuals.[5] And while the press has carried prominent articles about the need for strong judicial measures on behalf of the state in

---

[4] W. Freeman, *Society on Trial* (Springfield, Ill: Charles C Thomas, Publisher, 1965), Preface.

[5] W. Amos and C. Wellford, *Delinquency Prevention* (Englewood Cliffs, N. J.: Prentice-Hall, Inc., 1967), p. 208.

every decade for the past 50 years,[6] only recently has general concern focused directly on court reconciliation of grievances between the state and individuals.

A traditional role of law enforcement in constitutional forms of government is *apprehending* law violators, while leaving *punishment* to the judicial process. Philosophically, at least, such a role permits crime *prevention* to be a mutual, although secondary, responsibility of both police and courts. But in recent times, police and courts are increasingly faced with "crimes" stemming from growing demands for social reform, rather than merely from the violation of criminal statutes. One apparent reaction by the courts, particularly the Supreme Court, has been a number of decisions tending to have great impact on police procedure in general, and on the relationship of police to social change in particular. In effect, the Supreme Court has handed down rulings that judge not only the lower courts' functions but the police function as well.

Much of the basis of the increasing Supreme Court assessment of police practice is the Fourth Amendment and to some degree the Ninth Amendment. The implications of the Fourth Amendment to the police function have received more than adequate concern in the literature.[7] Nonetheless, a brief review of the highlights of the more significant court decisions may serve to clarify these implications.

In 1914 the United States Supreme Court ruled in *Weeks United States* that a federal court could not accept evidence that was obtained in violation of search and seizure protection, which is guaranteed by the Fourth Amendment. In 1963 the Supreme Court ruled on the appeal case of *Gideon* v. *Wainwright*. The effect of this ruling was that a new trial could be demanded by anyone convicted of crime who did not have legal counsel. Moving closer to the function of the police, in 1964 a decision was handed down in the case of *Escobedo* v. *Illinois*. This decision, based on a five to four majority, held it the constitutional right of an indigent to be provided with legal counsel at the time of police interrogation. In June, 1966, again by a five to four majority, the Court ruled on the case of *Miranda* v. *Arizona*. The *Miranda* decision had the effect of providing legal counsel during police questioning for persons *suspected* of crimes. Since this and the previous rulings were made on the basis of "constitutional rights," law enforcement found itself compelled to regard many traditional investigative methods as unconstitutional. Yet if con-

---

[6] R. W. Winslow, *Crime in a Free Society* (Belmont, Calif.: Dickenson, Pub. Co., Inc., 1968).

[7] E. L. Barrett, "Personal Rights, Property Rights, and the Fourth Amendment," in *1960 Supreme Court Review* (Chicago: University of Chicago Press, 1961), p. 65. See also, C. R. Sowle, ed., *Police Power and Individual Freedom* (Springfield, Ill.: Charles C Thomas, Publisher, 1962); and W. H. Parker, "Birds Without Wings," in *The Police Yearbook, 1965* (Washington. D. C.; International Association of Chiefs of Police, 1965).

stitutional rights are violated by certain heretofore practiced police methods, the question becomes one of alternate approaches.

Alternate approaches are at best difficult when the overall function of the courts is undergoing change, resulting from Supreme Court interpretations of the United States Constitution. One of the definitive assessments of the court role in an era marked by social change appears in the introductory section entitled "The Courts" in *The Challenge of Crime in a Free Society*:

> Some Constitutional limitations on the criminal court are based on principles common to most civilized criminal systems. One is that criminal penalties may be imposed only in response to a specific act that violates a pre-existing law. The criminal court can not act against persons out of apprehension that they may commit crimes, but only against persons who have already done so. Furthermore, the basic procedures of the criminal court must conform to concepts of "due process" that have grown from English, common law seeds. Unquestionably, adherence to due process complicates, and in many instances handicaps, the work of the courts. But the law rightly values due process over efficient process. And by permitting the accused to challenge its fairness and legality at every stage of his prosecution, the system provides the occasion for the law to develop in accordance with changes in society and society's ideals.

After elaborating these points, the report goes on to state:

> Nevertheless, these limitations on prosecution are the product of two centuries of Constitutional development in this country. They are integral parts of a system for balancing the interests of the individual and the state that has served the nation well.[8]

If *the goal* of the judicial process is "a system for balancing the interests of the individual and the state," then the definition of what these interests actually are becomes important. The particular importance of such a definition to law enforcement is clearly implied in the evolution of Supreme Court decisions geared to relieve social problems—relief frequently requiring police to abandon traditional police methods.

Regardless of the importance of defining interests, such a task cannot be easy in an era of articulate yet divergent explanation of interests. The difficulty is increased still more by Supreme Court decisions that influence not only the definition of what *due process* is but also the definition of the *interests* served through due process. Nevertheless, defining *interests* remains crucial to law enforcement.

CIVIL RIGHTS AND POWER

Supreme Court decisions since World War II have influenced a number of interest definitions—particularly, in terms of educational

---

[8] President's Commission on Law Enforcement and the Administration of Justice, *The Challenge of Crime in a Free Society* (Washington, D. C.: Government Printing Office, 1967).

opportunity and civil rights. In the majority of Supreme Court treatments of these areas, there is an implied definition of the individual's interest in political power. For indeed, *insofar* as constitutional government is concerned, there is little value in guaranteeing equal distribution of educational opportunity and civil rights if there is not a corresponding equality in the power to influence both. Put another way, the individual cannot gain equality either in educational opportunity or in civil rights unless and until he also commands political power—as much as is guaranteed to all—to modify both.

In discussing this, a Lutheran minister, Reverend Joseph R. Barndt, writes:

> The central problem of the ghetto is powerlessness, and its result is a physical and emotional paralysis. The deepest need of the ghetto resident, as an individual and as a part of the whole community, is the power of self-determination.

> The first tragic mistake we make in analyzing the needs of the ghetto is to confuse the symptoms with the disease, to fail to separate cause and result. The symptoms are poor education, over-crowded housing, unemployment, and underemployment, welfare, etc. But these are the results and not the causes of the ghetto resident's deep distress. If the four R's—rats, roaches, rape, and lack of recreation—were eradicated tomorrow by the magic wave of a wand, along with the rest of the symptoms of ghetto living, the disease would not be cured, the ghetto would not disappear. The ghetto will disappear only when the disease itself is dealt with efficiently, when power is returned to the people from whom it has long been withheld.

> The second mistake we make is to pretend there is no sickness, but only a lack of will. A medical doctor who fails to diagnose illness in a patient, and who in addition, accuses the patient of pretending to be sick, should be sued for malpractice at the very least. A society that fails to diagnose the existence of a serious illness of the black slum ghetto, but instead accuses the patient of pretending or being lazy, is committing the same inexcusable action. The only possible explanation for our failure to diagnose the sickness is that if we did so, we would have to recognize ourselves as the cause of the illness.

> We have all too often and far too long been inaccurate in describing the condition of a person born and raised in the low income, minority ghetto. He has been portrayed as an ambitionless, lazy man, lacking the initiative necessary to raise himself to the same level of success as his middle and upper income brothers. The premises on which such a portrayal is based—that he has equal opportunity, that no preventive forces restrict him, and that the fault lies within people inside the ghetto walls—are false. In order to portray the resident of the low income minority ghetto accurately, we must understand this falsity. The ghetto resident is prevented from improving his own situation simply because he has been rendered powerless by, and is controlled by, outside forces. Although these forces are frustratingly invisible to the ghetto resident, some of their representatives are visible daily, performing their various tasks inside the ghetto walls. They include the slumlord, the case worker, the inspector, the politician, *the policeman*, the War on Poverty worker, and many, many more. In any other community, these people would at

least represent cooperative forces that join the individual to assist him in the self-determined directions of his life. In the ghetto, however, these forces completely determine the individual's life, leaving him powerless for self-determination.

Furthermore, these outside forces effectively determine not only the life of the individual but also that of the collective community.[9]

Social problems of any kind are remedied or relieved through power —political and economic power. The absence of such power almost assuredly leads to resentment among those on whom social problems have their greatest direct impact. This resentment, whether expressed or implied, is of critical interest to law enforcement in an era when Supreme Court decisions and civil rights legislation often tend merely to dramatize the frustration in achieving the power needed to influence one's own destiny. Constitutional government's dealing successfully with frustrations in gaining such power has emerged as the greatest singular social problem having direct impact on law enforcement in a changing community.

Summary

As an extension of Chapters 1 and 2, this chapter undertook the presentation of the impact of social problems on law enforcement, and the influence of constitutional government on the solution of such problems.

Various limitations and restrictions on law enforcement were considered in the context of "free" constitutional government, and these included property rights; free speech, with the right of dissent; and the right to seek alternate methods of affording an orderly environment— orderly environment being discussed as a primary responsibility in all forms of government.

Unrest was discussed as a consequence of disparity between the interests or needs of individuals and governmental methods of dealing with such interests or needs. In this regard, student concern with "relevance" was presented as a model for examining various social problems. Such terms as *extremists* and *activists* were discarded in favor of assessing the degree or level of the demand for social change.

The influence of both legislative and judicial process in constitutional government was considered, with judicial influence cited as having the greater immediate impact on law enforcement in a changing community. The United States Supreme Court decisions were reviewed in terms of, first, their immediate consequence on law enforcement and then, their indirect impact of decisions that tend to call attention to the gross limitations of political and economic power available to some indi-

[9] J. Barndt, *Why Black Power* (New York: Friendship Press, 1968), p. 31.

viduals—often individuals seeking such power merely to achieve solutions to social problems. Power was equated with educational opportunity and civil rights and was presented as a prime requisite in remedying chronically unresolved social problems in constitutional government.

QUESTIONS

1. What are the obligations of a free constitutional government to the individual who permits his behavior to be controlled?

2. Name five social consequences of World War II. Discuss the relationship of each to law enforcement.

3. What is the most significant difference between current student unrest and student nonconformity of the past?

4. Discuss the role of police in solutions to social problems in general. In demonstrations, in particular.

5. What bearing have Supreme Court decisions on social problems in general? On police, in particular?

6. How is the acquisition of power by minorities an advantage for the majority? For law enforcement?

ANNOTATED REFERENCES

Amos, W., and C. Wellford, *Delinquency Prevention*. Englewood Cliffs, N.J.: Prentice-Hall, Inc., 1967, Chapters 9, 10, and 11 deal effectively with the relationship of economics, police, and the judicial process in the community.

Barndt, J., *Why Black Power*. New York: Friendship Press, 1968. An excellent treatise of value to law enforcement officers which identifies and isolates the *positive* value of political and economic power for minorities.

Eldefonso, E., A. Coffey, and R. Grace, *Principles of Law Enforcement*. New York: John Wiley & Sons, Inc., 1968. Chapter 8 elaborates on the direct police role in community relations within the framework of police organizational restrictions.

Freeman, W., *Society on Trial*. Springfield, Ill.: Charles C. Thomas, Publisher, 1965. An exceptionally detailed review of modifications in modern judicial process.

May, E., "The Disjointed Trio: Poverty, Politics, and Power," *National Conference on Social Welfare: Social Welfare Forum*, 1963, pp. 47–61. An excellent discussion of the relationship of power to poverty through the medium of politics.

Nordskog, J., E. McDonagh, and M. Vincent, eds., *Analyzing Social Problems*. New York: The Dryden Press, Inc., 1950. A fine collection of contributions affording a classical analysis model for virtually all modern social problems.

President's Commission on Law Enforcement and Administration of Justice, *The Challenge of Crime in a Free Society*. Washington, D.C.: Government Printing Office, 1967. The *summary* on pages v through xi gives an excellent context for the law enforcement role in the changing community. See also from the same commission, *Task Force Report: The Police* and *Task Force Report: The Courts*.

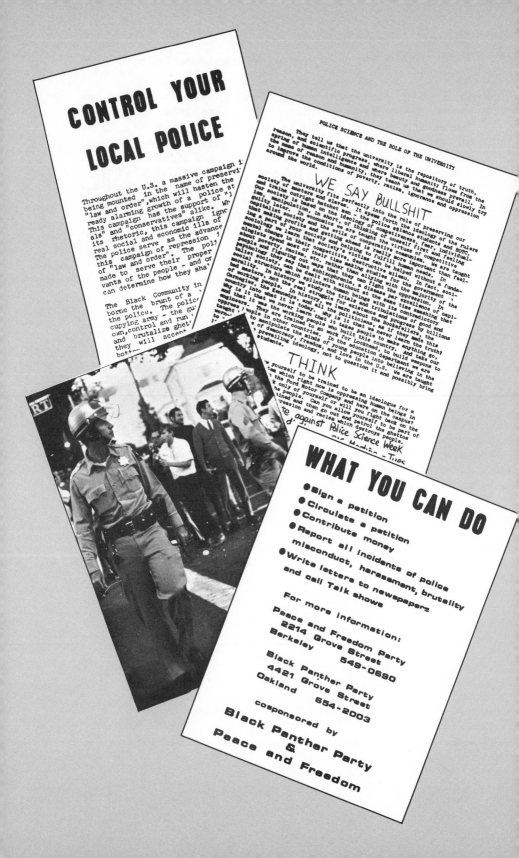

CHAPTER FOUR

THE PROBLEM OF THE POLICE IMAGE IN A CHANGING COMMUNITY

Figure 4.1 *There is no doubt that the law enforcement officer is under "attack" from special "interest groups." Therefore, it is incumbent upon each individual policeman to be concerned about the image* he *projects and the problems of police image in our changing community. Photo courtesy of Berkeley Police Department, Berkeley, California.*

POLICE ACROSS THE NATION ARE CONFRONTED WITH THE MOST DIFFICULT
TASK IN THE HISTORY OF LAW ENFORCEMENT. We live in an era of growth,
expansion, and change that is unprecedented. Law enforcement is more
directly affected by the changes than perhaps any other agency of government.

Numerous methods used by the police in the past have been declared
unconstitutional. Decisions handed down (discussed in Chapter 1 and
Chapter 3) by the Supreme Court and new laws make the work of the
police in protecting the general public much more difficult.

In the nation's large cities and in many small cities and towns as
well, the need for strengthening police relationships with the communities they serve is critical today. Negroes, Puerto Ricans, Mexican
Americans, Indians, and other minority groups are taking action to
acquire rights and services which have historically been denied them. As
the most *visible* representatives of the society from which these groups
are demanding fair treatment and equal opportunity, law enforcement
agencies are faced with unprecedented situations which require that they
*develop policies and practices governing their actions when dealing with
minority groups and other citizens.*

*Even if fairer treatment of minority groups were the sole considera-
tion, police departments would have an obligation to attempt to achieve
and maintain a positive public image and good police-community relations.*
In fact, however, much more is at stake. Police-community relationships
have a direct bearing on the character of life in the cities and on the community's ability to maintain stability and solve its problems. At the same
time, the police department's capacity to deal with crime depends to a
large extent upon its relationship with the citizenry. Indeed, no lasting
improvement in law enforcement is likely in this country unless police-
community relations are substantially improved.

It is not the intention of this chapter to address itself to police-
community relations *programs*; this is a major topic of chapter 12.
Instead, emphasis will be on the effect of a negative police image and
the problems confronting law enforcement agencies in developing and
maintaining a positive police image. As indicated in Chapter 1, "a good
police image tends to affect favorably the individual's willingness to
observe the law voluntarily. Therefore, police retain a vital interest in
good image."

Social Control[1]

Social control among homo sapiens is based upon custom. The system of social control consists of those mechanisms and techniques used
to regulate the behavior of persons to meet societal goals and needs. All

[1] R. L. Derbyshire, " The Social Control Role of the Police in Changing Urban Communities," *Excerpta Criminologica,* Vol. 6, No. 3 (1966), pp. 315-16.

cultures provide adequate control over behavior. Controls are initiated either formally or informally. *Informal controls* usually start in the family and consist of orders, rebukes, criticisms, reprimands, ridicule, blame, praise, rewards, etc. How an individual responds to informal and formal social control in the community frequently depends upon the consistency and certainty of controls in the family experience while he was growing up. Most frequently, informal controls are used by primary groups. Primary (two or more people involved in an intimate and durable relationship) affiliations require emotional reciprocity; therefore, they are quite subject to informal control.

Formal controls are those sanctions instituted by the body politic and its agencies. Since emotional attachment is seldom a part of secondary associations, laws, sanctions, and punishments are explicitly stated and theoretically apply to everyone, no matter what his position, in the social structure. Schools, hospitals, welfare agencies, and the *police* are examples of secondary socializing agencies which use formal social control methods.

Theoretically, a continum of social control exists from unregulated to institutionalized behavior. Unregulated behavior is unknown to contemporary man. Even within one's most intimate thoughts and during one's most isolated conditions, pressures from the social system both inhibit and stimulate behavior. Fantacies, hallucinations, and delusions of persons whose behavior appears most unregulated (e.g., the psychotic) are determined by sociocultural experiences.[2]

Unregulated and unrestricted behavior is detrimental to society. Societies are unable to maintain equilibrium without some form of social control. Each person's understanding of himself as a vital contributor to society stems from his early experiences with social control systems. Behavior inhibitions start in the family and are developed and modified as the growing child interacts and interprets his relations with family, peers, neighbors, the community, and all the beliefs, attitudes, and values available through his experience.

Studies have shown that the more homogeneous and stable the people and the belief systems, the fewer the transgressions. In other words, violations of folkways, mores, and laws most frequently occur under conditions of transcience, heterogeneity, and instability—where social relationships most frequently display anonymity, impersonality, and superficiality.[3] Social control systems operate most effectively and efficiently, the police notwithstanding, where there is constant and unified, overt and covert, cultural and social *support* from all control agencies. This support must be unambiguously stated in the value systems of

[2] M. K. Opler, ed., *Culture and Mental Health* (New York: The Macmillan Company, 1959).

[3] R. K. Merton, *Social Theory and Social Structure* (New York: The Free Press, 1957), pp. 131-94.

families, community, and the *greater society* of which the individual is a functional part.

THE COMMUNITY AND POLICE IN CONFLICT

Many police officers today sense that they are held in low esteem by the very communities they are serving. Responsible people are not likely to march up to a policeman and start listing, point-blank, such-and-such reasons why they do not regard their town's police force with fondness. If they did, their complaints might range anywhere from annoyance over a traffic ticket they once got to vague, general charges about police corruption.[4]

Historically, the police have always been used for political and social control. In the past they have done their work with almost unanimous support from the middle and upper class. *Now this is not so.* Many of those who oppose the police are children of the rich and the suburban well-to-do. These young people make up most of the amorphous cultural entity called the New Left. This goes a long way toward explaining the furor over police actions during the Democratic Convention in Chicago. The demonstrators were not blacks nor factory workers fighting in obscure parts of the city; they were the sons and daughters of influential people battling "downtown."

Figure 4.2 *At times, the taking into custody of a demonstrator may require physical force. During these occasions, in order to alleviate as much confusion and delay as possible, as many officers as are necessary should assist in making the arrest. Photo courtesy of the San Francisco Police Department, San Francisco, California.*

[4] "Storm Around U. S. Policemen," *Senior Scholastic* (January 14, 1965), p. 12.

Furthermore, this new breed of demonstrator is willing to do battle, usually, but not always, in a nonviolent fashion, particularly if they have law enforcement officers on anything like equal terms. These are rough youngsters from the suburbs; most are in superb physical condition. Anyone who thinks they are a group of timid draft dodgers would change his mind if—like the Chicago police and the law enforcement officers who confronted the dissenters at San Francisco State College, the University of California, Columbia University, etc.—he had an encounter with them.

THE PUBLIC

Ten years ago a study concerning public attitudes toward the police was conducted in Los Angeles.[5] It revealed a number of prejudices common in urban communities which are useful as a guide to an understanding of the problems of the police.

Since it is the primary duty of the police to enforce laws that restrict behavior and the very nature of their work leads to both private and public resentment:

> Really favorable conditions will never be provided so long as misuse of police authority continues to bulk large in the public mind. Notwithstanding the rapid extension of a policy of moderation in the exercise of law enforcement powers, the tide of general opinion still runs strongly against the police. The reasons for this condition are easily identified. Universal use of the automobile invites an increasing volume of restrictions upon the motoring public, and the old easy division of the community into law breakers and law observers is thereby destroyed. Today, all are law breakers, and a large and important minority are deliberate offenders.[6]

Therefore, the frequency of police contact with the whole population (usually through the mass media) has thrown enforcement of the law into sharp collision with general standards, to which neither police nor public has reacted well. The public has—because of occasional "lawless" enforcement of the law (police abuse of constitutional rights)—become cynical about its own police officers and its legal system. This, in turn, has resulted in an almost universal phenomenon: peace officers have isolated themselves from the community they serve and have banded together in condemning anyone who levels criticism at them. Because of the policeman's possible aloofness and egotistical and arbitrary demeanor, each "collision" results, on the one hand, in a swelling of his authority complex and, on the other hand, in a *new* birth of antagonism in some large (or "minority group") groups.

There is a strong belief (a belief somewhat dispelled by Albert

---

[5] K. Davies, "Police, Law and the Individual," *Annals of The American Academy of Political and Social Science,* 1954, p. 145.

[6] B. Smith, *Police Systems in the United States* (New York: Harper & Row, Publishers, 1949), p. 10.

J. Reiss, Jr.'s study "Police Brutality—Answers to Key Questions")[7] among many members of nonwhite minority groups that they get rougher treatment at the hands of the police than whites do. A 1961 report by the U.S. Civil Rights Commission declared that although "most police officers never resort to brutal practices," the victims of police abuse, when it does occur, are almost always those "whose economic and social status afford little or no protective armor—the poor and racial minorities."

Police spokesmen have protested angrily against the charges of brutality raised against them. Quinn Tamm, executive director of the International Association of Chiefs of Police, declared that he knew of "no period in recent history when the police have been the subject of so many unjustified charges of brutality, harassment, and ineptness." Tamm contended, "Never, have we been signaled out so mercilessly and so wrongfully as the whipping boys by demonstrators for so-called sociological evolution and by out-and-out hoodlums who have abandoned the banner of civil rights to engage in senseless insurrection."

Yet, many believe that all the denials and explanations in the world will not dispel the deeply seated suspicion that police sometimes practice a double standard in dealing with minorities. Press reports of police dispersals and arrests of civil rights demonstrators—particularly but by no means exclusively in the South—are said to have reinforced in many people a view of the policeman as the defender of the in-group and the oppressor of protesting minorities. Many civil rights leaders remain unconvinced, to put it mildly, that policemen always act in strict "line-of-duty" terms in racial cases. As a result, hostility toward the police has become an increasing problem in neighborhoods having large minority populations.

But the problem involves more than minority group relations. There is increasing evidence that Americans of all races, creeds, and income groups share in present-day reservations about their town's police. Some of these are for the "obvious" reasons which have always plagued the police: the fact that most people tend to come in direct contact with them only under rather unhappy circumstances—when they have parked the car "just a little bit illegally," when caught while driving faster than the posted speed limit, or when they were involved in some "innocent" horseplay that misfired. Coupled with this is the old adage: "When you happen to need a policeman, there's never one within miles." Either way, the police image comes out scarred.

According to a noted author, H. H. Toch,[8] it is the broader connotations of police actions rather than their direct impact that may promote most of the antagonism on the part of society. Although these connotations probably can be ameliorated through stronger emphasis on

[7] Albert J. Reiss, Jr., "Police Brutality—Answers to Key Questions," *Trans-Action* (July-August 1968).

[8] H. H. Toch, "Psychological Consequences of the Police Role," *Police*, Vol. 10, No. 1 (September-October 1965), 22.

police courtesy and public relations, they can hardly be completely eradicated. Ultimately, the social and psychological control role of law enforcement is relegated to one in which there is essentially one-way communication against a backdrop of latent power.[9]

If limited to this type of contact, the police role as a controlling agent within the community will be damaged. Furthermore, according to Toch, such one-way contact ultimately will prove psychologically harmful to the police as well as to the public. The policeman exaggerates the prevalence of apathy and projects hostility even where there is none. He interprets public antagonism as an indication of his inevitable separation from the "mainstream" of the community.[10]

The violence that scarred the Democratic Convention is an excellent example of a complete lack of communication between the two most antagonistic social groups in the country—police and youthful demonstrators. Such a "collision" in conditions of high tension and publicity as reported by *Life* and in D. Walker's *Rights in Conflict* further aggravated divisions across the country.

"The whole world is watching," screamed the demonstrators as the Chicago police moved in, and they were right. The four violent days of the Democratic Convention in August must go on record as the most widely observed—though far from the bloodiest—riot in history. In the great law and order debate it has become a symbol and a cause, used to defend police and to attack them, to decry protest, and to sympathize

Figure 4.3 Confrontation: *Police enforcing the right of students to attend classes at San Francisco State College. Photo courtesy of the San Francisco Police Department, San Francisco, California.*

[9] E. Eldefonso, A. Coffey, and R. C. Grace, *Principles of Law Enforcement* (New York: John Wiley & Sons, Inc., 1968), p. 14.

[10] *Ibid.*

with protestors' injuries. Yet, for all the emotional—press and T.V.—attention the rioting received, nobody knows much more about what really happened.[11]

The confrontation and violent by-products can be attributed to an antagonism between the rising middle class of upper-income whites and the archaic middle class of lower-income whites. The young people who protested are typical products of the rising middle class. They are educated and without major economic worries. They are full of confidence and high aspirations, particularly for the achievement of peace and equality for the Negro. But they have no sympathy for whites who do not have their educational and economic advantages. They express their contempt by demonstrations, by words, by dress, and by their central political tactic. That tactic is "play the game my way or else there will be trouble."

THE POLICE

The police who controlled the demonstrators are typical expressions of the middle class or more commonly the conservative. The policeman, according to a Berkeley criminologist, Gordon Misner, "pictures himself as the crime fighter standing alone against the Mongol hordes, without the support of the public, the politicians or the courts. You don't often find a liberal in policing."[12]

In many respects, law enforcement officers represent the most typical beliefs and attitudes of their communities, including what former Los Angeles Chief of Police, Thomas Reddin deplores as a moralistic tendency to see things in terms of either/or.

Not surprisingly, police tend to be appalled by abnormal behavior and rebellions against authority. Most scorn long hair, and homosexuality horrifies them. With their ingrain respect for work, they take a dim view of people living on welfare. Perhaps the most irritating to cops are the antiwar protestors, most of them collegians who have rejected advantages that policemen themselves lacked and toil to give their own children....[13]

"The police consider the beatniks spoiled darlings of society," says Berkeley economist Margaret Gordon, who serves on the City Council. "Their rage and frustration can break out uncontrollably even in the historically well-disciplined and polite Berkeley Police Department."[14]

The are engaged in traditional occupations, which are being loaded down with new requirements because of the changes brought on by the Negro colonization of the central cities. The October, 1968, issue of *Time* truly captures the problem:[15]

---

[11] "Corruption Behind the Swinging Clubs," *Life*, Vol. 65, No. 23 (December 6, 1968), p. 35.

[12] Time Essay, " The Police Need Help," *Time*, (October 4, 1968), p. 26.

[13] *Ibid.*

[14] *Ibid.*

[15] *Ibid.*

Nothing is tougher than being a policeman in a free society. For one thing, the U.S. Constitution guarantees as much individual liberty as public safety will allow. To uphold that elusive ideal, the policeman is supposed to mediate family disputes that would tax a Supreme Court Justice, soothe angry ghetto Negroes despite his scant knowledge of psychology, enforce hundreds of petty laws without discrimination, and use only necessary force to bring violators before the courts. The job demands extraordinary skill, restraint and character—qualities not usually understood by either cop-hating leftists who sound as if they want to exterminate all policemen, or by dissent-hating conservatives who seem to want policemen to run the U.S. in a paroxysm of punitive "law and order."

The U.S. policeman is forbidden to act as judge and jury—for that way lies the police state. Yet, he also has enormous discretion to keep the peace by enforcing some laws and overlooking others. How does he exercise that discretion? Largely on the basis of common sense and common mores, plus his own private attitudes. Unfortunately, he faces an era of drastically changing mores that challenges his most cherished creeds and conceptions. . . .

The "Time Essay" continues by stating that the American public is confused as to their expectations of the role of law enforcement officers in the United States.

We ask our officers to be a combination of Bat Masterson, Sherlock Holmes, Sigmund Freud, King Solomon, Hercules and Diogenes," says Rocky Pomerance, Miami Beach Police Chief. Indeed, the U.S. often seems lucky to have any cops at all. Plato envisioned the policeman's lofty forebear as the "guardian" of law and order and placed near the very top of his ideal society, endowing him with special wisdom, strength and patience. The U.S. has put its guardians near the bottom. In most places, the pay for an experienced policeman is less than $7,000 a year, forcing many cops to moonlight and some to take bribes. Fear and loneliness are routine hazards.

The "Time Essay" concludes its analysis of the basic police problem by commenting that "the average cop feels that he is unappreciated or even actively disliked by the public he serves. Very often, he is right—and thus, all the more prone to confine his entire social, as well as professional, life to his fellow cops, a group that all too often see the world as *we* and *they*."

Image:
Police and Demonstrators

Because of a rapidly changing American society, police are constantly on the defensive. They are unable to adequately communicate with the Negro or members of other minority groups. And it is not unusual for police officers to return the contempt felt by militants.

Under these circumstances, it was inevitable that any naked confrontation between police and militant young protestors would be violent.

In one confrontation during the Chicago Democratic Convention, the demonstrators were shouting at the police, "Pigs, pigs, pigs." And some of the police were shouting back, "Kill, kill, kill."

It is contended[16] that overreaction on the part of some policemen, although provoked, may indirectly (and often, in the cases of countless "race" riots, directly) serve not to control, but to exacerbate what is already an explosive situation.[17]

> Where police react to groups of people, and not to the problem of crime, this will inevitably happen. The ghetto inhabitant's resistance to being forced to see himself through the eyes of a white policeman is an attempt to salvage some sense of dignity in his imposed restricted world—to reject rejectors. Police disposition to react violently on sensing danger, plus the subject's recalcitrance, express an overwhelming potentiality for danger.[18]

Understanding Provocator's Tactics

In order to promote or maintain good police image, it is of paramount importance that police officers thoroughly understand the community which they seek to serve. As this chapter and other chapters unfold, it is hoped that such understanding will develop. Because of the increase in campus and other types of unrest and demonstrations, it appears appropriate, as well as important, for police officers to understand the manipulative abilities of the small minority that once again (Chicago) was able to manipulate a situation for ends totally at odds with the concepts of justice, order, and free expression of views. A handful of professional agitators was able to *weaken public support* not only for the all-important rights of assembly and protest but for their *local law enforcement agencies as well.*

Will those who inadvertently cooperated with the extremists in Chicago in further polarizing national opinion learn from this experience? Or will the next carefully staged act in the politics of confrontation again yield a victory for the proponents of division and discord? The answer cannot, of course, be predicted. But the grim alternatives to drawing the right conclusions from the Chicago tragedy can.

It is important, first of all, that law enforcement officials, in Chicago and throughout the nation, understand the tactics used by radical provocators so that responses to future confrontations can be mastered.

[16] For a candid and provocative analysis of police reaction to large groups see : D. J. Dodd, "Police Mentality and Behavior," *Issues in Criminology*, Vol. 3, No. 1 (Summer 1967), pp. 47-67, School of Criminology, University of California, Berkeley, Also see E. Hopkins, *Our Lawless Police* (New York : The Viking Press, Inc., 1963), and W. Westley, "Violence and the Police," *American Journal of Sociology*, Vol. 59, No. 34 (1953).

[17] *Ibid.*, p. 59

[18] *Ibid.*

It was no secret that organized troublemakers intended to try their disruptive techniques in Chicago. Many of these persons were known to the police, and authorities had ample time to prepare plans for the anticipated eruptions. But although the police were ready in numbers, they were not prepared by adequate training or psychologically geared to control the challenge they faced. To be sure, the vicious amount of physical and verbal abuse inflicted upon the police—152 of whom were injured—may, perhaps, explain the breakdown in discipline. But this explanation cannot be used to justify what followed. Sworn to uphold the law, *some* police joined in breaking the law in an explosion of anger and frustration.[19]

The results were precisely what the radical agitators sought. The police *appeared*, in the streets of Chicago and on the television screens around the world, as a repressive, brutal force bent on denying a constitutionally sanctioned group its right to assemble and protest. The most visible symbol of governmental authority was made to look like armed rabble. As a consequence, respect for peace officers and orderly processes was further eroded. This is just what the anarchists and "others" who were responsible for the demonstration wanted. Their main tactics are to foment incidents which would lead to disrespect and distrust of the law through contempt for the law's instruments—the police.

If they are *not* to continue this inadvertent cooperation with those who intend the nation no good, police must learn to be tolerant ("keep their cool") even in the face of intense provocation. *Police must: (1) use techniques that will maintain order by means of legitimate controls; (2) uphold the law by steadfastly using the law; and (3) be able to isolate and arrest those guilty of illegal acts without indiscriminate attacks upon the innocent.* And similarly, local officials should be prepared to display flexibility and good sense in dealing with demonstrations.

Some Factors Inherent in a Riot Situation That Affect Police Conduct

Still more relevant to understanding police conduct under stressful and frustrating situations—conduct at times resulting in complaints by citizens—is this excerpt from a report from the office of the City

---

[19] "Corruption Behind the Swinging Clubs," *Life,* pp. 35-38; see also, *Rights in Conflict,* a report (Submitted) to the National Commisson on the Causes and Prevention of Violence. (New York: Bantam Books 1968). This study, coordinated by D. Walker, took 53 days to complete. With a staff of 212, 12,000 still photographs as well as 180 hours of film were reviewed. The FBI assisted Walker's staff in interviewing 3,437 witnesses and participants—20,000 pages of testimony was amassed (*Life,* December 6, 1968).

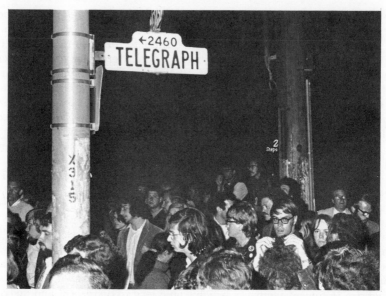

Figure 4.4 *The magnitude of unrest in our society is being expressed by violent outbreaks on many campuses. The Telegraph Avenue Demonstrations of August, 1968 serve as a particular example.*

Manager of Berkeley, California, William C. Hanley. The report was directed to the mayor and the members of the City Council of Berkeley following The Telegraph Avenue Demonstrations of June 28 through July 3, 1968. Mr. Hanley offered rather candid general observations on some factors inherent in a riot situation that affect police conduct:

> A municipal police department is organized essentially to deal with single incidents. It is staffed by men experienced largely in "one-to-one" relationships. It is not an army, and is not normally employed in massive actions. In Berkeley, there are usually no more than 25 or 30 officers on duty at any given time, and they are deployed as individuals. Despite training in group actions, and occasional brief experience in such police functions, the preponderance of a municipal peace officer's experience consists of single and non-violent actions. In a riot situation, the equivalent of squads and platoons are formed, and the chain of command takes on characteristics to which officers are not accustomed.

> For instance, under normal conditions, one sergeant may supervise as many as ten or twelve officers, and only by "remote control," that is, by radio. When a small police department is placed under riot conditions, there are not enough sergeants, or officers with supervisory experience, to accompany each squad or detail and maintain an effective level of command supervision.

> On the other hand, a riot situation is not analogous to a conventional military operation in that it is extremely difficult to distinguish between participants and observers; the opposition doesn't wear uniforms or arm

bands. A great number of the complaints received about Berkeley's recent disturbances came from individuals who stated they were "just watching" or "came to see what was going on." However, most of them knew that violence was erupting or that a curfew had been declared. While many could be considered innocent victims of the circumstances of their proximity to the violence, many others consciously chose to enter or remain in an area of danger.

The police officer charged with clearing the streets to restore order is not asked to sort the violent from the non-violent; he is directed to clear the streets. For this reason, every effort must be made to warn all persons in the area to be cleared. In this instance, a full hour of announcements and requests by the police preceded any use of tear gas or physical contact with the crowd on Friday evening. On succeeding evenings, only a miniscule fraction of the population could legitimately claim to be unaware of the conditions that existed in Berkeley. I am unable to offer any simple solution to the problem of possible inconvenience or injury to "innocent bystanders," except reasonable restraint and patience on the part of law enforcement personnel, and reasonable discretion and cooperation on the part of citizens.

Unfortunately, two factors were evident in these disturbances, which probably tended to increase the unnecessary involvement of innocent residents. First, as the days and nights wore on, our officers became physically and emotionally fatigued to an extreme degree. Second, the disturbing growth of an attitude of non-cooperation and hostility toward authority, particularly prevalent in the South Campus area but recognized as a nationwide trend, has diminished the level of mutual respects and cooperation between officer and citizen. With all the recent public discourse on this factor, it may seem redundant to discuss it, but it cannot be brushed away with platitudes. A general demand for law enforcement officers to uniformly behave as saints cannot be fulfilled within a milieu of mounting antagonism and distrust. No human being can achieve and maintain perfection in his dealings with other humans if he is regularly subjected to taunts, epithets, derision and physical abuse.

Another significant factor affecting police conduct, as the conflict continued, was the increasingly lethal character of the weaponry evidenced in the riot area—fire bombs, guns, Molotov cocktails, dynamite and other explosives—coupled with an all too apparent willingness to use them. Inevitably, an officer's attitude is affected as it becomes more and more manifest that any encounter may entail extreme physical risk. From this vantage point, the attributes of cordiality, sensitivity and patience tend to become luxuries that are difficult to maintain, particularly when there is neither the possibility nor the time to distinguish between the passerby and the ill-intentioned.

Finally, it must be borne in mind that there is a vast difference in perception of the situation between the individual who is involved in one incident and the law enforcement personnel who are aware of the total mosaic of which that incident is a tiny piece. From the widely divergent perceptions of the setting in which the incident occurs, there frequently flow two completely unrelated expectations of the behavior pattern that should follow. The result may then be an adverse encounter that would never have developed if both had started from the same perceptual base. Having said all this, however, I want to emphatically assert that none of it has been presented as justification for any act of unnecessary force or other improper conduct on the part of any law enforcement officer.

These comments are solely in the hope that they may contribute to some increased understanding of the inevitable human frailties that emerge under protracted and intolerable stress.

There is no question in our minds that individual acts of unnecessary force or other improper conduct did occur. We have and are still diligently investigating every one of the 85 complaints that we have received, and we will conduct our inquiry to a conclusion on each of them. The only limitation on that effort will be inaccessibility to the facts essential to an informed judgment. At the conclusion of each investigation a judgment will be reached on the basis of all the facts and any appropriate administrative action will be taken. In addition, we are reviewing all of the complaints to obtain any insights that we can toward improvements in training, procedures, departmental policies and tactics. Some areas of this concern are set out in the next section.

GENERAL COMMENTS AND RECOMMENDATIONS:

A number of problems, deficiencies and areas of concern were revealed by our review of the events of June 28 to July 3, 1968. Some of them have been alluded to or discussed in some more detail earlier; some have not. Some developed from a post-mortem of our plans, procedures, tactics and actions; some from review and consideration of complaints. Some have yielded obvious courses of improvement to be followed; others are not susceptible of easy solution. In any event, I would like to comment on them briefly:

1. *It is clear that one of our over-riding needs in circumstances of civil disorder is for a substantial additional number of supervisory personnel in the field to provide continuity of direction and command.* This is essential to secure the uniform implementation of overall tactical decisions and to insure continuing adherence to basic departmental policies even under conditions of intense stress. There is, unfortunately, no easy answer to this need, short of a substantial increase in personnel and several years of training and experience. We are studying intensified training of our officers and will seek other methods of increasing supervisory experience.

2. As I indicated earlier, in a small department like Berkeley's, sheer *fatigue is a major problem* when mass confrontations occur over a sustained period of days. Here again, apart from a massive increase in manpower (and, by massive, I mean at least doubling the size of the force) there are no easy solutions. An even heavier and earlier reliance on mutual aid from other agencies appears to offer the only alternative, and this presumes the capacity and willingness of surrounding agencies to supply it.

3. These events revealed again the *deficiencies* of the Department's individual portable radio transceivers for which we have already initiated replacement. *There were occasions when communication with units on foot was impossible and effective coordination and control suffered as a result.* This will be corrected shortly.

4. A number of complaints concerned the difficulty of *identifying* individual officers and we are arranging to have distinctive highly visible numerals afflxed to helmets to correct this problem. In addition, although not directly related to this concern we will secure

uniform nameplates for more personal identification under normal conditions.

5. From a tactical standpoint, we believe that we should have shifted earlier from a dispersal technique to an *arrest deployment.* To do so, however, requires a significant increase in manpower on the streets plus a massive gearing up of related agencies including the courts, the district attorney's office, the County jails and prisoner transportation vehicles. We had hoped the first two nights to resolve the conflict without mass arrests. It proved impossible to do so.

6. There has been some criticism of the number of officers used. At no time were there more than 350 law enforcement personnel deployed in the city and that number was reached only on Sunday evening. During the height of the violence on Saturday, there were no more than 270 men on duty. Rather than too many, it is our judgment that *too few* officers were employed, considering the range and duration of the disorder.

7. A City Staff Committee, under the leadership of the Director of Social Planning, has initiated a series of *meetings with representatives* of students, merchants, "street people," ministers and University to explore the wide variety of problems, interests and concerns of the Telegraph Avenue area. They are discussing physical improvements of the street including the Mayor's plaza proposal and others, the drug problem, the mounting crime and violence, and a wide variety of other matters. It is a beginning. We are confident that practicable proposals for constructive programs to serve the area will be flowing out of those meetings in the near future.

8. One final, fundamental observation needs to be made. The Berkeley Police Department is designed and developed as a professional organization with skill, training, knowledge and capacity in the highly complex fields of crime prevention, crime detection and law enforcement. In all these respects, it has a richly deserved nationwide reputation for excellence. *It is not an army designed to deal with mass confrontation and riot.*
   Disregarding all other factors, the basic and inescapable limitation is that the department simply is not big enough to function this way. *New York City* experience has shown that the most peaceful and effective results in these situations are obtained when the number of demonstrators is matched by the number of officers. If the crowd numbers 500, then 500 officers are dispatched to insure civil peace and orderly conduct; if there are 2,000 demonstrators, 2,000 officers are used. But *New York City has 30,000 police officers, while the size and scope of the demonstrations there do not differ markedly from those we face in Berkeley.* If the responsibility for preserving the peace of the community in this kind of situation is to be repeatedly thrust upon small, individual departments in the Bay Area like Berkeley, the only real answer may be a regional law enforcement agency. I hope not.

9. Despite the amazingly few serious injuries and the relatively small number of complaints about specific actions, when considered in the context of literally tens of thousands of contacts between officers and citizens, the general and widespread charges of brutality deserve

comment. Police deployment during these disorders was not intended nor organized to be punitive. Incidents of unnecessary force and improper conduct were *individual errors* in judgment, not part of any command decision. To the extent that increased training and provision for better supervision may reduce such individual cases of poor discretion, those efforts will be made.

10. Let there be no misunderstanding about one central point. *This whole, contrived affair had nothing to do with the constitutional guarantees of free speech and public assembly.* No community anywhere provides more opportunities and facilities for freedom of speech and the right to peaceably assemble than does the city of Berkeley, and no city government more fully supports the free exercise of those fundamental rights. Sproul Plaza and Civic Center, or "Provo" park are internationally known as the "Hyde Parks" of the San Francisco Bay Region. There are many other University, School District and city facilities that are easily accessible and regularly used with no limitation on the content of the meeting. City owned areas in the immediate campus vicinity, like the Sather Gate and Durant parking lots, are available and have been used by groups like the Port Chicago Vigil for rallies and public discussion. The difference is that these groups were sincerely interested in the subject and purpose of their rallies and not in contriving the elements of the riot. We continue to give unqualified support of the ready availability of public facilities for the exercise of free speech, regardless of content. We do not believe that it is an essential element of free speech that it be exercised in the middle of Telegraph Avenue, University Avenue or the on-ramp to the Bay Bridge.[20]

Although City Manager Hanley's report to the mayor and the City Council deals primarily with an "incident" in Berkeley, California, it seems reasonable to assume that police conduct, as well as that of *some* citizens in other communities, under *similar circumstances*, would be identical with that of the Berkeley Police Department. Because Hanley's observations and recommendations would be applicable to most law enforcement agencies, his analysis should thoroughly be reviewed.

Complaints of Harassment and Brutality As They Affect the Police Image

As previously indicated, professionalization has not resolved the problem of police personnel's sensitivity to public criticism. Identification with fellow officers is reinforced, *"forging a social bond among them, at the same time it generates a great deal of mutual suspicion."*[21]

---

[20] Italics are supplied by the authors of this text.
[21] Dodd, "Police Mentality," pp. 56-57.

The fact that the policeman, owing to fear of physical injury (statistics indicate that there is a definite increase in assaults against policemen), must constantly be "on his guard" may tend to contribute to the policeman's isolation and view of his community—a view which is seeing

> everything taking place around him as a configuration of events designed to attack him. His natural reaction is to strike first. This idea of the *symbolic assailent* illustrates one of the two principal variables which make up the working personality of a police officer—reaction to danger. The other is his reaction to authority.... His natural suspicion, plus his conception of his work as a way of life, reinforce the tendencies previously noted, and draw him further away from the public he intends to serve and protect."
>
> ... This is especially so in the lower class areas, where the cop is seen as standing for the interests and prejudices of dominant (white) society in the role of the oppressor, and where each party sees the other as a misfit.[22]

Since a community's attitude toward the police is influenced by the actions of individual officers on the streets, courteous and tolerant

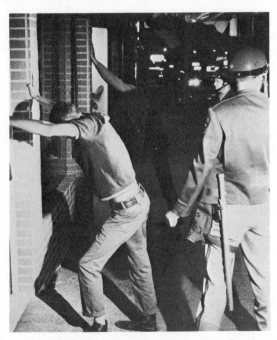

Figure 4.5 *Although "shakedowns" (under certain situations) are a necessary part of police activity, a courteous demeanor—a professional approach to the task—is mandatory. Photo courtesy of the Berkeley Police Department, Berkeley, California.*

[22] Dodd, "Police Mentality"

behavior by policemen in their contacts with citizens is a must. According to a report by the President's Commission on Law Enforcement and Administration of Justice,[23] there have been instances of unambiguous *harassment and physical abuse.* Nelson A. Watson, project supervisor of the Research and Development Division, International Association of Chiefs of Police, gave the following report at a police administrators' conference regarding police action:[24]

> So far as police *action* is concerned, there are things that come to my attention on that, too. I hear of the incidents from police and from civil rights workers. I read about them in the press, in magazines, and books. I cannot vouch for the accuracy of these reports because we all know how easily things can get distorted and misintepreted. But accurate or not, it is vitally important that we all remember that people form opinions and take action on the basis of what they hear and what they believe without checking its accuracy. Things like the following illustrate what people are saying, what they believe, and what is back of the way they behave:
>
> *Case No. 1*
> "The cops pulled us over and came up to the car with guns in their hands. This one cop (incidentally, the officer was a Negro) told me to show him my license and registration. When I asked him why, he told me to do as I was told and not get smart. Then they made us all get out of the car while the other guy looked inside. When they couldn't find anything wrong, they told us we could go. I asked them what it was all about, and the one cop said they had a lot of stolen cars around there lately so they had to check up."
>
> *Case No. 2*
> A newspaper reported that a man had complained about the actions of an officer which he felt were uncalled for. It was reported the officer had arrested a man and had handcuffed him. For some reason, the man fell to the ground and the complainant said the officer then put his foot on the man's neck. The complainant said the arrested man was not fighting the officer and, after all, he was handcuffed. He cited this as an example of police brutality.
>
> *Case No. 3*
> An officer patrolling a beach where kids had caused trouble approached a teen-aged boy who was sitting by himself on a bench drinking from a bottle. Drinking liquor by minors was forbidden by law. The officer asked the boy what he was drinking and the boy replied that it was Coke. The officer took the bottle and smelled the contents. Finding that it contained no liquor so that he had no basis for arrest, the officer poured the remainder of the drink onto the sand and ordered the boy to move along.
>
> *Case No. 4*
> A man reported a fight in progress and said some shots had been fired. He later complained that it took the police nearly an hour to respond and

---

[23] President's Commission on Law Enforcement and Administration of Justice, *The Challenge of Crime in a Free Society* (Washington: D. C.; Government Printing Office, 1967), p. 102.

[24] N. A. Watson, "The Fringes of Police-Community Relations." Paper read at Police Administrators Conference, June 29, 1966, at Indiana University. (Mimeographed).

charged that the same report from a white neighborhood would have brought them on the double.

Case No. 5
A Negro who witnessed a robbery was asked by two officers to come with them to see whether he could identify a suspect who was working in a gas station. The place was miles away across town. When they got there, the suspect had left. The officers put the witness out of the car saying they were too busy to take him back home.

Case No. 6
A Negro was observed walking in a white neighborhood one evening about 10:00 o'clock. Two officers stopped and asked him to explain his presence there. He told them it was none of their business, that he had a right to walk on any street any time he felt like it. He refused to answer questions so they took him to headquarters for further interrogation. It turned out he was a minister who was very active in the civil rights movement. He had no criminal record and had done nothing to sustain any charge in this instance. He complained that the officer's action was indicative of the attitude of police toward all Negroes.

Case No. 7
With respect to the Puerto Rican disturbances in Chicago recently, the *Christian Science Monitor* reported as follows: "There was little doubt that the presence of police—and their handling of Puerto Ricans over a period of several years—was the center of the controversy in this conflict. We heard no other argument or issue in the seven hours we worked the streets.... Despite careful guidelines, police tactics were not uniformly discreet. One instance took place before we began breaking up the congestion at Division and California. Most of the young men had gone, and we had been thanked by the sergeant on the corner. Suddenly a police captain with a dozen blue-helmeted men stormed across the street. I was standing inside a restaurant at the time because the street was virtually clear. The captain and three men pushed into the restaurant where more than 50 people, in family groups, were quietly eating their evening meal. In a loud voice, he demanded to see the owner. Moving to the kitchen, he demanded that she clear the place and close up. Then he stalked out, shaking his fist and shouting: "I'll give you 15 minutes to get everybody out of here, you understand. Fifteen minutes." Then he slammed the door with such force the storefront windows rattled. In less than a minute, he had changed quietness into anger.... A spokesman for the police department said it was only one of several complaints about the same captain. At 10:50 P.M., only a handful of people were left on the street. A lieutenant and a group of policemen raced to the upper floor of a three-story building on Division Street and hauled out two men who someone said had been seen with crude anti-police signs in a window. Then the police closed a restaurant below where there were a number of young Puerto Ricans. Those in the restaurant scattered as ordered. But two youths, walking slowly a block away were spotted by a sergeant who cursed them, saying to the lieutenant: "Those guys were in the restaurant. Let's go get them." At this point, the only incident of undue physical roughness I observed during the entire night took place. Two police searched one of the youths, and then gave him a hard shove that sent him sprawling toward the police wagon. The lieutenant and sergeant stood on the curb discussing what they could charge the two youths with since they had only been walking down the street...."

Watson concluded this portion of his address to the conference by stating:

Now, as I said, I cannot vouch for the accuracy of these reports. I suspect there is a considerable bias in them. I also realize that when they are shaved down in the retelling, there may be significant facts omitted. *But the point is that these are the kinds of things people hear and it is on the basis of such stories they form their opinions about police.* Then, when approached by an officer they expect rough, inconsiderate, impolite treatment.

I know and so do you that it sometimes takes pretty strong talk and forceful action to get the police job done. However, I am sure we can agree that an officer who uses profanity is definitely out of line. So is one who is so prejudiced that he cannot treat the objects of his prejudice as ordinary human beings. An officer who generates resentment, who makes people rise up in anger by the things he says or does or the way he acts toward them is a source of trouble. An officer who would stand by and watch someone being beaten is violating his oath. One of the things that we must attend to in our effort to improve relations with the people in our communities, therefore, is the way our officers are doing their job on the street day in and day out. This is not to say that *all* the fault lies in police behavior, but, to the extent that *any* of the fault lies there, we must accept the blame and correct it.

The President's Commission observed that physical abuse is only one source of aggravation in the ghetto. In nearly every city surveyed, the commission heard complaints of harassment of interracial couples, dispersal of social street gatherings, and stopping Negroes on foot or in cars without an objective basis. These, together with contemptuous and degrading verbal abuse, have great impact in the ghetto—impact in the area of attitudes toward law enforcement personnel. (The psychology and significance of attitudes will be discussed in Chapter 8.) Such conduct, relates the commission, strips the Negro of the one thing he may have left—his dignity, "the question of being a man."

Harassment or discourtesy, according to the President's commission, may not be the result of *malicious or discriminatory intent* of police officers. Many officers simply fail to understand the effects of their actions because of their limited knowledge of the Negro community. Calling a Negro teen-ager by his first name may cause resentment because many whites still refuse to extend to adult Negroes the courtesy of the title "Mister." A patrolman may take the arm of a person he is leading to the police car. Negroes are more likely to resent this than whites because the action implies that they are on the verge of flight and may degrade them in the eyes of friends or onlookers.[25]

Commission observers *also* have found that most officers handle their rigorous work with considerable coolness. They have found that there is *no* pronounced racial pattern in the kind of behavior just described. Because this topic will be discussed in Chapter 8, suffice it to say that the most discernible tendency is for officers, white and black,

---

[25] President's Commission on Law Enforcement and Administration of Justice, Challenge of Crime, p. 102.

to treat "blue-collar" citizens, *regardless* of race, in such a fashion. However, all such behavior is obviously and totally reprehensible, and when it is directed against minority-group citizens, it is particularly likely to lead to bitterness in the community. The fact that provocation and physical danger do exist does not excuse an intolerant demeanor on the part of police officers.[26] As O. W. Wilson, recently retired Chicago police superintendent and distinguished author of numerous law enforcement textbooks, once stated in his text, *Police Administration*:

> The officer must remember that there is no law against making a policeman angry and he cannot charge a man with offending him. Until the citizen acts overtly in violation of the law, he should take no action against him, least of all lower himself to the level of the citizen by berating and demeaning him in a loud and angry voice. The officer who withstands angry verbal assaults builds his own character and raises the standards of the department.[27]

These views are accepted by all responsible police officials. Although all departments have written regulations setting standards of decorous behavior by its members, in many departments the regulations are too generalized.[28] Where "standards" are violated, there should be a thorough investigation of complaints and prompt, visible disciplinary action where justified.

A Survey of Public Attitudes Toward the Police

Of course, to say that there is much distrust of the police among members of minority groups is not to say that all members of minority groups distrust the police or to imply that only members of minority groups do so.

A National Opinion Research poll showed that on the question of police conduct, 63 percent of the whites polled said they believe the police are "almost all honest" while 1 percent said the police are "almost all corrupt." Comparable figures among nonwhites were 30 percent and 10 percent. The difference of opinion by race reflects, in part, the complexities of race relations in the United States.[29]

Nationwide Gallop polls indicate that *35 percent* of Negro men be-

---

26 *Ibid.*

27 O. W. Wilson, *Police Administration.* (New York: McGraw-Hill Book Company, 1963)

28 President's Commission on Law Enforcement and Administration of Justice, *Challenge of Crime.*

29 "Crime and Lawlessness—Who's to Blame, the Police or the Public?" *Senior Scholastic,* Vol. 92, No. 3, (February 15, 1968).

lieve there was police brutality in their areas, *7 percent* of whites thought so. A University of California at Los Angeles study of the Watts area found that *79 percent* of the Negro males believed police lack respect for Negroes or use insulting language to them and *74 percent* believed police use unnecessary force in making arrests. In 1967, an Urban League study in Detroit found 82 percent of the Negro population believed there was some form of police brutality.[30]

Police misconduct—whether described as brutality, harassment, verbal abuse, or discourtesy—cannot be tolerated even if it is infrequent. It contributes directly to the rash of civil disorders. Besides demeaning respect for law enforcement as a profession, it is inconsistent with the basic responsibility and function of a police force in a democracy. Police departments have rules prohibiting such misconduct and these rules should be objectively and vigorously enforced. Police commanders must be aware of what takes place in the field and use firm methods to correct abuses.

Police:
Symbol of Social Problems

As Deputy Inspector Joseph Fink, commanding officer of the Ninth Precinct of the New York City Police Department, pointed out in a recent article,[31] the police are encountering strong resistance in their attempts to rectify deteriorating public support.

Conflict between the police and the residents of the city slums and ghettos—the very neighborhoods that need and want effective policing the most—has, on occasions, broken out into "open warfare." In these areas there is much distrust of the police, especially among boys and young men, among the people the police most often deal with. It is common in those neighborhoods for citizens to fail to report crimes or refuse to cooperate in investigations. Often policemen are sneered at or insulted on the beat. Indeed, everyday police encounters in such neighborhoods can set off riots, as many police departments have learned.

It may be paradoxical that the same people who are most victimized by crime are most hostile to the police, but it is not remarkable. It is not remarkable because the policeman is the *symbol* of middle-class society and values. He generally comes from a middle-class community in the suburbs where he lives a well-regulated life according to middle-class standards of ethics and morality. But he works at law enforcement in an area populated largely by people who are alien to him. He finds

---

[30] *Report of the National Advisory Commission on Civil Disorders* (New York: Bantam Books, Inc., 1968), p. 302.

[31] J. Fink, "Police in a Community—Improving a Deteriorating Image," *Journal of Criminal Law, Criminology, and Police Science,* Vol. 59, No. 4, (December 1968), p. 624.

the language, customs and resentments of Puerto Ricans, Mexicans, Negroes, and other minority groups strange, hostile, and aggravating. There is no doubt that both the people of the community and the police find themselves misunderstood, mistreated, and much maligned. Under such circumstances, it is no wonder that antagonisms develop to such a point that distrust and dissatisfaction on both sides take the place of more logical thinking and conduct.[32]

In a fundamental sense, however, it is wrong to define the problem solely as hostility to police. In many ways, the policeman only symbolizes much deeper problems. Responsibility for apathy or disrespect for law enforcement agencies would be more appropriately attributed to:

> ...a social system that permits inequities and irregularities in law, stimulates proverty and inhibits initiative and motivation of the poor, and relegates low social and economic status to the police while concommitantly giving them more extraneous non-police duties than adequately can be performed.[33]

To a considerable extent, then, the police are the victims of community problems which are not of their making. For generations, minority groups and the poor have not received a fair opportunity to share the benefits of American life. The policeman in the ghetto is the most visible *symbol* of a society from which many ghetto residents (particularly the Negroes) are increasingly alienated.[34]

> At the same time, police responsibilities in the ghetto are greater than elsewhere in the community since the other institutions of social control have so little authority: The schools, because so many are segregated, old and inferior; religion—which has become irrelevant to those who have lost faith as they lost hope; career aspirations, which for many young Negroes are totally lacking; the family, because its bonds are so often snapped. It is the policeman who must deal with the consequences of this institutional vacuum and is then resented for the presence and measures this effort demands.[35]

The policeman, furthermore, has unfortunately become a *symbol* not only of law but of the entire system of law enforcement and criminal justice. As such, he becomes the tangible target for grievances against shortcomings throughout that system: When a suspect is held for long periods in jail prior to trial because he cannot make bail, when he is given inadequate counsel or none at all, when he is assigned counsel that attempts to extract a financial settlement from him or his family even though he is indigent, when he is paraded through the courtroom in a

---

[32] *Ibid.*

[33] Derbyshire, "Social Control Role of the Police," p. 319

[34] President's Commission on Law Enforcement, *Challenge of Crime in a Free Society*, p. 150; see also, The National Advisory Commission on Civil Disorders, p. 157.

[35] *Report of the National Advisory Commission on Civil Disorders* (Washington, D. C.: Goverment Printing Office, 1968), p. 157.

group or is tried in a few minutes, when he is sent to jail because he has no money to pay a fine, when the jail or prison is physically dilapidated or its personnel brutal or incompetent, or when the probation or parole officer has little time to give him, the offender will probably blame, at least in part, the police officers who have arrested him and started the process.[36]

The policeman assigned to the ghetto is a *symbol* of increasingly bitter social debate over law enforcement. The Commission on Civil Disorders noted that one side, disturbed and perplexed by sharp rises in crime and urban violence, exerts extreme pressure on police for tougher law enforcement. Another group, inflamed against police as agents of repression, tends toward defiance of what it regards as order maintained at the expense of injustice.[37]

Because the police are a *symbol* of society's "social ills," it is incumbent upon them to take every possible step to allay grievances that flow from a sense of injustice and increased tension and turmoil.[38]

Eliminating or Reducing Influences Contributing to the Bad Image

Since public attitudes toward the police are mostly the result of personal contacts rather than of a knowledge of police methods, the public is not only ill-informed concerning the caliber of its police generally but it also lacks appreciation of the conditions under which the police must operate. It is therefore of great importance to police departments to spend a considerable amount of time in public relations and the building of a favorable image. However, only in Utopia would every citizen feel respect and friendliness toward the police. A certain amount of resentment on the part of the public is natural, and must be expected. James J. Skehan paints a word picture of the crux of the whole problem :

> A police force gains the respect of the community it serves by carrying out its functions in a spirit of toleration, human kindness, and good will toward all men. This is a difficult task, because people in every community have many standards of morality, and although they are willing to obey some of our laws, they are determined to violate others. Therefore, the policeman is never popular with all classes of persons. He is, of course, looked upon by the vicious and lawless as their natural enemy. He is considered to be an obstructionist by every arrogant and selfish citizen who desires to indulge his own self-seeking whims and inclinations, to the annoyance or the disadvantage of others. He is often and will continue to be used as a footstool by every crack-brained reformer whose ideas are born of emotionalism. And the reputation of the fine,

[36] *Op. cit.*
[37] *Op. cit.*
[38] *Op. cit.*

manly, decent men who comprise the overwhelming majority of police organizations will probably continue to be besmirched by the bad conduct of the comparatively few in police organizations who prove false to the trust placed in them.[39]

Policemen, then must be realistic—they must realize that the people they serve will not universally like or respect them:

Today's policemen are the heirs of that frightful legacy of ill will built up over many years—the man who walks the street bitter at the police may still be harboring a grudge of forty years' standing. The policeman who embittered him then may long ago have gone to his reward, but his successors must suffer the consequences.[40]

Bearing this in mind, the problem becomes one of today creating the most favorable image possible, being the finest law enforcement officers possible.

It is extremely difficult for police organizations to construct codes or rules dictating the specific manner in which all police tasks shall be performed. As Don Kooken, in his book *Ethics in Police Service* pointed out, "the problems of police service are many, and they are subject to the influences of the constant development of public administration. . . ." Furthermore, peace officers are continually deluged with new orders, directives, and advice, much of it conflicting and confusing. "Be firm but fair." . . . "Use caution." . . . "Assert your self and be consistent." . . . "Address everyone as Mister, Miss, or Mrs." . . . "You will be expected to attend community-relations classes."

However, in view of the importance, complexity, and delicacy of police work, it is necessary that police administrators develop and articulate clear policies aimed at guiding and governing the way policemen exercise discretion on the street.

Human Relations and Ethics[41]

It might be said then that the use of the principles of human relations by police should begin with an attempt to eliminate or at least reduce influences contributing to a bad image. Creating and maintaining a good police image, for the majority of the community, requires little more than conscientious adherence to the standard *Law Enforcement Code of Ethics*:

As a Law Enforcement Officer, my fundamental duty is to serve mankind; to safeguard lives and property; to protect the innocent against deception, the weak against oppression or intimidation, and the peaceful

[39] J. J. Skehan, *Modern Police Work* (New York: 1951), Francis M. Basuino, pp. 8–9.
[40] E. Adlow, *Policemen and People* (Boston: 1947), William J. Rockfort, p. 17.
[41] Eldefonso, Coffey, and Grace, *Principles of Law Enforcement*, pp. 165–67.

against violence or disorder; and to respect the Constitutional rights of all men to liberty, equality and justice.

I will keep my private life unsullied as an example to all; maintain courageous calm in the face of danger, scorn, or ridicule; develop self-restraint; and be constantly mindful of the welfare of others. Honest in thought and deed in both my personal and official life, I will be exemplary in obeying the laws of the land and the regulations of my department. Whatever I see or hear of a confidential nature or that is confided to me in my official capacity will be kept ever secret unless revelation is necessary in the performance of my duty.

I will never act officiously or permit personal feelings, prejudices, animosities or friendships to influence my decisions. With no compromise for crime and with relentless prosecution of criminals, I will enforce the law courteously and appropriately without fear or favor, malice or ill will, never employing unnecessary force or violence and never accepting gratuities.

I recognize the badge of my office as a symbol of public faith, and I accept it as a public trust to be held sc long as I am true to the ethics of the police service. I will constantly strive to achieve these objectives and ideals, dedicating myself before God to my chosen profession ... law enforcement.

Personnel selection, training, and supervision geared to maintaining strict adherence to this code usually ensure public respect, because strict adherence eliminates marginal practices such as accepting gratuities for individually selective enforcement methods and related activities that generate disrespect for policemen. And, needless to say, strict adherence to the code eliminates the more obviously corrupt practices as well.

As FBI Director J. Edgar Hoover stated in the January, 1966, *FBI Law Enforcement Bulletin*:

Public trust is built on respect and confidence inspired by outstanding service. In discharging its responsibilities, law enforcement can follow the objectives and ideals of professional police service to avoid a breach of this trust.

But in spite of high ethical standards and conscientious performance of duty by police, certain members of the community often require further persuasion, or "selling," to eliminate a bad police image in their minds.

Obviously, the press continues to retain all of the significance implied in Chapter 7. The question of whether the press creates or reflects the police image cannot be ignored. For the purpose of discussing image in terms of human relations, an unknown degree of influence by the press will be assumed while still other influences are being examined.

In returning to the subject of promoting or "selling" respect for police goals to certain members of the community, once again, some consideration might be given the apparent reasons for this disrespect. It seems reasonable to assume that a person brutally mishandled by one policeman may have difficulty in "seeing" how helpful most policemen really are. This possibility alone should afford a convincing argument for the elimination of force wherever possible. Behavior scientists believe a kind of "selective perception" sets in which causes an unjustly abused individual to look for and "see" only those incidents that "prove" that the police are brutal. Years and years of looking for and seeing such incidents, combined with reassurances from other persons doing the same thing create a bad police image. This area, "rewarding misbelief," is discussed in Chapter 11 and offers a piece of human understanding that is of singular value to law enforcement.

The Development of Guidelines for Police Action

Many police departments have published "general order" or "duty" or "rules, regulations, and procedures" manuals running to several hundred pages.[42] Quite properly, they deal extensively with the personal conduct of officers on and off duty, with uniform and firearms regulations, with the use of departmental property, with court appearances by officers, with the correct techniques of approaching a building in which a burglary may be in progress. They instruct an officer in taking a suspect into custody and transporting him to the station, in dealing with sick or injured persons, in handling stray dogs, in cooperating with the fire department, in towing away abandoned automobiles—with, in short, dozens of situations in which policemen commonly, or uncommonly find themselves. What such manuals almost never discuss are the hard choices policemen must make every day: whether or not to break up a sidewalk gathering, whether or not to intervene in a domestic dispute, whether or not to silence a street-corner speaker, whether or not to stop and frisk, whether or not to arrest. Yet these decisions are the heart of police work. How they are made determines to a large degree the safety of the community, the attitude of the public toward the police, and the substance of court rulings on police procedures.

No doubt there are several reasons for the failure of the police to set forth consistent law enforcement policies. One is that it is an extremely hard thing to do. For example, defining the amount of objectively based suspicion that justifies a "stop," in such a way that the definition will be of some help to a patrolman on his beat, takes much thought and much expertise: However, it is by no means impossible. The *Bulletin of the New York State Combined Council of Law Enforcement Officials* affords the patrolman practical guidance for his actions, including examples, factual variables, and guiding principles. In effect, this carries a

---

[42] President's Commission on Law Enforcement, *Challenge of Crime In a Free Society*, pp. 103–4.

New York "stop and frisk" statutory provision into the street situations in which it is administered, and the administrative guidance supplements the general legislative policy.

Another reason that law enforcement policies are seldom stated is that many of them would turn out to be, if clearly set forth, highly controversial. For example, if the police announced publicly that non-disorderly drunks would be arrested only if they had no home to go to, they might be accused of discriminatory treatment.

Probably the most pervasive reason that the police do not articulate policy formally is that they usually do not realize that they make policy informally every day. The police are not accustomed to thinking of them-selves as employees of an agency that much more often enforces laws administratively than by invoking the formal criminal process through arrest. Yet a decision by a policeman to order a sidewalk gathering to "break it up," or to take a delinquent youth home rather than arrest him. or to "cool off" a drunk in a precinct lockup rather than formally charge him, is an administrative decision. Not only should policemen be guided by departmental policy in the making of such delicate decisions, but the people who will be affected by these decisions—the public—have a right to be apprised in advance, rather than ex post facto, what police policy is.

Police departments should, then, establish policies that outline in detail proper and improper police practices. Such policies should be stressed in *training, reviewed fully with all officers, and publicized* in the community at large.

The Los Angeles County Sheriff's Department's *Manual of Policy and Ethics* is replete with human relations considerations. Each officer receives many hours of instruction from this manual. The regulations are designed to set forth specific responsibilities for each member of the department. Violations can result in oral or written reprimands, suspension or dismissal, depending upon the gravity of the situation.

Excerpts from those regulations most particularly concerned with human relations are as follows:

1222. ... members shall strive to gain public support and win friendly citizen cooperation in the Department programs and procedures in order to facilitate the accomplishment of the Department's objectives. The attitude of each member shall be one of service and courtesy.... In non-restrictive situations, the member should be pleasant and personal....

1435. No member of the Department shall at any time, or for any reason, willfully subject any person ... to cruel treatment or willfully neglect the necessary humane action which the circumstances may require.

1436. He shall not use uncomplimentary terms of speech in referring to any prisoner or another person, or intentionally antagonize any person with whom he comes in contact.

1446. A member of the Department shall give all proper information to persons requesting the same, carefully, courteously, and accurately, avoiding all unnecessary conversation and controversy.

1507. Members shall be respectful, courteous, and civil with the public
... and shall not use coarse, profane, or insolent language toward any
individual.

1512. Members of the Department shall not engage in political or religious discussions to the detriment of good discipline, and shall not speak
disparagingly of the nationality, color, creed, or belief of any person.

68. All ... officers ... shall at all times treat the public with whom they
come in contact with utmost courtesy. Any violation of this rule shall be
punishable by suspension without pay not to exceed ten days.

Improving the Police Image: A Personal Challenge

Each and every peace officer must accept the winning of public
support and respect as a personal challenge. Lip service to this goal is
readily obtained; however, failures to follow through are legion. The
Los Angeles Sheriff's Department[43] and many other law enforcement
agencies consider the factors listed below basic if the police are to establish and maintain acceptance.

Attitude: The attitude of the individual officer is perhaps the primary factor in community relations. The International City Managers'
Association points out, that:

> Action is determined by frames of mind, and the police should scrutinize
> their own point of view to assure that it is a proper one. Their attitude
> will be determined by their concept of the police function—of their duty
> toward the public. They should recognize the line of demarcation between
> the police function and the court function. They should realize that the
> essence of a proper police attitude is a willingness to serve. They should
> distinguish between service and servility, courtesy and softness. They
> must be firm, but at the same time, courteous; they must avoid an
> appearance of rudeness. They should develop a friendly, impersonal and
> unbiased manner, pleasant and personal in all non-restrictive situations
> but firm and impersonal on occasions calling for regulation and control.
> They should understand that the primary police purpose is to prevent
> violations—not to arrest offenders.[44]

By its very nature, police work requires an officer to be suspicious;
this typifies a basic problem in attitude development:

> By nature, training or experience, policemen are *suspicious*. Being sus-
> picious helps to make you a good policeman. But this desirable quality
> can become a *rock in the roadway* to your getting along with people.[45]

---

[43] P. J. Pitchess, *Police Community Relations* (Los Angeles, Calif: Los Angeles County
Sheriff's Department, 1966), pp. 19–22.

[44] International City Managers' Association, *Municipal Police Administration* (Chicago:
International City Managers' Association, 1966), p. 323.

[45] D. Hollingsworth, *Rocks in the Roadway* (Chicago: Stromberg, Allen and Co.,
1954), p. 6.

Traffic: The most frequent personal contact a police agency has with the people is in the field of traffic. Remarks on the explosive and critical nature of this particular problem permeate this and countless other reports. We must bear in mind that police influence the public in proportion to the number of contacts made.

> ... Since the police make more public contacts in controlling traffic than in any other activity, it is especially important that continuous attention be paid to police attitudes in dealing with traffic offenders to increase respect and improve public relations.[46]

W. D. Ladd feels that there are two vital ingredients in a traffic program (or almost any police program) :

> They are Public Information and Organized Public Support. On the latter rests the entire structure of the program. It is the foundation which supports the official action. It gives organized backing to engineering, enforcement, and education. Closely allied with this is Public Information, its most valuable instrument in developing the necessary informed public opinion.[47]

Courtesy: There can be no substitute for police efficiency, in building a sound community relations program. Hand in hand with efficiency, goes courtesy in carrying out each assignment. This is a key factor in face-to-face contacts—police to citizen—whenever practical and possible. One area too frequently overlooked in this regard, is the fact that, "relatively few police contacts involve punitive action." Thus, we have an excellent opportunity for friendly and effective cementing of sound relationships that is often ignored, or just overlooked.

Appearance: Uniform and personal appearance of each officer tells those we serve of the care taken to present the police in the best possible light. Supervisors can materially improve the appearance of their men by holding preduty inspections daily, and seeing to it that the men are presentable and their equipment is in good order. When viewed by the numerous citizens each officer deals with during a tour of duty, an unsewn button or unshaven face can wreak havoc on an entire department.

This is not something which once done can be left alone. As is the case with the other elements dealt with, it requires continuous attention.

The Telephone: Many police authorities contend that the most frequent contacts a law enforcement agency has with the public are through letters and via the telephone. Letters must be courteous and informative. There is usually time to frame a reply that serves both purposes. The telephone, however, offers a dilemma for modern law enforcement:

> The most common form of police discourtesy is encountered in telephone conversations. Indeed public relations gets a jolt from which it is slow

[46] International City Managers' Assoc., *Municipal Police Administration*, p. 27 .

[47] W. D. Ladd, *Organizing for Traffic Safety in Your Community* (Springfield, Ill. : Charles C Thomas, Publisher, 1959), p. 69.

to recover when the telephone rings a number of times before one of our tired voices growls a "Yeah?" at the other end of the line. This kind of reception is a "slap in the face" to the caller who has telephoned concerning what is to him an important matter. We must constantly fight the discourtesy that exists through the use of the telephone.[48]

Summary

Historically, the police have always been used for political and social control, but in the past, they have done their work with almost unanimous support from the middle and upper class. Now this is not so. The children of the rich and the suburban well-to-do make up most of the amorphous cultural entity that is called the New Left. The character of the demonstrators thus goes a long way in explaining the furor over police actions during the Democratic Convention in Chicago.

The very nature of police work leads to both private and public resentment; a certain amount of resentment is natural and must be expected. Policemen, then, must be realistic—they must realize that the people they serve will not universally like or respect them. Bearing this in mind, the problem becomes one of creating the most favorable image possible, being the finest law enforcement officers possible.

In order to promote and maintain a good police image, it is of paramount importance that police officers thoroughly understand the abilities of the small minority who are extremely capable of manipulating a situation for ends totally at odds with the concepts of justice, order, and free expression of views. The police must be tolerant under all conditions—even in the face of intense provocation. Police must: (1) use techniques that will maintain order by means of legitimate controls; (2) uphold the law by steadfastly using the law; and (3) be able to isolate and arrest those guilty of illegal acts without indiscriminate attacks upon the innocent.

Chapter 4 briefly discussed the Telegraph Avenue Demonstrations of June 28 to July 3, 1968 as being relevant to understanding police conduct under stressful and frustrating situations. The city manager's report vividly reveals the problems confronting a relatively small police department attempting to control a riotous situation. It gave some rather candid observations and factors—factors generally conceded to be prevalent in most disturbances similar in nature—inherent in a riot situation that affect police conduct. The recommendations offered by W. C. Hanley should be thoroughly reviewed due to their relevancy to most police agencies.

Nelson Watson's report at a police administrators' conference indicates the "up-hill fight" confronting law enforcement officers' attempts to improve their image. Although the cases presented by Mr. Watson

[48] R. E. Clift, *A Guide to Modern Police Thinking* (Cincinnati: The W. H. Anderson Co., 1956), pp. 303–6.

may not be accurate, they, unfortunately, illustrate what people are saying, what they believe, and what may be in the back of the way they behave.

The President's Commission on Law Enforcement and Administration of Justice, when investigating complaints of harassment and brutality, observed that physical abuse is only one source of aggravation in the ghetto. In nearly every city surveyed, the commission found complaints of harassment in various forms. Chapter 4 discusses the degrading verbal abuse as well as its impact in the area of attitudes toward local enforcement personnel. Such harassment or discourtesy, according to the commission, may not be the result of malicious or discriminatory intent of police officers. Many officers simply fail to understand the effects of their actions because of their limited knowledge of the Negro community. Examples displaying lack of community understanding are presented in this chapter.

The winning of public support and respect is a personal challenge each and every peace officer must accept. The *attitude* of the individual peace officer is perhaps the primary factor in community relations. When carrying out an assignment—particularly during traffic control—*attitude, courtesy, appearance* and the efficient use of the *telephone* are extremely important in developing a favorable police image.

QUESTIONS

1. Discuss the system of social control (i.e., informal and formal controls).

2. Discuss the social and psychological control role of law enforcement as presented by H. H. Toch.

3. What are some of the factors inherent in a riot situation that affect police conduct?

4. What is suggested by, "the policeman *symbolizes* much deeper social problems?"

5. Discuss the steps individual police officers may take to promote a favorable image.

ANNOTATED REFERENCES

"Corruption Behind Swinging Clubs," *Life*, Vol. 65, No. 23 (December 6, 1968). A candid discussion of the Democratic Convention demonstrations and an analysis of the contributing factors.

Derbyshire, R. L., "The Social Control Role of the Police in Changing Urban Communities," *Excerpta Criminologica*, Vol. 6, No. 3 (1966).

Explores image of the police in the urban community, police power, and definition of role.

Devlin, P. A., "The Police in a Changing Society," *Journal of Criminal Law, Criminology, and Police Science*, Vol. 57, No. 2 (June 1966). An excellent discussion of impact of social change on traditional law enforcement roles.

Dodd, D. J., "Police Mentality and Behavior," *Issues in Criminology*, Vol. 3, No. 1 (Summer 1967), 47–67, School of Criminology, University of California, Berkeley. Affords a particularly good commentary on police culture and their view of the community they serve.

"Time Essay, The Police Need Help," *Time* (October 4, 1968), p. 26. The October 4 issue of *Time* truly captures the problem of law enforcement in a changing community.

PART TWO

EXPLORING RACIAL AND COMMUNITY TENSION:

Minority

Group

Crime

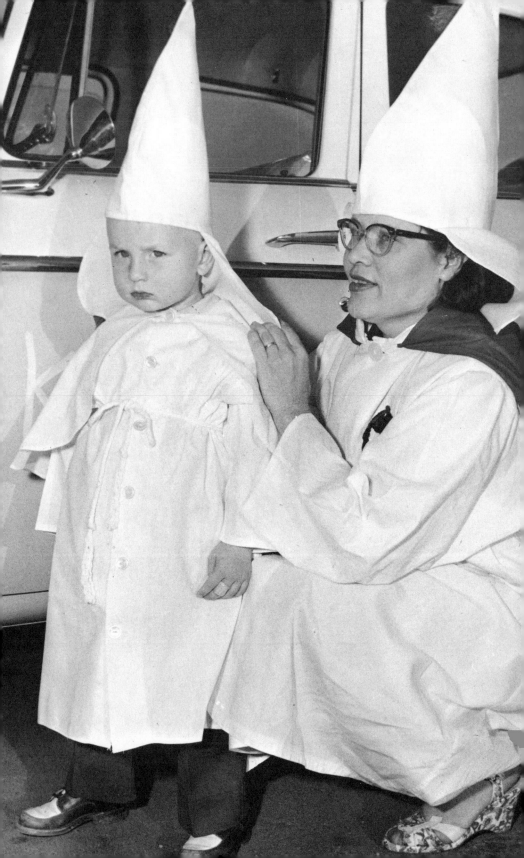

CHAPTER FIVE

SOME COMMENTS ON RACE AND PREJUDICE

Figure 5.1

MAN IS A COMPLEX ANIMAL—so baffling, in fact, that since the first syllable of reported time, the "man on the street" has responded to the riddle "What is man?" in terms of glib and totally erroneous generalizations. Not only is such erring all too human, it is further compounded by a set of genuine but contradictory facts; human behavior is characterized by (1) an *essential sameness* and (2) *multifold differences.*

Many fallacies have been attached to the term *race* and of all the standpat bromides, it has been far and away the most popular explanation of the differences which distinguish segments of mankind.

Race :
Myth and Reality

Race, as the term is popular defined, is traceable to a threefold origin: from (1) *mutations* (markedly different specimens that appear in a species for no apparent reason and then pass on their unusual characteristics to their offspring through hereditary forces); (2) *isolation* (whether geographical, self-imposed, or whatever, it results in interbreeding that tends to perpetuate and magnify original eliteness) ; and (3) *inbreeding* (the usual outcome of a combination of mutation and isolation factors).

The most frequently used criteria for racial identification are skin color; hair color; hair form; eye color; ratio, multiplied by 100, of head width to length (cephalic index) ; ratio of the nose width to nose height times 100 (nasal index) ; distribution of body hair and beard; stature; and prognathism (lower-facial projection). These particular criteria are used because it is assumed that they are: (1) relatively stable, that is, more or less unmodifiable by the environment and essentially inherent in the genes; and (2) easily measured.

But in studying the distribution of these characteristics in the human species, it has been discovered that there is a *wide variation* in each of them; thus, human types range through every conceivable combination of such factors. Are there not, however, large numbers of peoples who have a *combination* of these characteristics in common? Earlier research did suggest that the world population could be divided into three distinct "clusters" of people—each distinguishable by the fact that the individuals in it shared a combination of physical characteristics not shared by individuals in other clusters. The following types are suggested by such early theorists: (1) *Negroid*—long headed, wide nosed, dark skinned, dark haired, dark eyed, more or less hairless, tending toward tall stature, having tightly coiled hair, highly prognathous; (2) *Mongoloid*—medium stature, straight haired, yellow skinned, "slant" eyed (the mongolian fold is merely a drooping of the eyelids), medium headed, medium nosed, medium eyed, mildly prognathous and relatively free from body hair and beard; (3) *Caucasoid*—light haired, light eyed, light skinned, medium or tall stature, round to medium head shape, relatively hairy, long nosed, wavy or curly haired, nonprognathous. Those

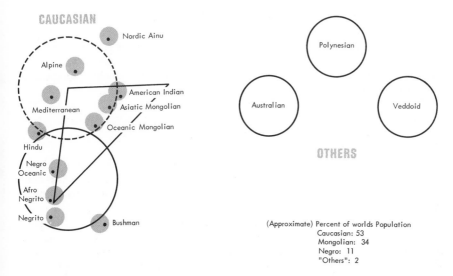

Figure 5.2 *That "races" differ from one another only slightly and through a continuing series of gradations (i.e. differences of degree or intensity—not of kind) is apparent. From the strictly genetic standpoint there can be no such thing as a pure race or human type because every single individual is literally a mixture of genes. The graphs above indicate the general groupings—and subracial groupings—of mankind. There are some groups ("Others") which defy accurate classification due to overlapping of physical characteristics.*

groups of individuals that did not "fit" into any of these clusters were either ignored or squeezed into one of the three racial pigeonholes, regardless of their lack of fit.

We now know that no individual fits exactly into the definition of a particular race because the definition itself is a *statistical average* of traits of the whole group. Thus, if we say a man is a Negroid, we imply that, to some degree, he has all of the Negroid characteristics listed above. In actuality, we find among the so-called Negroids, the tallest and the shortest people on earth; people with light-tan skins and bluish-black skins; those with long, thin noses and flat, broad noses; and people having heads which are elongated and heads which are "round." The same scattered array of racial traits marks the Mongoloid and Caucasoid. And in the last analysis, more people do *not* fit these type-descriptions than do fit them! In reality, most people are neither distinctly Mongoloid nor Negroid nor Caucasoid but show some mixture of all the listed characteristics. Whatever the origin of man—multiple or single—biologists and anthropologists concur on one point: *there is no "pure" race.* A pure race could exist only if its people had lived throughout its history in complete and total isolation—with *no* crossbreeding whatsoever with other groups.

We find, then, that there are no pure races in any serious sense of the word and no large numbers of people who are reasonably identifiable as distinct types (who share numerous characteristics in common). We are left, therefore, only with the fact of the existence of many small groups who may share in common certain genetic features by which they are identifiable and distinguishable. The biological fact of race and the myth of "race" should and must, then, be distinguished. *For all practical social purposes "race" is not so much a biological phenomenon as a social myth.* We cannot, therefore, scientifically account for differences in group behavior in terms of differences in group biology. The events overwhelmingly point to the conclusion that "race" and "race differences" are not valuable concepts for the analysis of similarities and differences in human group behavior.

Whatever classification[1] of races an anthropologist might concur with, he never includes *mental characteristics* as part of the classifications. It is generally recognized in today's social science circles that *intelligence tests* do not in themselves enable us to differentiate safely between what is due to innate capacity and what is the result of environmental influences, training, and education (the usual estimate: 65–70 percent inheritance). In fact, wherever it has been possible to make allowances for differences in environmental opportunities, the tests have shown essential similarity in mental characteristics among all human groups. One of the more famous studies in this area provided conclusive data on the point: Negroes newly arrived in New York City from the Deep South obtained far lower intelligence quotients than did American-born whites when they first arrived in the city. But several years later —acclimated to the city's competitive, literacy-stressing, fast-geared environment—the same Negroes' IQ's were statistically identical with the whites! As another example of the huge role of cultural conditioning in structuring intelligence, consider the numerous well-documented cases of identical twins (who have identical intelligence) reared apart. IQ differences of 20 and 30 points have separated twins reared in favorable versus unfavorable environments. *In short, given similar cultural opportunities to realize their potentialities, the average achievement of the members of each and every ethnic group is virtually identical.*

Not only are there no innate cultural, social, or intellectual differences among the races, but there is no evidence whatsoever that race mixture produces biologically "bad" results. As was stated earlier, each race is in fact an intricate amalgam of crossbreeding with other racial strains. No race (or nation), then, is biologically any more or less pure than any other; races are "inferior" only in the sense that they are defined as inferior by the ethnocentric values of people of the "white supremacy" class.

A TRAGIC ERROR

The idea of race, as one authority has noted, represents one of the

[1] For more detailed and illustrative data on the weakness of racial classifications, see R. W. Mack, *Race, Class, and Power* (New York: American Book Company, 1963), pp. 33–94, and H.~S. Becker, ed., *Social Problems: A Modern Approach* (New York: John Wiley & Sons, Inc., 1967), pp. 339–56.

greatest—if not the greatest—error of our time, and the most tragic. Everyone seems to know, and is only too eager to tell, what race is. Well-intentioned or otherwise (the latter is most often the case), the mythical "man on the street" is abysmally ignorant and almost totally ill-informed on the matter. For the student, in particularly, the facts must be put straight.

"Though the concept of race is genuine enough," famed anthropologist Clyde Kluckhohn once observed, *"there is perhaps no field of science in which the misunderstandings among educated people are so frequent and so serious."* One of the basic misunderstandings to which Kluckhohn refers is the confusion between *racial* and *ethnic* groupings of mankind.

ETHNIC GROUP

Where race refers, of course, to hereditary ties, the term *ethnic* connotes social and cultural ties. Thus, when people confuse racial and ethnic traits, they are confusing what is *given* by nature and what is *acquired* through learning. What, then, is an ethnic group? The Jews, the American Indians and the Nordics are *not* racial entities—but ethnic units—in the sense that they largely *share a common cultural heritages* and set of values. But even the label ethnic is conducive to gross oversimplification. Take for example, the category Jew. The German, Russian, Spanish, English, and Polish Jew (which together comprise some 95 percent of American Jewry) differ radically from one another not only in cultural terms but in the realms of religious belief and dogma, too. Further, there is a profound split within the Jewish religion—among Orthodox, Conservative, and Reformed. Also in America fewer offspring of Jewish parents are Jews in the *religious* sense than are the children of Protestants Protestant or of Catholics Catholic. Similarly, the generic term *Indian* encompasses a people whose original tribes differed from one another linguisticaly and culturally as much as modern Americans differ from ancient Chinese.

Racial Prejudice

We have all known people whom we can justly label prejudiced. Many of the readers of this book, in fact, are in all probability quite intolerant toward one or more of the ethnic or racial groupings—toward Jews, Negroes, or some other group of "foreigners." Prejudice toward outsiders (out-groups) is so frequent an aspect of American society—of all known societies—that it is literally a universal phenomenon. Despite the contention of many racialists, however, prejudice is *not* inherent in man as man; it is *not* a biogenic trait. To effectively probe the how and why of prejudice, then, it is crucial that we recognize that like stature or IQ, prejudice is not a thing that a person either has or does not have, but is a matter of degree and intensity. We cannot, for example, legitimately assert that a man who is 6 feet tall is "tall" and a man who is 5 feet, 11 inches is "short," or that a person with a recorded IQ of 140 is "near-genius," while one whose IQ is 139 is merely "bright." Nevertheless, there are tall people, geniuses, and highly prejudiced persons. And the authors' concern throughout the remainder of this chapter will largely be with the highly prejudiced.

DEFINITION OF PREJUDICE

Prejudice is, specifically, thinking ill of a person or a group without sufficient justification; a feeling (favorable or unfavorable—though we shall be concerned with the latter aspect here) is prior to, or not based on, actual experience. It is of course not easy to say how much "fact" is required to justify a judgment. A prejudiced person will almost certainly claim that he has sufficient cause for his views. He will tell of bitter experiences he has had with refugees, Koreans, Catholics, Jews, or Negroes. But, in most cases, it is evident that his facts are both scanty and strained. He typically resorts to a selective sorting of his own memories and mixes them up with hearsay and then he overgeneralizes. No one can possible know *all* refugees, Koreans, Catholics, etc. Hence, any negative judgment of these groups as a whole is, strictly speaking, an instance of thinking ill without warrant, or justification. We can further elaborate our basic definition of prejudice to include an avertive (avoiding) or hostile attitude toward a person who belongs to a group, simply because he belongs to that group and is, therefore, presumed to have the objectionable qualities ascribed to the group. Another essential attribution of prejudice is that of giving and applying a stereotyped name or *label of difference* to members of a given group.[2]

TARGETS OF PREJUDICE

Historically, the targets of prejudice have been determined by the particular configuration of conflicting values and opposing groups; they have been determined largely by the particular cultural and social situation of the time and place. *And the most evident targets of prejudice have been those particular group relationships which are marked by competition or other forms of opposition.* Often a group may be singled out for a period of time and then be replaced by another group.

At the outset of our history, the first targets of strong prejudice were the British who opposed our efforts toward independence. But there was also a certain amount of sectional division among the states. As the struggle for the extension of slavery became more and more a factor in national politics, a split between the industrial North and agrarian, slave-geared South became evident. After the Civil War, the whole situation changed in the South, with the appearance of the color-casts system, which still continues. Later, as the Negro moved into the North in response to sordid conditions at home and the lure of freedom and economic

---

[2] A *stereotype* is a conception of a particular group held by the general public in the absence of specific knowledge of the characteristics of the individual members of that group. Stereotypes function, in a sense, as a substitute for knowledge.

betterment, he came into direct competition with the northern urban white. And a certain amount of anti-Negro prejudice began to emerge in such places as Chicago, Detroit, Los Angeles, and New York City. Then, with the flood-tide of immigrants fleeing poor political and economic conditions in Europe, new objects of prejudice took their place in the sun.

The Negro and immigrant groups constituted a handy set of specific targets of intolerance, discrimination, and prejudice on the part of native-born or longer-established American citizens. While economic competition was a crucial factor in the earlier outbreaks of prejudice (for immigrants willing to work for lower wages often eased American workers out of jobs in this era of rapid industrialization and explosive capitalism), one of the symbols of hostility pertained to an ideological conflict between the Protestantism of the Americans and the Catholic faith of the immigrants. This was especially true after 1890, when southern Europeans began to outnumber immigrants from Germany, Britain, and Scandinavia. The Protestant-Catholic friction—with native enmity less often directed toward Catholicism per se but toward the very "different" southern European brand of culture—erupted in the growth of "native American" or nativist movements. Foremost of those movements was the Ku Klux Klan.

TWO BASIC TYPES OF PREJUDICE

Granted that prejudice is so widespread that it is "normal," who are the persons likely to manifest the *most* prejudice? Although prejudice is essentially a matter of degree, there are two basic types of prejudice: culture-conditioned and character-conditioned.[3]

Culture-Conditioned Prejudice We shall consider the former first, for it is by far the most typical. As its name might imply, culture-conditioned prejudice is primarily learned or acquired in the *normal* process of social interaction. Thus it is the rare southerner who views the Negro without antipathy. For he has been taught—deliberately and by subtle examples—that the Negro is both different and inferior; he has known no other explanation from childhood on. It cannot be overemphasized that *typically* the formation of prejudiced attitudes is not a product of "distorted" personality development. Prejudiced attitudes are, in fact, formed through the same process as other attitudes; they are derived from group norms. Within a group where patterns of prejudice prevail, it is the individual who *conforms* to the group (i.e., the most "normal" or "well-adjusted" person) who is likely to be the most prejudiced; conversely, lack of prejudice in such a group (for example, in the Deep South) implies nonconformity. And studies of the growth of ethnic prejudice in children

---

[3] For a lucid analysis of *culture-* and *character-conditioned prejudice*, see T. W. Adorno, *et al.*, *The Authoritarian Personality* (New York: Harper & Row, Publishers, 1950); G. Allport, *The Nature of Prejudice* (Reading, Mass.: Addison-Wesley Publishing Co., Inc., 1955); and H. M. Hodges, Jr., *Social Straitification* (Cambridge, Mass.: Schenkman Publishing Co., Inc., 1964).

indicate that such prejudice arrives largely through contacts with prevailing social norms rather than through individual contacts with members of the out-group in question. Once a small child accepts the prejudicial norms of his parents, and, through osmosis, of his schoolmates, the negative outgrowth stereotypes he has learned become internalized; that is, they slide into his subconscious and become a functioning part of his personality configuration. In his adult years when he "feels" an aversion for the out-group he learned to dislike in childhood, he will defend his attitude with all manner of "reasonable" rationalizations.

There are, however, differences in susceptibility to the culture-conditioned brand of prejudice even among individuals reared in the same general culture. Thus, the more highly prejudiced person, in contrast those less prejudiced, is more likely (1) to be older; (2) have had less formal education; (3) be either a farmer or in an unskilled or semi-skilled occupation; (4) live on a farm or in a very small town; (5) take less interest in civic affairs, be less informed on public issues, and vote less often, and (6) earn a lesser income. Many of these sociological factors, it is apparent, are intercorrelated; that is, they almost automatically "go with one another" (e.g., education, age, income, occupation, etc.). Closer analysis has revealed that of all these sociological variables *formal education* is the most crucial. Other social cultural determinants appear to be downward mobility and social-economic insecurity.

The particular target of prejudice will depend upon a number of factors; but it is currently most likely to be the Negro in the North and South; the Puerto Rican, Mexican, and Jew in large urban areas; and in the more rural sectors of the Middle West, the big-city eastern intellectuals or "aristocrats." The particular *scapegoat* or object of prejudice will often, however, be a group sanctioned as "inferior" by people in general or a person or group too weak to strike back when attacked.[4]

Culture-conditioned prejudice *can* be "unlearned"; although the process is not as effortless as many well-intentioned and naïve people believe. Because such attitudes are not formed in a piecemeal way and they are usually deeply ingrained within the personality structure, attempts to legislate prejudice out of existence, on some occasions, have had the opposite effect. Almost as unsuccessful have been efforts to "educate" people, to shame them (by appeals to their religious ethics or Americanism), or to bring them into "contact" with minority groups. Lecturing, like legislation, requires expert and subtle direction, if it is to avoid alienating its subjects. Social contact and situations such as living in an interracial housing project have often, when poorly handled, increased friction and hostility. Because the particular highly prejudiced individual is conformistic and cautiously attuned to his group's values, he is unlikely to alter his basic beliefs unless the group's beliefs change

---

[4] Scapegoating has always been with us; people have traditionally found it uncomfortable to blame themselves when "things are going wrong." Projecting blame onto another source (displaced aggression) has long been a popular way to ease such unpleasant tensions.

too.[5] To lessen prejudice with any degree of effectiveness, then, we must either change the basic values or attitudes of entire groups, or we must somehow transfer the prejudiced person's allegiance to another group (or "reference group"). Educating the young child is, of course, a far simpler undertaking than changing ossified adult attitudes. However, such educational programs must reach the child during his lower-elementary school years, must be skillfully handled (preferably with the help of visual aids), and must strongly compete against extracurricular influences, such as the family and lower-cultured values, which are frequently enormously potent.

Character-Conditioned Prejudice is quite firmly imbedded in the personality makeup, and attempts to rid people of it must be, quite needless to note, far more formidable than the just-cited techniques for eradicating culture-conditioned prejudice. As will become clearer later in this chapter, the person victimized by character-conditioned prejudice almost *has* to hate, and if one of his scapegoats or objects of venom is somehow eliminated from focus, he will inevitably seek out some other victim.

A psychologically prejudiced person (one having character-conditioned prejudice) is more dangerous than the sociologically prejudiced or culture-conditioned prejudiced person in a twofold sense; he is (1) present in all areas of the population—among the educated, the wealthy, and influential as well as the poor and ill-educated, and (2) is more likely to be actively prejudiced and in a position whereby he can translate his hatred into effective political or social action. Postwar studies of the more avid Nazis and of potent native American Fascists have uncovered all the earmarks of the *character-conditioned* brand of prejudice.

Like culture-conditioned prejudice, the character-conditioned variety has its roots in childhood. But unlike the former, specific sets of prejudice, such as anti-Negro or anti-Semitic, are seldom acquired in the early years. Rather, a basic outlook on life is learned during this formative period—an outlook that will warp the entire life of its victim. How does the childhood of such psychologically prejudiced persons differ from the normal person's? It differs at many—and as the subconscious will affirm—crucial points. It is worth recalling, at this juncture, how vitally important the formative years are in shaping one's entire personality.

DEVELOPMENT OF A PSYCHOLOGICALLY (CHARACTER-CONDITIONED) PREJUDICED PERSON

As one might suspect, the parents of such children are, in large part, the guilty parties in the genesis, or beginning, of such prejudiced personalities. They are certainly not "normal" adults. They are highly

[5] The authors do not intimate that such legislation (Civil Rights Act, 1964) is inappropriate; active government intervention in areas of unjustified ethnic prejudice is an absolute "must." However, such efforts will only cause frustration or "false hopes" if there are "unenforceable" laws or if such laws are not intelligently executed.

concerned with status, social position, the "right" occupation, friends, and neighborhood; are "proper"; social decorum plays a vital role in their lives. In rearing their children, they often accept the dictum that "Children should be seen but not heard," and when their children misbehave, they use harsh and rigid forms of discipline to keep them in line. Perhaps after an initial period of futile revolt, the children of such parents tend to submit to, rather than accept and understand, such harsh demands. Although on the surface these children are inclined to idealize their parents, they lack genuine and spontaneous affection. As the child grows up, this authoritarian-in-the-making is increasingly prone to put heavy emphasis on conformity to social norms. He tends to define the perfect boy as being "polite," "having good manners," "being clean," in contrast to "being a good companion," "being fun." This trend toward outward conformity in the prejudiced child finds expression in his frequent endorsement of statements like: *"There is only one right way to do anything." "Appearances are usually the best test." "One should avoid doing things in public which seem wrong to others, even though one knows that these things are really all right."*

Furthermore, authoritarian children accept the parental emphasis on rigid discipline to such an extent that they describe the "perfect" father in terms of the punitive and restrictive aspects of parent-child relations, rather than in terms of love and understanding. Because the relatively unprejudiced child is more likely to be treated as an equal and given the opportunity to express feelings of rebellion or disagreement, he more typically thinks of his parents as companions. In contrast, the prejudiced child tends to view his parents more as punishing disciplinarians—more or less as strict masters. The relatively unprejudiced child learns at home an equalitarian and individualized approach to people, whereby the prejudiced child learns an authoritarian way of thinking. The authoritarian child submits to the demands of a harsh and strict parent because of fear of punishment. The originally forced submission to parental authority, however, leads later in life not only to a continued demand for autocratic leadership but also to an acceptance of a system of strict discipline and punishment.

Further clues relating to the parent-child relationship in the genesis of prejudice are revealed by the beliefs of mothers of prejudiced children. In contrast to parents of unprejudiced children, they more often agree that, *"Obedience is the most important thing a child can learn;" "I prefer a quiet child to one who is noisy;"* and *"A child should never be permitted to set his will against that of his parents."*

What does such a style of child training do to a child? For one thing, it puts him on guard. He has to watch his impulses carefully. Not only is he punished for them when they counter his parents' convenience and rules, as they frequently do, but at such times, he feels that love is withdrawn from him. When love is withdrawn, he is alone, exposed, desolate. Thus, he comes to watch alertly for signs of his parents' approval or disapproval. It is they who have power and they who give or withhold their conditional love. Their power and their will are the decisive agents in the child's life.

What is the result? First of all, the child learns that power and authority dominate human relationships, not trust and tolerance. The stage is thus set for a hierarchical view of society. Equality does not really prevail. But the effect goes even deeper. The child mistrusts his impulses; he must not disobey his parents; he must not have temper tantrums; he must not be naughty. He must fight such evil in himself. Through a simple act of projection, the child comes to fear evil impulses *in others*. Others have dark designs; they are not to be trusted.

In all cases of intense character-conditioned prejudice, there is a common factor, which one social psychologist has called "threat orientation." Underlying insecurity seems to lie at the root of the personality. The individual cannot face the world unflinchingly and in a forthright manner. He seems fearful of himself, of his own instincts, of social change, and of his social environment. Since he can live in comfort neither with himself nor with others, he is forced to organize his whole style of living, including his social attitudes, to fit his crippled condition. His specific social attitudes are not malformed; rather it is his ego that is crippled.

Other aspects of the victim of character-conditioned prejudice, as pointed out by authorities in the field of racial prejudice, are:

1. He is characterized by repressed feelings of weakness and rejection.
2. To him the world appears to be a jungle, in which everyone is the enemy of everyone else.... People are out for themselves, and are not basically interested in others.
3. The ensuing distrust of others is coupled with the absence of secure emotional attachments, disturbances in his feelings of belonging. He is unclear about his role and place in society.
4. He emphasizes strength and toughness as supreme values, considers love and sympathy signs of weaknesses. Security can be obtained only through domination or submission, not through love and co-operation.
5. In line with his feelings of weaknesses, he overrates the power of some and exaggerates the weaknesses of others. He divides the world into the weak and the strong, into born leaders and born followers.
6. Doubt in his ability to carry things through to their successful completion leads to an unwillingness to accept responsibility for his own deeds and an avoidance of taking the initiative.
7. Lack of ego strength, expressed in more or less unconscious doubt about his own worth, is coupled with high dependency needs, the desire to lean upon and submit to a strong personal group.
8. In more democratic societies, submission to the dictates of the group, an almost blind conformity, takes the place of submission to a strong leader.

9. Protest against the leader in authoritarian societies, violation of the group rules in democratic societies, are experienced as powerful threats to the security of the weak individual, which is based on submission.
10. The reaction to such submission, the giving up of individuality, leads to the generation of strong hostile tendencies which need release.
11. The ensuing hostility has to be displaced because such a person cannot afford to attack those on whom he is dependent.
12. Hostility tends to be displaced toward those who are weak and non-conformist, often against minority groups.

Such prejudice is, then, "functional"; that is, it serves a profound personality need; without the crutch of such hatred for out-groups, the prejudiced personality would flounder in an anchorless world.

The necessity of the psychologically (character-conditioned) prejudiced person of seeing the world in terms of black and white, good and bad, strong and weak, appears to go back to a specific way of thinking. While he does not differ from the sociologically (culture-conditioned) prejudiced person in intelligence, his thinking is characterized by greater rigidity and lack of capacity for abstract and creative thought. Such persons tend to generalize too rapidly and too broadly. They are puzzled by ambiguous situations and prefer clear-cut issues. When there are positive and negative aspects to an issue, they are bewildered. In other words, they like the villains to be villainous and the heroes to be heroic—with no confusing in-betweens. The psychologically prejudiced person also tends to be less productive intellectually, less original, and less responsive emotionally. Such a lack of creativity stems in part from the discouragement of independent thinking early in life. The emphasis on power also interferes with their capacity to enjoy life. While sex is important to the psychologically prejudiced person, it is experienced as overpowering or submitting and is disassociated from affection. This is not surprising if we remember that such personalities have received little affection and are therefore less able to give it. Similarly, the emphasis on success, with its corollary stress on duty, interferes even with the genuine enjoyment of one's worth. It is easy to see how the lack of gratification from major areas of life contributes to frustration and, hence, aggravates hostility.

It is abundantly clear, in summation, that the more deeply prejudiced person—one who looks down on *many* minority groups rather than one or two specific out-groups—is marked by a distinct personality makeup. He is, in short, a "sick person." His sickness is not of his own doing but rather is the outcome of a strict and undemocratic upbringing. As a result, his entire life will be marred by deeply imbedded frustrations, vague hatreds, and insecurity. He is already a target for demagogues of the far Right and far Left. He will be unhappy with both the Republicans and the Democrats, and can only be satisfied with a totalitarian order.

Forms of Prejudice

What is racism? The word has represented daily reality to millions of black people for centuries, yet it is a difficult term to define. *Racism* may be defined as: the predication of decisions based on considerations of race. Furthermore, such decisions or policies are intended to subjugate a minority racial group for the purpose of maintaining or exerting control of that group.

Minority problems are problems of intergroup relations, in which each minority is the subject of prejudice and discrimination by the majority. The majority itself is made up of many minorities and, indeed, is sometimes but the dominant minority or a group of minorities holding key positions. As previously indicated, prejudice is an attitude arrived at without sufficient exploration of the facts. It is prejudging, in the sense of making a judgment before or independently of the relevant facts in the matter. *Discrimination*, although related to prejudice, is, however, *not* the same thing. Discrimination implies the unequal treatment of different people according to the group to which they belong.

DISCRIMINATION AGAINST MINORITY GROUPS

Discrimination takes several forms, as it applies to minority groups. *Economic discrimination* involves unequal treatment, in the economic sphere, of individuals who are members of certain minorities. For example, the Negro finds that many types of occupations are not open to him because he is a Negro. In many instances, he is paid lower wages than a white person doing the same type of work. *Social discrimination* (to be discussed) may operate along with economic discrimination to the Negro's disadvantage by preventing him from making the friendships which often aid in business matters.

Black communities are becoming more and more economically depressed. In June, 1968, the Bureau of Labor Statistics reported on the deteriorating condition of black people in this country. In 1948, the jobless rate of nonwhite males between the ages of fourteen and nineteen was 7.6 percent. In 1967, the percentage of unemployment in this group was 22.6 percent. In the ten-year period from 1957 to 1967, the total employment for youth between the ages of fourteen and nineteen increased from 2,642,000 to 3,612,000. There were 970,000 *new* jobs offered during this period; nonwhite youths obtained only 36,000 of these.

In 1967, unemployment rates were higher for nonwhite high school graduates than for white high school dropouts. According to the Department of Labor, a white man with four years of high school education can expect to earn about $253,000 in his lifetime. For a nonwhite with five years or more of college this figure is $246,000.

Educational discrimination is closely allied to economic discrimination. Certain minority groups are discriminated against educationally. When such groups are numerous in a locality, they are sometimes segregated in the schools, and the facilities available to them are greatly inferior to those of the dominant group. This is particularly true in the case of the Negro in the South, but it is also true of other minorities, for example, the Spanish-speaking Mexican Americans in the Southwest. In addition, members of minority groups often find themselves discriminated against when they apply for admission to institutions of higher learning.

Political discrimination is exercised against various minority groups, notably Negroes in the South, despite constitutional amendments designed to assure citizens the right to vote. Political discrimination is particularly important because it is largely through federal legislation that minorities can expect to gain protection against the many other types of discrimination.

Another aspect of political discrimination is the manipulation of political boundaries and the devising of restrictive electoral systems. In areas where the Negro does vote, it is not unusual for the political "machinery" of the dominant group to have gerrymandered black neighborhoods so that their true voting strength is not reflected in political representation.

Social discrimination is perhaps the most difficult form to eliminate through legislation. This may be attributed to the strong belief of many people that it is their basic democratic right to associate with whom they please and to bar whom they please from membership in associations to which they belong. So, for example, many fraternities will not admit members of certain minority groups. Also, restrictive convenants in housing operate to exclude minority groups from certain residential areas. The recent United States Supreme Court decision regarding open housing has not eliminated this problem, nor has the Rumford Act in California. Social discrimination is important because it hinders a closer association between the members of different groups and thus reinforces stereotyped prejudicial thinking which arises through ignorance.

Although racial prejudice and discrimination have been a problem to other racial groups, Negroes have been so victimized by discrimination that they have been referred to as second-class citizens and the "underdog's underdog." Negroes make up roughly 12 percent of the population of the United States. The *difference* in life expectancy of Negroes and whites is perhaps the best indication of the condition of Negroes as a minority group. The average nonwhite male, according to the United States Department of Health, Education and Welfare, has a life expectancy at birth nine and one-half years less than that of the average white male. The corresponding figure for the average nonwhite female is nearly eleven years less than for the white female.

THE FUNCTIONS OF PREJUDICE

Among the functions which prejudice against minority groups may perform are the following:

1. It provides a source of egotistic satisfaction, through invidiously comparing others with oneself.
2. It affords a convenient grouping for people one is ignorant of. Lumping people one is ignorant of together under a popular stereotyped description saves time and thought and affords a convenient grouping.
3. It provides a convenient group or person to blame when things go wrong in one's personal life or in the community (scapegoatism).
4. It provides an outlet for projecting one's tensions and frustrations onto other people.
5. It symbolizes one's affiliation with a more dominant group.
6. It owes justification for various types of discrimination which are thought to be of advantage to the dominant group.[6]

THE FUNCTIONS OF DISCRIMINATION

Among the functions performed by discrimination against minority groups are the following:

1. It tends to reinforce prejudice concerning the group's alleged inferiority.
2. It assures members of the majority group various types of economic advantages.
3. It limits the effectiveness of possible competition from members of the minority group in business, education, political office, and so forth.
4. It affords an avenue to economic exploitation of the minority group.[7]

WORKING TO ELIMINATE PREJUDICE

Since much prejudice is based on *stereotyped* thinking, education in the matter of group differences—where they are found—should provide the necessary intellectual basis for a change of attitude with regard to prejudice. It is for this reason that various organizations like the National Conference of Christians and Jews, the National Association for the Advancement of Colored People, the Urban League, and the Anti-Defamation League carry on extensive educational programs. However, as was mentioned in an earlier section, prejudice is almost by definition an irrational attitude. Knowledge is not enough. A change of attitudes

---

[6] For a thorough analysis of minority group problems see J. S. Roucek and R. L. Warren, *Sociology, An Introduction* (Totowa, N. J.: Littlefield, Adams & Company, 1956), pp. 146–48.

[7] *Ibid.*

—attitudes conditioned by norms found acceptable by the group—must be the ultimate goal. Several "techniques" were found to be successful in achieving this goal: (1) changing group norms (values, folkways, mores) through discussion, lectures, and the use of communication media (TV, newspapers, books, radio, etc.); and (2) encouraging association with members of the minority group. Quite often, the removal or suspension of discrimination subsequently provides an opportunity for experiencing mutual social participation and leads to a reconsideration of the *prejudiced* conception held by majority group members. Since prejudice is largely irrational and emotional in nature, emotional appeals to the alleged values of democracy are sometimes effective, though they frequently have little permanent effect. Educational campaigns seem to be effective over a longer period of time.[8]

THE REDUCTION OF DISCRIMINATION

Most sociologists and social psychologists are of the opinion that the attempt to eliminate prejudice under conditions of widespread discrimination is almost destined to failure:

> ... For it separates verbal symbols and behavior, and the verbal symbols of tolerance and understanding are largely ineffective if daily life reinforces habits of discrimination. Hence, many people see the resolution of the problem in a constant agitation to defeat discrimination wherever possible, and to make it illegal where this is within the power of the law.[9]

Therefore, despite the emotional outcries of, "Slow down, the time is not ripe; you can't outlaw prejudice and discrimination," anti-discriminatory laws have proven to be effective, although not without conflict. There are *some* indications of an improvement in the conditions surrounding minority groups—particularly the Negro. The U.S. Supreme Court has made several important decisions pertaining to desegregation, i.e., education, housing, use of public facilities, and voting. Furthermore, because the Negro is becoming much more sophisticated politically and his vote is growing larger with every election, politicians are taking cognizance of the Negro's plight. Also many new types of employment were opened up for large numbers of Negroes during World War II, the Korean Conflict and the Vietnam War: These jobs have "opened the door," and labor unions have displayed a willingness to admit Negro workers to their membership. Nevertheless, the range of discrimination is still great and constitutes a challenge to any country claiming to be a democracy.

Prejudice:
Related Effects

Two Negro assistant professors of psychiatry at the University of

---

[8] *Ibid.* (Roucek)
[9] *Ibid.* (Roucek)

California Medical Center, William H. Grier and Price M. Cobbs, conclude in their recent book[10] that riots express personal pain and rage provoked by the severe psychological and emotional pressures of living in a racist society. Many other authorities in the field of race relations are of the same opinion. The psychological pressures and fear derived from a history of oppression and capricious cruelty. This is clearly pointed out by Louis E. Lomax:[11]

> The American Negro spent the first half of the twentieth century adjusting to and recovering from the all-pervasive reality of legalized segregation. Fear of white people being advanced was the basic motivation of Negroes during those years, and I suppose there is some validity in the analysis. But I doubt that fear was the only force shaping Negro activities and behavior; self-realization in an essentially hostile world, I suggest, is a more accurate description of what the Negro was about. Fear, to be sure, was one of the techniques of that self-realization. After all, when the entire legal structure is against you and your very life is in daily peril, fear is an understandable emotion. Denied modern weapons with which to defend yourself, and hauled before openly hostile courts when you fight back with sticks and stones, you will do well to pretend fear even when you are not afraid.

Not surprisingly, according to Grier and Cobbs, paranoid psychosis (or persecution complex—quite exaggerated) is the most typical type of serious mental illness among Negroes. The authors assert that the problem has its genesis during the formative years at the most crucial stage of development—sexual identity. A Negro mother, relates Grier and Cobbs, because she is afraid of the "penalties" of white society, will strive to maintain stringent control of her son. She must "intuitively cut off and blunt his masculine assertiveness and aggression lest they put the boy's life in jeopardy." Furthermore, this pattern of attempting to eliminate assertiveness and creativeness does not stop when the child reaches the adolescent stage but continues under the guise of the parents' discouraging of education. Negro families, the authors write, tend to discourage their sons from seeking a degree by using hostility, scorn, and hatred as well as praise. Black families feel that having a degree may force their children into direct and dangerous competition with whites.

Unable to withstand the pressure of daily living in the ghetto, many Negro families are simply unable to function. This disintegration can be seen in the high percentage of fatherless homes. Sociologist Daniel P. Moynihan, in a well-publicized report, argued that lack of job opportunities prevents the black father from asserting authority in his household, so that, *psychologically emasculated* and humiliated, he leaves his

---

[10] W. H. Grier and P. M. Cobbs, *Black Rage* (New York: Basic Books, Inc., Publishers, 1968). Also, for information relating to this topic, see E. E. Thorp, *The Mind of the Negro* (Baton Rouge, La.: Ortlieb Press, 1961), and F. K. Berrien, *Comments and Cases in Human Relations* (New York: Harper & Row, Publishers, 1951).

[11] L. E. Lomax, *The Negro Revolt* (New York: Harper & Row, Publishers, 1963), p. 42.

family. The emasculating force is not economic but social, the father feels impotent and helpless because, living in prosperous American society, he is unable to provide for his family and protect it from harm.

For many Negroes self-respect has become almost impossible. Traditionally, a large number are preoccupied with hair straighteners, skin bleaches, and the like, which illustrates a most tragic aspect of American racial prejudice—Negroes have come to believe in their own inferiority. Recently, however, there have been some encouraging signs; for instance, Blacks have begun to advocate the "beauty of dark skin and kinky hair." And there has developed a new culture pride (e.g., natural Afro hair styles and African style of dress) which has had a positive effect on their mental health.

Summary

Race, as the term is popularly defined is traceable to a threefold origin: (1) *mutations*, (2) *isolation*, and (3) *inbreeding*. We find that there are no *pure* races in any serious sense of the word and no large numbers of people who are reasonably identifiable as distinct types (who share numerous characteristics in common).

The biological fact of race and the myth of "race" should and must, then, be distinguished; *for all practical social purposes "race" is not so much a biological phenomenon as a social myth.* We cannot, therefore, scientifically account for *differences* in group behavior in terms of *differences* in group biology; the events overwhelmingly point to the conclusion that "race" and "race differences" are not valuable concepts for the analysis of similarities and differences in human group behavior. Whatever classification of races the anthropologist might concur with, he never includes *mental* characteristics as part of those classifications. Furthermore, intelligence tests do not enable us to differentiate safely between what is due to innate capacity and what is the result of environmental influences, training, and education.

Where *race* refers, of course, to hereditary ties, the term *ethnic* connotes social and cultural ties. Thus, when people confuse racial and ethnic traits, they are confusing what is *given* by nature and what is *acquired* through learning.

We can define *prejudice* as thinking ill of others without sufficient justification—a feeling (favorable or unfavorable) toward a person or group which is prior to, or not based on, actual experience.

Essentially, there are two basic types of prejudice: *culture-conditioned* (sometimes individuals affected are referred to as sociologically prejudiced), and *character-conditioned* prejudice. The latter produces psychologically prejudiced individuals. This chapter discusses fully the manifestations of such prejudice and analyzes the personality makeup of the persons infected with this social disease.

QUESTIONS

1. Briefly discuss mutations, isolation, and inbreeding.
2. Is there a pure race? Discuss.
3. Discuss the difference between ethnic groups and race.
4. Define prejudice.
5. Discuss culture-conditioned and character-conditioned prejudice.

ANNOTATED REFERENCES

Adorno, T. W., *et al., The Authoritarian Personality.* New York: Harper & Row, Publishers, 1950. This book presents a classic study of authoritarianism and, using a statistical scale, measures prejudice.

Allport, G., *The Nature of Prejudice.* Reading, Mass.: Addison-Wesley Publishing Co., Inc., 1955, pp. 79, 80, 282. Excellent discussion in the area of the biased and bigoted. This book provides information on "adopting" and "developing" prejudice, which is similar to the culture- and character-conditioned prejudice discussed in this chapter.

Berrien, F. K., *Comments and Cases in Human Relations.* New York: Harper & Row, Publishers, 1951. Deals with conditions and circumstances affecting interpersonal relations, using material from sociology, psychology, and anthropology. It includes case histories of disturbances in interpersonal relations typical of those one might meet.

Christie, R., "Authoritarianism Re-Examined," in *Studies in the Scope and Method of "The Authoritarian Personality,"* eds. R. Christie and M. Jahoda. New York: The Free Press, 1954. An analysis of the person victimized by prejudice. Discusses his personality, philosophy, and interpersonal relationships.

Grier, W. H., and P. M. Cobbs, *Black Rage.* New York: Basic Books, Inc., Publishers, 1968. Discusses reasons why Blacks who are "well off" are among the ones who loot and burn. The social emasculation of the Negro male is thoroughly discussed, along with an intuitive explanation of the severe psychological injury suffered by the Negro male and female.

Hodges, H. M., Jr., *Social Stratification.* Cambridge, Mass.: Schenkman Publishing Co., Inc., 1964, pp. 210–12. Provides detailed information on culture- and character-conditioned prejudice.

CONSTITUTION of the UNITED STATES

PREAMBLE

ARTICLE I.
Legislative Department

ARTICLE II.
Executive Department

ARTICLE III.
Judicial Department

ARTICLE IV.
The States and the Federal Government

ARTICLE V.
Amendments

ARTICLE VI.
Other Provisions

ARTICLE VII.
Ratification of Constitution

AMENDMENTS

ARTICLE I.
Restrictions on Powers of Congress

ARTICLE II.
Right to Bear Arms

ARTICLE III.
Billeting of Soldiers

ARTICLE IV.
Seizures, Searches and Warrants

ARTICLE V.
Criminal Proceedings, Condemnation of Property

ARTICLE VI.
Mode of Trial in Criminal Proceedings

ARTICLE VII.
Trial by Jury

ARTICLE VIII.
Bails—Fines—Punishments

ARTICLE IX.
Certain Rights Not Denied to the People

ARTICLE X.
State Rights

ARTICLE XI.
Judicial Proceedings

ARTICLE XII.
Election of President and Vice-President

ARTICLE XIII.
Slavery

ARTICLE XIV.
Citizenship, Representation and Payment of Public Debt

ARTICLE XV.
Right of Citizens to Vote

ARTICLE XVI.
Income Taxes

ARTICLE XVII.
United States Senators

ARTICLE XVIII.
Liquor Prohibition

ARTICLE XIX.
Equal Suffrage

ARTICLE XX.
Changing Terms of Office of President and Assembling of Congress

ARTICLE XXI.
Repeal of Liquor Prohibition

Published by GEORGE BURR MacANNAN, Taft Building, Hollywood, California. For Best Results this Parchment Should Be Mounted on White Backing.

CHAPTER SIX

EQUAL JUSTICE AND MINORITY GROUPS

Figure 6.1 *Equal treatment by the courts and the police—as well as society in general—is a necessary ingredient in our American way of life.*

IN THE "PLEDGE OF ALLEGIANCE TO THE FLAG," that every school child in this country learns is the phrase, "liberty and justice for all." These words, if truly accepted as expressing a national goal, carry broad implications not only in regard to equal treatment by the courts, by the arm of the courts known as the police, but also in the general functions of society.

The courts and the police are the institutions of society generally examined with reference to injustice. However, it appears that it would be more logical to start an investigation of injustice by examining minority-group treatment within the general society. Because over 70 percent of minority-group people lived within ghettos by 1967,[1] the ghetto itself needs to be examined. A ghetto is defined by the *Report of the National Advisory Commission on Civil Disorders* as:

> ...an area within the city characterized by poverty and acute social disorganization and inhabited by members of a racial or ethnic group under conditions of involuntary segregation.[2]

If you keep that definition in mind, you realize that slum ghetto dwellers, through the limiting nature of the ghetto itself, do not enjoy liberty or freedom to pursue many of their goals. We need to undertake some study of ghetto life, including the limitations it imposes on its residents, if we are to better understand the subtleties of justice. For this purpose the black ghetto will be used. It is used here in the full knowledge that there are many ghettos with other ethnic compositions. The black ghetto was selected because the most recent research has been done on it, and it illustrates the many problems of the ghetto per se.

The Ghetto and the Concept of Equal Justice

The National Advisory Commission on Civil Disorders has made an extensive investigation into ghettos. The following is a summary of their findings, which was published in 1968.[3]

Almost every large city in the United States has a Negro ghetto. These ghettos are a constantly growing concentration of Negroes within the central city. A breakdown of the 21.5 million blacks in the United States today shows that approximately 15 million live in metropolitan areas, and of these, 12.1 million live in the central cities.

Indications are that, during the past three decades, there has been a great shift of Negroes from the rural southern area to the large cities

[1] *Report of the National Advisory Commision on Civil Disorders* (Washington, D.C.: Government Printing Office, 1968), p. 115.
[2] *Ibid.*, p. 6.
[3] *Ibid.*, pp. 115–20.

of the North and West. In 1910 the number of Negroes in metropolitan areas was 2.7 million, or approximately 28 percent of the Negro population. Today the 15 million Negroes who live in metropolitan areas represent approximately 69 percent of the black population.

One of the most significant findings of the commission was that approximately one percent of the total population of the nation consists of poor Negroes who come from disadvantaged neighborhoods. However, this 1 percent represents 16 to 20 percent of the total Negro population in the central city. Therefore, within the central city, there is a high concentration of very poor persons of a particular ethnic background.

These population shifts, with the resultant formation of large Negro ghettos, have been caused by three factors: (1) the migration of southern Negroes to the cities in pursuit of employment (this has accelerated since World War II); (2) the concentration of Negroes in segregated big-city neighborhoods; and (3) the rapid growth of the black population because of better medical care coupled with a high fertility rate among Negroes.

To get a more accurate picture of the concentration of black Americans, note that by 1966 approximately one-third of all Negroes who lived outside the South were residents of our twelve largest central cities— New York, Chicago, Los Angeles, Philadelphia, Detroit, Baltimore, Houston, Cleveland, Washington, D.C., Milwaukee, St. Louis, and San Francisco. For the most part, they lived in ghetto-type segregation. According to the Civil Disorders Commission's report, there are several reasons for this. Like other migrants and immigrants, Negroes first moved into the oldest sections of the cities. Unlike immigrants from Europe, the black man's color barred him from leaving these poor neighborhoods even when he became financially able to do so. The predominantly white society which has absorbed the immigrant has, by and large, refused to absorb the black man. Until quite recently, this was effected by local housing ordinances and real estate codes. It was even done by violence and intimidation. Often when a black man moved into a white neighborhood, whites moved from the area, causing vacancies which were, in turn, filled by black citizens, and the whole character of the neighborhood was changed. Unscrupulous real estate agents often used this so-called "block busting" technique to increase sales and, consequently, real estate commissions.

Racial segregation has existed in American cities for decades; however, recently it has increased to a high degree in every large city in the United States. A study by Karl and Alma Taeuber shows this quite graphically.[4] These authors devised an index to measure the degree of residential segregation. This index indicated the percentage of black

[4] K. Taeuber & A. Taeuber, *Negroes in Cities* (Chicago: Aldine Publishing Company, 1965).

Americans who would have to move to other blocks from the block where they live to bring about a perfect proportional unsegregated distribution of the population. The average segregation index for 207 of the largest cities in the United States in the year 1960 was 86.2. This means that an average of over 86 percent of all Negroes would have to relocate to create an unsegregated population distribution.

Considering the unequal population distribution, an examination of minority housing might well be in order at this point.

Ghetto Housing

The Commission on Civil Disorders (Kerner Commission) found that approximately two-thirds of black Americans living in cities reside in neighborhoods characterized by blight and substandard housing. Despite the fact that federal housing has been in existence since 1934, it has not solved the problem of the urban poor.[5] Substandard housing, still is one of their greatest problems. It is defined by the Department of Housing and Urban Development as:

> ...that housing reported by the U.S. Census Bureau as (1) sound but lacking full plumbing, (2) deteriorating and lacking full plumbing, or (3) dilapidated.[6]

Figure 6.2

It should be noted that the actual number of urban whites in substandard housing is two and a half times the number of urban blacks in such housing. However, the important thing is that the proportion of the black population in inferior dwellings as of 1960 ran from a low of 18.1 percent in Los Angeles to a high of 58.9 percent in Pittsburgh.

[5] *Report of the National Advisory Commission on Civil Disorders*, p. 257.
[6] *Ibid.*, p. 257.

Approximately 25 percent of the Negro population living in central cities lived in substandard housing, compared with 8 percent of all Caucasians. Furthermore, in six of the fourteen largest cities in 1960, 40 percent of black housing was below standard. The Commission Report[7] also indicated that Negro housing is far more likely to be substandard and aging than white housing—and far more likely to be overcrowded, too. In 1960, in fact, 25 percent of all Negro housing in American cities was overcrowded. (This means that each room contained 1.01 or more persons.) This figure for overcrowding—8 percent as against 25 percent—is approximately three times that for white housing—as a matter of fact, in many cities more than 25 percent of the Negro population live in overcrowded housing.

This overcrowding is directly related to the fact that Negroes tend to get far less for their housing dollars than whites do. Often they cannot get housing similar to that of whites without paying much more for it. According to the Kerner Commission report, when Negroes pay the same amount of money as Caucasians, they get worse houses. However, they generally pay more than Caucasians. Seemingly, this situation prevails in most racial ghettoes. This plus the predominantly low incomes earned by black ghetto-dwellers results in a large percentage of the family income being spent for housing. As a matter of fact, in many cities Negroes use from 35 to 40 percent of their income for housing. Needless to say, having to pay such percentages for housing severely cuts into ghetto residents' funds for other items.

Black people tend to live in ghetto housing that is substandard, overcrowded, and old. Furthermore, the cost of this housing is exceedingly expensive when compared with housing generally available to white persons. Landlords often victimize ghetto residents by ignoring building codes; probably because they know, by and large, that their tenants are restricted, by economics or ethnic background, to living in the ghetto. Broadly speaking, these circumstances, along with others that will be expanded later, are those that minority groups refer to when they state that they are being treated unjustly by society.

There is some feeling that ghetto dwellers might have a better chance of leaving the ghetto if they were able to earn a better income. With this thought in mind, job possibilities are minority-group members should be examined.

THE PROBLEM OF JOBS FOR THE GHETTO RESIDENT

Unemployment and underemployment are among the most serious and persistent problems of the disadvantaged minorities; they contribute mightily to civil disorder in the ghetto. Beginning with the

7 Op. Cit.

Employment Act of 1946, when the national goal of a useful job at a reasonable wage for all who wish to work was set, the United States government has made persistent efforts to solve these problems. Despite many efforts and despite sustained economic prosperity, this goal has never been met. Possibly because of the growing demand for skilled persons in industries that are becoming more and more automated, attaining full employment has become even more difficult.

Even more important than unemployment is the related problem of the undesirable nature of many jobs open to Negroes. Negro workers most often are concentrated in the lowest-paying and lowest-skilled jobs in the economy. These jobs often involve substandard wages, great instability, and uncertainty of steady employment. As a result, the income of black families remains far below that of white families. In 1966 the median family income for blacks was 58 percent of the median income for whites.

Because of these factors, residents of Negro ghetto neighborhoods have been subject for decades to social, economic, and psychological disadvantages. The result tends to be a cycle of failure. The employment disabilities of one generation breed similar problems in the following generation.

So far we have seen that the ghetto is a portion of the central city which is characterized by poor housing. Persons who live there tend to have less education and consequently fewer job opportunities and, in general, are poorer than the average American. These problems seem to be related to high crime rates, insecurity, and poor health and sanitation in the ghetto. We will examine these problems next.

CERTAIN SOCIAL AND HEALTH PROBLEMS OF GHETTO

For years criminologists have known that crime rates are always higher in poor neighborhoods, whatever their ethnic composition. The Negro ghetto is no exception to this. The black residents' sense of personal security is certainly undermined by the frequency of crime in the big-city ghettos. The Kerner Commission found that crime rates in the ghettos are much higher than elsewhere in the city. For example, one very low income Negro district had 35 times as many serious crimes against persons per 100,000 residents as did a high income white district.

Crimes in the ghetto are commited by a small minority of the residents. And most of the victims are law-abiding black people. It is quite difficult for middle-class whites to understand how insecure these law-abiding ghetto dwellers feel. In poor areas Negroes are probably 75 percent more likely to be victims of a major crime than are residents of most higher income areas. They are about 3.5 times more likely to be robbed. And Negro women are probably 3.7 times more likely to be raped.

Because of this high crime rate, many Negroes have bitter feelings toward the police. They feel they do not receive adequate protection from law enforcement agencies. Many black people believe that the police do not offer them adequate protection, and this tends to be one of the black person's principal grievances against the police. This latter point was reiterated because it is important that law enforcement personnel be cognizant of it.

Ghetto residents tend to have other problems also. Poor families are usually found to have poor diets, poor housing, poor clothing, and poor medical care. Generally speaking, about 30 percent of such families suffer from chronic health problems that have adverse effects upon employment possibilities. Although Negro ghetto residents have many more health problems, they spend less than half as much per person on medical services as white families with comparable incomes. Apparently the reasons for this are: (1) Negro families are usually *larger* than white families; (2) necessities often cost Negroes *more* than whites, e.g., housing costs for Negroes versus housing costs for whites; (3) *fewer* medical facilities and personnel are available to poor Negroes, generally because doctors prefer to practice in higher-income areas; and (4) general environmental conditions in the Negro ghetto are not conducive to good health. Among these are *poor* sanitation and overcrowding, the lack of decent facilities for storing food, as well as serious rodent problems.

The one bright hope most Americans in earlier periods had for their future generations lay in the school. Schools in Negro ghettos leave a great deal to be desired. An examination of educational facilities in the ghetto appears to be appropriate at this time.

EDUCATION IN THE GHETTO

A good education has traditionally been the means by which people have escaped from poverty and discrimination and, consequently, from the ghetto. Therefore, education within the ghetto is a particularly acute problem. However, by and large, schools in black ghettos have failed to liberate the people from their plight. This failure has caused resentment and grievances by the Negro community against the schools. This resentment is not wholly unfounded.

As time passes, the record of public education for ghetto children seems to be becoming worse. In the critical verbal skills of reading and writing, Negro students fall further behind with each year of school completed. The U.S. Department of Health, Education and Welfare published a report in 1966 which indicated that on the average, minority group children from the ghetto are somewhat below white children with respect to educational level upon entering first grade. However, by the sixth grade, standard achievement tests indicate that Negro students are 1.6 grades behind, and by twelfth grade, they are 3.3 grades behind the white students who started school with them.[8]

As a result of this, far more Negro students (minority students in general) than white students drop out of school. Negro students are three times as likely to do this as white students. Unfortunately, a very high proportion of the dropouts are not equipped to enter the normal job market, and when they do, they tend to get low-skilled, low-paying jobs.

The vast majority of inner-city schools are involved in *de facto* segregation. Racial segregation in urban public schools is principally the result of residential segregation, combined with widespread employment of the neighborhood school policy. This, of course, transfers segregation from housing to education. Many of the students in the segregated schools are poor. Many come from families whose adults were products of inadequate rural school systems of the South, which had low levels of educational attainment. Children from these families most often have limited vocabularies and are not well equipped to learn rapidly. When these disadvantaged children are racially isolated in ghetto schools, they are deprived of a significant ingredient of a quality education—exposure to other children who have strong educational backgrounds. Most educators and sociologists believe that strong socioeconomic background of pupils in a school exerts a powerful impact upon the achievement of other students in that school. By the nature of the ghetto school, this is denied to most minority-group pupils.

Furthermore, generally speaking, ghetto schools are inferior to schools in predominantly white neighborhoods in many respects. Indications are that the teachers are less qualified and have less experience than teachers in suburban schools. Ghetto schools typically have overcrowded classrooms; the buildings are old and poorly equipped; and the books and supplies are inadequate, if not in short supply. And the money which could eliminate these conditions has not been available.

Teachers in inner-city schools say they have many emotionally disturbed, retarded, and maladjusted students and few facilities to deal with these students. Another valid criticism of ghetto schools is that the curricula and materials used there are ordinarily geared to middle-class white suburban students, and textbooks make no reference to Negro achievements and contributions to American life. Because the schoolwork has little or no relevance to the ghetto youngster's life experience, the youth tends to conclude that education is not relevant to his life.

Many Negro residents of the inner city are angry about the inadequacies of their schools. Unfortunately, communication between the com-

---

[8] Department of Health, Education and Welfare, *Equality of Educational Opportunity* (Washington, D. C.: Government Printing Office, 1966), p. 20.

munity and the school administrators is likely to be quite poor. Probably this is because the teachers and administrators live outside the ghetto and do not fully understand its problems. On the other hand, most ghetto parents lack much formal education and generally believe they have little voice in changing school matters. However, they do feel that the schools are not providing an adequate education for their children, and they regard this as unjust.

Schooling, employment, crime, health problems, and housing are all factors that reflect upon the nature of ghettos. Taken together, they could be termed *the world of the ghetto.*

SOME THOUGHTS REGARDING A TYPICAL GHETTO FAMILY

As stated before, the majority of the poorest people in the United States are found in ghettos. The Report of the National Advisory Commission on Civil Disorders indicates that in 1966 approximately 12 percent of the country's white families were poor; this was true of approximately 41 percent of the Negro families in the United States. Of the Negro poor, about 70 percent, or nearly 12 million live in inner cities, which are known as ghettos.

Poverty, which seems to be the result of underemployment and unemployment, has many effects on the ghetto family. Because often the men of the family cannot obtain good jobs enabling them to support their wife and children, their status and self-respect are affected. Frequently wives are forced to work; they frequently make more money than their husbands can earn. This has the effect of making the husbands feel inadequate and, consequently, they separate from or divorce their wives. This, in turn, leads to more and more Negro families being headed by females rather than males. Almost three times as many Negro families are fatherless as white families—a situation which has great impact on the children.

Furthermore, Negro families headed by women are twice as likely to live in poverty as those headed by men. In the poorest Negro ghettos the problem of fatherless families has many side effects. Many children, with their fathers gone and their mothers working to support the family, spend much of their life in the streets where crime and violence are commonplace. In the streets where the children grow up the men tend to be "hustlers," thieves, dope peddlers, pimps, and numbers operators rather than honest laborers. In such an atmosphere these fatherless Negro children probably do not attend school regularly, and they are very likely to become delinquent, to contract venereal disease, or be responsible for illegimate births.

The real injustice of the ghetto system is that the future is not promising for many of the children. A great majority are growing up in poverty under conditions that make them better candidates for crime and civil disorder than for jobs that would provide an entry into the mainstream of the American economy.

Conditions in the ghetto are a reflection of the general social structure of the society and its lack of concern for equal justice among minority groups. The institutional structure of the courts and their history has had a telling effect upon the present social structure of the ghetto. Lest one get the idea, however, that the courts have been wholly responsible for the situation, one must remember that to a large extent the courts have been responsible for some of the changes for the better that are happening in regard to minority groups in this country.

Equal Justice in the Courts

The courts are quite important even though relatively few cases reach trial. It should be noted that those that do so, establish the legal rules for all cases and vitally affect the public image of justice.[9] The great majority of persons accused of crime in this country are poor. The system of criminal justice under which they are judged is rooted in the idea that arrest can be made only for cause and that those arrested are presumed innocent until proven guilty. By and large, the accused are entitled to pretrial freedom to aid in their own defense. A plea of guilty should be voluntary, and all the allegations of antisocial behavior are to be submitted to the adversary system that is referred to as the bar of justice.

To examine this system as it relates to minority-group members, some consideration should be made of the history of the courts' treatment of minority groups. Certain historical highlights regarding this will therefore be examined at this point.

Highlights in the Courts' Treatment of Minority-Group Members

The most appropriate place to start examining minority-group treatment before the courts is with the Dred Scott[10] decision, which was handed down by the Supreme Court in 1857. This case concerned Dred Scott, a Negro slave who had lived with his master for five years in

[9] President's Commission on Law Enforcement and Administration of Justice *Task Force Report: The Courts* (Washington, D. C.: Government Printing Office, 1967).
[10] *Dred Scott* v. *Stanford*, 19 How. 393 (1857).

Illinois and the Wisconsin Territory. At the time these were free and the southern states were slave states. The Court decided that Dred Scott was a Negro slave and therefore not a citizen; consequently he could not sue in court.

This decision quite plainly indicated that a little over one hundred years ago peoples of a minority group had no rights whatsoever in court. However, in 1868 the Fourteenth Amendment to the Constitution was passed, and it stated in part:

> All persons born or naturalized in the United States, and subject to the jurisdiction thereof, are citizens of the United States and of the State wherein they reside. No State shall make or enforce any law which shall abridge the privileges or immunities of citizens of the United States; nor shall any State deprive any person of life, liberty, or property, without due process of law; nor deny to any person within its jurisdiction the equal protection of the laws.

This amendment clearly established that members of a minority group were to be treated equally under the law. However, for many years following this, the courts interpreted the law in the light of a doctrine which was known as separate but equal rights. The case of *Plessy v. Ferguson*,[11] decided by the United States Supreme Court in 1896, upheld this doctrine as it related to the civil rights of American Negroes. In many areas, especially with schools, the doctrine of *separate* was prevalent but the facilities were far from *equal*. Obviously, facilities for the minority group were inferior. On the other hand, however, in certain specific situations, minority-group members were afforded equal treatment.

A study by Guy B. Johnson,[12] which covers the years 1930 to 1940, indicates that in most southern courts Negroes who committed offenses against other Negroes were dealt with no more severely than white persons who committed crimes against other white persons. Differentiation was made when a Negro perpetrated a crime against a member of the Caucasian race; at this point he was dealt with quite severely. The Johnson study did not take into account the probability that more accused persons of the Negro race were convicted than were members of the Caucasian race. A great deal of the reason for this has to do with the fact that Negroes, in general, tend to be poorer than Caucasians, and the greatest discriminating factor in criminal justice is whether or not the accused has sufficient monetary means. Persons who have money

---

[11] *Plessy v. Ferguson*, 163 U. S. 537 (1896).

[12] G. B. Johnson, "The Negro and Crime," in *The Sociology of Crime and Delinquency*, eds., M. Wolfgang, L. Savitz, and N. Johnson (New York: John Wiley & Sons, Inc., 1962), pp. 145–53.

are much more likely to be treated leniently by the courts than persons who do not.

Recently, the Supreme Court has made some rulings which should change this. Some of these cases were discussed in Chapter 1, but they will be discussed again here in reference to the particular problem of minority-group members and the probability that they have less money than persons of the majority group.

In one such case, the United States Supreme Court in 1954, by a famous ruling known as *Brown* v. *Board of Education*[13] declared that the separate but equal doctrine that had been used to segregate the public schools was unconstitutional. *Brown* v. *Board of Education* was specifically concerned with the Board of Education of Topeka, Kansas. Similar cases regarding the states of Virginia, Delaware, and South Carolina were decided at the same time. This ruling by the Supreme Court began the process of correcting injustice to minority-group members.

The Supreme Court has actively led this country toward a fuller understanding of the high ideals set forth in the Constitution. Through various decisions the Supreme Court has begun to equalize a poor person's chances before the bar of justice with that of someone who has more money. This is most important to minority-group members because they tend to be poorer than members of the white majority. Among the cases that probably did most for minorities in this indirect manner was *Gideon* v. *Wainwright*,[14] decided in 1963. Essentially, Gideon was charged with breaking and entering a poolroom. At his trial in Florida he asked the court to appoint a lawyer for him, but the judge refused. When the U.S. Supreme Court reviewed the case they responded by stating that legal assistance is the right of one charged with a crime and is fundamental to a fair trial. (It should be noted that when Gideon, with competent counsel, was later re-tried he was found not guilty.)

A second case of interest is *Miranda* v. *Arizona*.[15] This case, decided by the Supreme Court in 1966, concerned a confession admitted as evidence in a rape charge. It developed that Miranda had not been informed of his constitutional rights to remain silent and to have legal counsel. The Supreme Court reversed his conviction, on the grounds that a person arrested for a crime should be given a fourfold warning before he is questioned. These warnings are that one has a right to remain silent; that anything he says may be used against him; that he has a right to have present an attorney during the questioning; and that if he is indigent, he has a right to have an attorney furnished to

[13] *Brown v. Board of Education*, 347 U. S. 483 (1954).
[14] *Gideon v. Wainwright*, 372 U. S. 335 (1963).
[15] *Miranda v. Arizona*, 384 U. S. 436 (1966).

him without charge. (It should be noted that Miranda was re-tried and again found guilty of the crime of rape.)

A third case which probably did a great deal to afford equal justice to minority groups was one decided in 1967 and known as In re *Gault*.[16] Gault, a minor, was found to be a "delinquent youngster" and committed to a state facility in Arizona. However, at the time of his arrest he was not given the forewarnings that the Court felt reasonable for an adult; furthermore, he had not been provided an attorney, and he had no opportunity to face his accusers. All these rights had, before this time, been spelled out for adults. In the Gault case, the Supreme Court indicated that they should also be applied to minors being tried in a juvenile court. The Gault case is important because from 40 to 50 percent of the persons arrested for crime in the United States are juveniles. In addition, as with adults, in a disproportionate number, they come from minority groups who tend to be the poor ghetto residents.

Another process of the court system which poses some inequities is the bail system.

INEQUITIES OF BAIL AND SOME ATTEMPTS TO RESOLVE THIS PROBLEM

Traditionally, criminal cases begin with an arrest; this is followed by detention until a magistrate can decide on the amount of bail the accused may post before trial for his release. In its present form the bail system discriminates against, and consequently punishes, the poor. The affluent can afford to buy their freedom, while the poor go to jail. Because of this, the defendant without monetary funds may lose his job and his present earning capacity. All this transpires before the trial and before there has been a determination of guilt or innocence. This, in effect, may result in a person's being punished rather severely for being poor.[17] Many changes are, however, taking place in the bail system, and these show promise for more equal justice for the poverty-sticken and, consequently, minority groups in general.

More and more, law enforcement agencies are coming to the conclusion that in certain circumstances there are alternatives to arrest. There is no question that arrest and detention is needed if the crime is serious or if there is danger of the defendant's fleeing from court jurisdiction. Furthermore, the police may feel that the defendant needs to be fingerprinted and photographed as well as searched and questioned. However, generally speaking, an arrest followed by detention is not used

---

[16] In re. *Gault*, 387 U. S. 1 (1967).
[17] R. Goldfarb, *Ransom: A Critique of the American Bail System* (New York: John Wiley & Sons, Inc., 1965).

in traffic matters and there is reason to believe that arrests for certain other offenses do not need to be followed by detention. Offenses involving petty crimes and local code violations may well be handled in another matter.

Alternatives to routine arrest and detention have been developed by several state and federal courts. These alternatives generally take two forms. In the first situation, a judicial officer issues a summons upon complaint of the prosecutor. In the second situation, a police officer issues a citation or notice to appear, much like a traffic ticket. In *Task Force Report: The Courts*[18] a description of the extensive use of citations for all misdemeanor offenses in San Francisco and Contra Costa County, California, is described. In this area, unless an arrest is necessary to protect the community, the court process, or the defendant, a misdemeanor suspect is released at the scene of the offense upon identifying himself. The arresting officer decides upon the summons process after he checks with headquarters through the computer-based Police Intelligence Network System. The federal courts in Washington, D.C., as well as many state courts, have been experimenting with the process of releasing persons on their own recognizance rather than having them post bail. Generally speaking, such moves by the courts have tended somewhat to improve chances of the defendant without monetary funds for equal treatment before trial.

As far as can be determined, in many matters of criminal justice, the courts have been starting to treat minority-group members more fairly as of late. It is possible however, that the emphasis on criminal court problems has somehow screened out the need for reforms in our civil courts, particularly as they involve the poor.

POSSIBLE INEQUITIES INVOLVING THE POOR IN CIVIL COURTS

According to Thomas E. Willinge, law professor at the University of Toledo,[19] the major barrier between poor people and justice is expert legal counsel. He indicates that while adequate counsel is a necessity for successful litigation, our efforts to provide good counsel for the poor have not worked out very well. For example, a poor person who believes that his landlord may be right or that the alleged debt which he owes is just, usually does not bother to show up in court. Those who do come to court feel that they have been treated unjustly and, therefore, they come to court in what they think is a good case. For the most part, lawyers

---

[18] President's Commission on Law Enforcement and Administration of Justice, *Task Force Report: The Courts*, pp. 40–41.

[19] T. E. Willinge, "Financial Barriers and the Access of Indigents to the Courts," *The Georgetown Law Journal*, Vol. 57, No. 2 (November 1968), pp. 253–306.

represent the businessman, in this case, the landlord, and they usually win judgments against the bewildered, intimidated poor. Too often, the poor leave the courtroom as losers, without any feeling that justice has been done.

A *second* factor, of course, is the financial barrier between poor litigants and justice. Under our system of justice, the Constitution guarantees free access to civil court for all citizens. However, many poor people are frightened by the court system, which they view as rigged against them, because they are frequently unsuccessful litigants and, therefore, are faced with loss of time and money as well as court costs upon losing the case.

After some brief examination of the society and of the courts, we should finally turn our attention to law enforcement agencies and their handling of minority groups as they relate to equal justice.

Police, Minority Groups, and Equal Justice

In most instances the decision to initiate criminal prosecution is a matter of police judgment. Supposedly, this judgment is based upon the legal definition of crime. However, it is quite apparent that in many instances in which a violation of the law has occurred and the police know of that violation, the police do not act. Some of the factors which cause this discrepancy are: (1) the *volume* of criminal law violations and the limited resources of the police, (2) the *enactment of laws* which define criminal conduct in a most generalized manner, and (3) various *pressures* reflecting the attitudes of a particular community.

An example of this dilemma is social gambling. In most jurisdictions gambling is illegal. However, there is good reason to believe that complete enforcement of antigambling laws is neither expected nor intended. Consequently, law enforcement agencies are left with the responsibility of enforcing antigambling statues in a particular community. Because of this, Bingo may be tolerated at church functions, while bookmaking is not. Also, the police may be confronted with the problem of deciding when gambling in a private home constitutes a violation of the anti-gambling statutes. For the average white middle-class American, a small game of poker within the confines of one's own home is possible because the indoor living space is adequate. On the other hand, in the crowded ghetto, where indoor living space is at a premium, games of chance are often moved to a dead-end street or alleyway.

When police are informed that such a game is taking place, they generally respond and arrest the players. Police justify their intervention by saying that these arrests serve to prevent crime because past experience shows that card games in the ghetto frequently end in fights;

those played in suburban areas generally do not.[20] Consequently, although the police's intention may be quite noble, this practice gives the appearance of improper class and racial discrimination.

A *second* example is law enforcement's handling of assaultive-type offenses. These offenses come to the attention of law enforcement agencies quite frequently because they occur in public, because police wish to intervene before more harm is done, or because the victim is found to be in need of medical aid by a patrol unit. While the perpetrator of the assault is known to the victim in a large percent of the cases, frequently there is no arrest, or if an arrest is made, it is followed shortly by release of the alleged assailant without prosecution. Seemingly, this is especially true in ghetto areas owing, according to law enforcement personnel, primarily to an unwillingness on the part of the victim to cooperate in the prosecution. Even if the victim should cooperate during the investigation stage, based on past experience, the police believe this willingness to cooperate will disappear at the time of trial. It might be possible for police to achieve some success in assaultive cases by subpoenaing the victim to testify. However, the subpoena process is seldom used. Instead, the path of least resistance—the decision not to prosecute—is followed when the victim appears unwilling to testify. Police justify this action by pointing out the high volume of cases and other compelling demands made upon the agency, which would be increased if victims needed to be subpoenaed as routine policy. This decision is further rationalized on the grounds that the injured party was the only person harmed and he does not wish to pursue the matter. Cases of this sort can be written off statistically as cleared cases, which are an index of police efficiency.

These kinds of police practices, particularly in the ghetto, raise the question, To what degree does police tolerance of assaultive conduct result in the formation of negative attitudes on the part of ghetto residents toward law and order in general?[21] Also, how can a ghetto resident consider law enforcement fair, when an attack by a ghetto resident upon a person residing outside the ghetto generally results in a vigorous prosecution.

According to the *Report of the Commission on Civil Disorders*, Negroes firmly believe that police brutality and harassment occur repeatedly in black neighborhoods. The reader is reminded that Chapter 4 also dealt with the problem of police brutality, but from the standpoint of its effect upon the police image; our concern here is with its relationship to equal justice and/or the treatment of minority-group members.

---

[20] President's Commission on Law Enforcement and Administration of Justice, *Task Force Report: The Police*, (Washington, D. C.: Government Printing Office, 1967) pp. 21–2.
[21] *Ibid.*, p. 22.

This belief that police tend to be unduly brutal when they arrest minority-group members may well be one of the main reasons for minority-group resentment against the police. To a large extent, research seems to show that these beliefs are unjustified.

> One survey done by the Crime Commission suggests that when police-citizen contacts are systematically observed, the vast majority are handled without antagonism or incident. Of 5,339 police-citizen contacts observed in slum precincts in three large cities, in the opinion of the observer, only 20—about three-tenths of 1 per cent—involved excessive or unnecessary force. And although almost all of those subjected to such force were poor, more than half were white.[22]

In another study conducted by the Center of Research on Social Organization[23], the data seemed to support the same kind of conclusion as in the study done for the Crime Commission. In the study done by the Center, observations of police arrests were conducted in Boston, Chicago, and Washington, D.C., seven days a week for seven weeks during the summer of 1966. Professional observers accompanied policemen on their calls and to the stations where bookings and lockups were made. There were 643 white suspects and 751 Negro suspects in the sample of this study. Twenty-seven of the whites and 17 of the Negros experienced undue use of force when they were arrested. This yields an abuse rate of 41.9 per thousand white suspects and 22.6 per thousand Negro suspects.

Physical abuse does not seem to be practiced against minority-group members in a greater degree than it is practiced against majority-group members. However, physical abuse is certainly not the only source of irritation to the ghetto resident. Any practice that degrades a citizen's status, restricts his freedom, or annoys or harasses him is felt to be an unjust use of police powers by law enforcement personnel. A policeman's talking down to a person or calling him names is particularly objectionable to most citizens. Black citizens complain that law enforcement personnel often talk down to them as if they had no name, calling them "boy" or "man." They feel that this type of treatment strips them of their dignity because they are shown no respect by law enforcement personnel. Other objectionable practices include the use of profanity and abusive language toward minority-group members. Police, too, are often inclined to command minority-group members to "get going" or "get home." Because homes in ghetto areas tend to be overcrowded, young ghetto residents are the most likely targets of this type of harassment. This is true especially during the hot summer months, when ghetto youths

---

[22] *Report of the National Advisory Commission on Civil Disorders*, p. 159.
[23] A. J. Reiss, Jr., "Police Brutality—Answers to Key Questions," *Trans-Action*, Vol. 5, No. 8 (July-August 1968), pp. 10–19.

spend most of their time in public places or walking the streets, as they have no other place to go.

In an article by Sam Blum[24] an incident that was felt to be police harassment was described. The incident, which happened in Washington, D.C., involved a man who had been arrested three times in two weeks' time—once for littering when he dropped a paper cup and twice for drinking in public. The latter occurred when the man was found drinking a beer while sitting behind a laundromat. Incidents of this type are generally regarded as police harassment by ghetto residents. Possibly this is because they tend to view their front or back steps as the suburbanite views his patio.

All parties agree that the elimination of charges of police misconduct requires selecting police for duty in ghettos with care. This is partly because police responsibility in these areas is particularly demanding and sensitive as regards ghetto residents' attitudes, and often it is rather dangerous as well. The highest caliber personnel is required to overcome feelings of inadequate protection and unfair discriminatory treatment by the police within the black community.

Summary

The inequities of justice for minorities were examined from three aspects: (1) minority treatment within the community by virtue of the minority-group member's being a ghetto resident; (2) minority-group treatment by the courts; and (3) minority-group treatment by the police.

The black ghetto is examined in some depth because the Negro represents the largest minority in the United States and most of the research studies have been done on the black ghetto. It was also felt that certain generalizations could be made about all types of ghetto residents from this examination. The student of police-community relations is cautioned to remember that other ethnic groups may be the predominant minority in his area. In a particular circumstance the information regarding another ethnic group may be somewhat different from that stated here, but it is felt that, by and large, generalizations stated here will apply.

A ghetto is a deprived, congested area of the city, characterized by poverty and social disorganization. Mainly because of poverty and segregation, much of the housing in ghetto areas tends to be substandard, overcrowded, aged, and deteriorating.

Underemployment and unemployment are critical problems for the

---

[24] S. Blum, "The Police" in *Violence in the Streets*, eds., S. Endleman (Chicago: Quadrangle Books, Inc., 1968), pp. 417–33.

ghetto dweller and may well be the key to his poverty. For example, twice as many black people as white people are unemployed, and black people are three times more likely to be underemployed. These circumstances help to strengthen the poverty cycle.

Poverty and family disorganization, as well as tension and insecurity, are part of the ghetto community, and crime rates in the ghetto are far higher than in better areas of the city. Narcotics addiction, juvenile delinquency, venereal disease, poor health services, and dependence on welfare are all prevalent in ghetto areas. The law enforcement student is reminded that the high crime rate causes ghetto residents to feel bitter toward the police because they believe they do not receive adequate protection from the police.

Another area which has caused a great deal of bitterness is education; ghetto schools tend to be the worst in any city's school system. The result of this is that far more minority-group students leave school before graduating than majority-group students. This is regrettable because a good education has traditionally been the means by which people have escaped from poverty and moved toward more equal treatment within society.

To examine equal treatment in society, the court processes of that society probably should be examined. This was done. A review of historic court decisions and statutes which changed the complexion of minority-group treatment was made. The starting point was the Dred Scott decision, wherein the Supreme Court decided that a black slave had no citizenship rights. This was changed by the enactment of the Fourteenth Amendment, but it was never completely implemented until the Supreme Court decision of *Brown* v. *Board of Education*. The courts enforced "Jim Crow" laws for almost 90 years before the *Brown* decision ended this in 1954.

Certain other Supreme Court decisions concerning the legal rights of indigent persons were discussed. Because minority-group members often are without monetary funds, these decisions should have a far-reaching effect on their treatment in the courts. A short critique of the bail system, as well as of the handling of civil cases by the courts and how these adversely affect persons without funds and consequently, minority-group members, was also made.

Police practices and their effect on equal justice regarding minorities were examined. Particular attention was devoted to the police tendency to enforce certain types of violations differently in the ghetto than elsewhere. An examples of this is the enforcement of antigambling laws in the ghetto as opposed to their lack of rigid enforcement in the suburbs.

Police brutality was reviewed, with the conclusion that acts of police brutality seemingly are not related to being a member of a minority ethnic group. Causes of police brutality seem to be more closely related to poverty than to ethnic background.

Finally, police harassment was discussed. This is often called police brutality by minorities and is a good example of the problems in communication between police and minority groups. Incidents of police harassment seem to be highest among the youth of ethnic minorities. It is felt that when each individual law enforcement officer understands some of the minority-group complaints regarding unequal justice, he will be better equipped to understand members of minority groups and to really communicate with them. It is the authors' contention that meaningful communication will lead to the solution of many problems in the area of police-community relations.

QUESTIONS

1. What is a ghetto?

2. What does a ghetto have to do with equal treatment for minorities?

3. Explain why it is felt that the courts have changed their attitude toward minorities over the past 100 years.

4. In what areas has the court been slow in acting in the best interest of minorities?

5. Explain the difference between police brutality and police harassment.

ANNOTATATED REFERENCES

Department of Health, Education and Welfare, *Equality of Educational Opportunity*. Washington, D.C.: Government Printing Office, 1966, p. 737. This report is an extensive study of the education received in ghetto schools as it compares with that of suburban schools. The chairman of the committee responsible for it was James S. Coleman. Therefore, the study is often referred to as the Coleman Report.

Endleman, S., ed., *Violence in the Streets*. Chicago: Quadrangle Books, Inc., 1968, p. 471. This is a collection of essays regarding violence and the police response to criminal behavior. The writers represented in this work seem to be from a broad spectrum of political persuasion.

President's Commission on Law Enforcement and Administration of Justice, *Task Force Report: The Courts*. Washington, D.C.: Government Printing Office, 1967, p. 178. This is part of the supporting material for the commission's report *The Challenge of Crime in a Free Society*. It provides a very good description of the criminal courts and how they function.

President's Commission on Law Enforcement and Administration of Justice, *Task Force Report: The Police*. Washington, D.C.: Government Printing Office, 1967, p. 239. This is also part of the supporting material for *The Challenge of Crime in a Free Society*. This report regarding police in the United States is quite good, and all law enforcement students should be familiar with it.

Report of the National Advisory Commission on Civil Disorders. Washington, D.C.: Government Printing Office, 1968, p. 425. This is a comprehensive study of several of the more recent riots in the United States, as well as an extensive investigation of conditions within the ghetto. Attention is directed toward these conditions particularly as they are related to civil disorders. The report is often referred to as the Kerner Report, for Otto Kerner was chairman of the committee responsible for the study.

CHAPTER SEVEN

SOCIAL CHANGE AND COMMUNITY TENSION

Figure 7.1 *America has changed in many ways. When there are changes in the very tangible world then changes in the social world should be no surprise. But change may not always be of a positive nature. Photo courtesy of the San Francisco Police Department, San Francisco, California.*

FOR THE MOST PART, EARLY AMERICAN CULTURE DEVELOPED IN THE RURAL AREAS. Farmers in the North depended mainly on the labor of their children, and the agrarian economy of the South depended on the labor of slaves. The main source of energy was human beings. Of course inventions in the field of agriculture and the use of tools helped to make human energy more effective, and early rural America enjoyed many labor-saving devices. Nevertheless, the primary source of energy was human effort.

The transition from agriculture to industry, known as the Industrial Revolution, tended to displace both the northern children and the newly freed southern slaves, forcing them to the cities. These same cities were busily replacing human labor with machinery, however, and at an even faster pace than farms were being mechanized.

One immediate result of the Industrial Revolution was increased leisure for many. In the case of those who worked, the mechanization of labor reduced the amount of time needed to achieve desired production levels. For those unable to gain employment in urban factories, leisure also increased dramatically, if not desirably—at least during periods when employment was being sought. In either event, the dawn-till-dusk workday of the farm began to fade from the American scene. With it also faded the security of the dreary but certain continuation of living out a predictable life on a farm or plantation. Several major wars and a never-ending elimination of jobs by machinery have done little to give the modern urban worker security similar to that of yesterday's farmer—in spite of, and perhaps because of, ever-increasing leisure.

Clearly, American has *changed* in many other ways, but it is the changes producing the greatest abundance of leisure time that become the sources of many community tensions.

Social Change

Perhaps the greatest clarity of the concept of *change* can be gained by first noting that change is *not optional*. The Grand Canyon is becoming deeper at the rate of one inch a year, whether people approve of such change or not. Scotland moves toward Ireland about eight feet annually, and Europe and the United States are moving about one foot apart each year. London sinks a fraction of an inch annually, while the North Pole moves southward one-half foot.

When you note such changes in the tangible physical world, then changes in the social world should be no surprise. Any difference in human behavior over a period of time is *change*, and differences in human behavior are constantly observable. But *change* may not always be of a positive nature. A brief discussion of leisure may illustrate this.

LEISURE

Many, if not most, would agree that leisure has a great number of positive factors. Discovery of tools and the use of animals along with numerous other sources of energy placed prehistoric man on a path ultimately leading to enough free time for the creation of the *arts and sciences*—neither of which was conceivable until sufficient leisure was available.

In this context leisure tends to gain a favorable connotation, probably because it can be equated either with *recreation* or productivity. But not all leisure is recreational or productive, and herein lies a source of community tension. Among the unemployed and underemployed of the ghetto, leisure may mean only having more time in which to get into trouble.

When American buying habits are examined, however, it might seem that the increasing leisure of affluence has been dominated by recreation. Beginning in the World War II decade of 1940 through 1950,[1] expenditures for sports equipment and toys increased threefold, musical instruments and sound equipment, fivefold, and for opera and legitimate theatre, doubled, with opera companies increasing in number from two to thirteen. In the same decade, twice as much money spent on books, the amount spent on foreign travel increased nearly nine times, and the number of classical music concerts held outside of New York City more than doubled. The twenty years that followed showed the same trend.

Such data imply widespread affluence in our country. But not everyone has enjoyed affluence to the same degree; some have not enjoyed it at all. One view of adversity that is dealt with in the literature is that it is more or less a "natural" consequence of "progress."[2] Of course, to accept such a view without challenge is to question the possibility or at least the advisability, of programs geared to alleviate the adverse consequences of social change. But if community tension is to be reduced, the negative results of social change that produce increased leisure *must* be conceived of as correctable. Correction, however, depends on a number of variables relating to the political and economic power discussed in Chapter 3—the key variable, in an increasingly automated society, being educational opportunity.

EDUCATION

The demand for education grows with social changes that result from increases in technical knowledge. With each discovery of new sources of energy and machinery to replace human labor, a corresponding demand for increased sophistication in methods of productivity occurs. *Automation, cybernetics*, and *electronic data processing* on the one hand, close many avenues of employment by displacing employees. On the other hand, they create many new and promising opportunities, but only for

---

[1] F. Turck, "The American Explosion," *Scientific Monthly* (September, 1952), pp. 187–91.

[2] H. Meissner, ed., *Poverty in Affluent Society* (New York: Harper & Row, Publishers, 1966), p. 19.

the well-trained and educated. The significance of education then necessarily increases.

Unemployment in America is traditionally a stigma. The moralistic Puritan ancestry that developed many of the American "work mores" drew heavily on the belief that labor was not only imposed by nature as a punishment for sin, but also that it is an ascetic discipline willed by God.[3] This Puritan heritage has led segments of the population to hold some quite rigid tenets. Individuals raised to believe in the necessity for and the value of work are likely to feel that persons who are not employed are simply lazy. Such an oversimplification, of course, ignores the vast complexity involved in examining the *true* nature of competition for meaningful employment. It also reduces the usual confusion in sophisticated analyses of the necessity of *access* to education in order to compete for jobs. But law enforcement personnel who are *increasingly confronted with the violent consequences of such oversimplifications must seek a far more sophisticated view of the causes of unemployment and the role of education in alleviating joblessness.*

Before examining equality of *access* to education, some thought might be given the concept of social change as it relates to education in general. The occupational field of law enforcement itself serves as a model of the lag between the growth of social institutions and the rate of change in modern America. In cities having growing populations, for

Figure 7.2 *Student unrest on campuses throughout the United States has had a tremendous effect on police tactics, manpower, and financial resources. Photo courtesy of the San Francisco Police Department, San Francisco, California.*

[3] H. Stein and R. Cloward, *Social Perspectives on Behavior* (New York: The Free Press, 1967) p. 273.

example, there are fewer police per 10,000 inhabitants than in cities with decreasing populations.[4] In like fashion, certain school programs for the disadvantaged child have lagged far behind the growth in the numbers of these children in the education system.[5] This lag has continued in spite of the compulsory school attendance that distinguishes the United States from much of the world.[6]

Social change, bringing increases in leisure, brings attention to education in two ways. As already noted, an increased demand for technical skill accompanies the discovery of new sources of energy and labor-saving machinery. Here there is, of course, an obvious role for education and training. But social change draws attention to the *length of time* necessary for a student to complete his education.

Both family and the public have traditionally been prepared to support a child's education through at least grade school and often through high school. But what about college? And how much college?

Prior to what is often referred to as the knowledge explosion, following the technical advances of World War II, college was not a requisite in most people's education. But automation, combined with government sponsorship through the GI Bill and other subsidized college programs, has rapidly focused attention on college training as a crucial part of the educational process. To many this social change has unveiled vast new horizons of opportunity. To others, it has even further widened the gap between affluence and poverty. For unlike the masses of middle-class families prepared and motivated to support children through the increasing expenses of education, poverty-stricken families necessarily consider the high-school-age child a potential source of income, or at least as some relief from the drain on limited family income. The relatively small number of college students from poverty backgrounds should not then be surprising, even in the rare instances in which *adequate* high school programs were available.

There are many sources of community tension, but none are so great as the social changes that increase the disparity of opportunity to control one's destiny. Education is increasingly the prime ingredient in the potential of ultimate control.

Community Tension

There are numerous causes of community unrest; many of these lie beyond the scope of law enforcement or of criminal justice. There is, nonetheless, a significant relationship between law enforcement and cer-

---

[4] W. Ogburn, "Cultural Lag as Theory," *Sociology and Social Research* (January-February 1957), pp. 167–74. Also, *Social Characteristics of Cities*, International City Managers Association, 1937.

[5] R. Kerckhoff, "The Problem of the City School," *Journal of Marriage and the Family*, Vol. 26, No. 4 (November 1964), pp. 435–39.

[6] E. Friedenberg, "An Ideology of School Withdrawal," *Community*, Vol. 35, No. 6 (June 1963), pp. 492–500.

tain aspects of unrest. As noted in Chapter 3, symptoms of unrest frequently foreshadow direct intervention by law enforcement agencies. Moreover, law enforcement may even become involved in various causal aspects of community tension. The relationship of law enforcement to such community unrest has been placed in excellent context by Frank Remington's comments on arrest practice:

> ... from the point of view of either the individual or the community as a whole, the issue is not so much whether police are efficient, or whether the corrective system is effective, but whether the system of criminal justice in its entirety is sensible, fair, and consistent with the concepts of a democratic society. . . .[7]

In this context, as already noted, at least part of the community tension can be thought of, first, as a disparity between various citizens in terms of their potential to control their own destiny. And, second, unrest may be thought of as a reaction to the method of enforcing conformity to a system that creates or permits this inequality. In other words, a system "that is unsensible, unfair, or inconsistent with democratic concepts" may become as much a source of community tension as the social changes that created the original disparity in potential.

DEMONSTRATING UNREST WITHOUT RIOTS

Of course determining what is "sensible, fair, and consistent with democratic concepts" may not be completely possible for law enforcement in an era of grossly divergent and constantly changing demands. But to whatever degree law enforcement is able to achieve a system having these attributes, to at least that degree is community tension likely to be reduced.

The significance of such a reduction is probably most perceptible in distinguishing between a demonstration and a riot. Throughout this book this distinction is discussed as the *behavior* of the group involved. And more often than not, the behavior itself relates directly to law enforcement. It would seem reasonable to generalize that rioters rarely conceive of law enforcement as "sensible, fair, and consistent," whereas possibly many demonstrators do not riot simply because they believe the police have nothing to do with social changes that cause tension. Obviously, this is not always true. In many instances there is overwhelming evidence that police have borne the brunt of violence erupting out of demonstrations protesting social problems having no connection with law enforcement. But it remains a valid area of conjecture that at least the *degree* of violence relates to the attitude of the rioter toward law enforcement.

Regrettably, having an enforcement system that satisfies Mr. Remington's criteria of making sense, being fair, etc. does not insure a favorable attitude toward law enforcement.

[7] F. Remington, Foreword, in W. La Fave, *Arrest* (Boston: Little, Brown and Company, 1965).

Figure 7.3 *A peaceful demonstration and a distinguishing lack of tension is noted among the demonstrators. It is incumbent upon police personnel that they be able to determine the mood, attitude, and overall demeanor of the demonstrators. Photo courtesy of the Berkeley Police Department, Berkeley, California.*

SENSATIONALISM

Elsewhere throughout this volume, the psychology, sociology, and even the economics of prejudice, bias, and discrimination are dealt with as areas of concern for police in the changing community. Other such areas are community-relations programs (to be dealt with in Chapter 12) and much of the police image (considered in Chapter 4). But in terms of attitudes toward police and their responsibilities in times of social change, the *sensationalizing* of problems and problem causes might be another area of concern.

Sensationalizing problems and the causes of problems tend to aggravate community tension not so much through the distortion of facts as through the distortion of perspective. In the myriad contacts of law enforcement with all segments of the public, some abuses of police power are real, some are fancied. Both are frequently reported. At the heart of the problem of perspective, however, is the newspaper addage that "a dog biting a man is not news, but a man biting a dog is news." Police are far more available and visible than any other symbol of government authority. But like "the dog biting the man," police authority used to support an orderly society is expected, and therefore of little news appeal. But "like the man biting the dog," police brutality, real or fancied, is not expected, and is therefore of great news appeal.

The "sensational news" of brutal policemen may serve two functions; law enforcement should be aware of both in its struggle for a "sensible, fair, . . ." system. *First*, sensational news is probably of high commercial value. *Second*, there is great attention-gaining value in sensationalism to any group seeking relief for actual or imagined social ills. Indeed, if government social programming accelerates in areas which have caused civil violence, then a motive to "sensationally discredit" police in order to foster riot conditions may evolve further.

As already noted, community tensions, in a large measure, reflect social changes over which the police have no control. But the sensationalism of contact between police and public is an area singularly susceptible to community relations programming. And just as *change* is not *optional*, the obvious methods of meeting the problems of change through awareness cannot be *unfeasible*. To remain of value, the manner in which all justice is dispensed, particularly in a changing community, must remain functional, problems of change or not.[8] But the function itself may ultimately depend on the very feasible problem-and-program awareness by police and public alike—with the ultimate initiative always falling on the shoulders of law enforcement when avoiding gross civil disruption is the goal.

Summary

This chapter discussed the concept of *social change* as it relates to unrest and tension in the community. *Change* was presented as an ongoing process, subject not to prevention but only to control. As an elaboration of the social problems discussed in Chapter 3, major social changes in society were discussed as being partially within the scope of law enforcement, and partially not.

The Industrial Revolution that changed America from a rural agrarian economy to a culture of urbanized automation was presented as a prime mover toward greater leisure—leisure proving of advantage to the employable and a disadvantage to those without employable skills. An ensuing demand for employable skills was discussed as part of the changing cultural focus on access to higher education—access to education isolated as not available equally and, therefore, an additional source of community tension.

The unemployment accompanying the Industrial Revolution was discussed in the context of Puritan ethics, with the suggestion that law enforcement acquire a more sophisticated understanding of the true factors in poverty if greater community unrest is to be avoided.

Community tension per se was presented as flowing from many social changes, the majority of which are beyond the control of law enforcement. Nevertheless, a system of enforcing law that is sensible,

---

[8] A. Coffey, "Correctional Probation: What Use to Society?" *Journal of the California Probation and Parole Association*, Vol. 5, No. 1 (1968), p. 28.

fair, and consistent with democratic concepts was discussed as one method of reducing community tension. In this regard, a distinction was suggested between the behavior of a demonstrator and a rioter.

The detrimental impact of sensationalizing alleged abuses of police power was discussed as singularly susceptible to correction through programs geared to reduce community tension (or at least to increase public confidence in the system of enforcing law—in a manner to be discussed in Chapter 12).

Finally, the response of law enforcement to social change and community tension was discussed as being either functional or ultimately unacceptable, with the weight of demonstrating the value of its function falling on law enforcement itself if gross civil disruption is to be avoided.

QUESTIONS

1. Discuss the concept of change. Of *social* change.

2. Discuss the sources of increased leisure in America, the variety of uses to which leisure is put, the nature of leisure.

3. Relate social change to community tension.

4. Relate community tension to law enforcement.

5. Relate community tension and the access to education.

6. Discuss education and automation as they relate to poverty.

7. What is the usual impact on community tension of sensationalizing alleged abuses of power by the police?

ANNOTATED REFERENCES

La Fave, W., *Arrest*. Boston: Little, Brown and Company, 1965. An extremely comprehensive coverage of the power boundaries of law enforcement in the community.

Meissner, H., ed., *Poverty in Affluent Society*. New York: Harper & Row, Publishers, 1966. A collection of contributions dealing with the many influences of poverty and on poverty in the community.

Minuchin, S., B. Montalvo, B. Guerney, B. Rosman, and F. Schumer, *Families of the Slums*. New York: Basic Books Inc., Publishers, 1967. Excellent coverage of the subject—particularly of corrective measures for the problems such families encounter.

Noel, D., "A Theory of the Origin of Ethnic Stratification," *Social Problems*, Vol. 16, No. 2 (Fall 1968), 157–72. A plausible explanation of the social separation of ethnic grouping.

Stein, H. and R. Cloward, *Social Perspectives on Behavior*. New York: The Free Press, 1967. A varied, comprehensive sociological coverage of the nature of human conduct.

ATTITUDES!

OPINIONS?

CHAPTER EIGHT

THE PSYCHOLOGY AND SIGNIFICANCE OF ATTITUDES

Figure 8.1

HOSTILE ATTITUDES OF CITIZENS TOWARD THE POLICE are probably as disruptive of order as police malpractice. Also, citizens probably will not get the complete protection their taxes are paying for until they change their viewpoint toward law enforcement officers. In many ways this presents a paradox in that, generally speaking, the people who display the most enmity toward the police need their protection the most. Many minority-group members harbor a resentment against authority and have doubts about American ideals. In consideration of the history of race relations as well as ghetto conditions in the United States, these by-products should be expected.

A report by the federal government in 1967 expresses this problem most succinctly:

> It is ... almost ... a truism that ghetto residents will not obtain the police protection they badly want and need until policemen feel that their presence is welcome and that their problems are understood. However, in the effort to achieve this state of affairs, the duty of taking the initiative clearly devolves on the police, both because they are organized and disciplined and because they are public servants sworn to protect every part of the community.[1]

The major problem with the police taking the initiative is that they first must have some understanding of people's motives and attitudes, how they were formed, and how they can be changed. The rest of this chapter will provide a basis for this understanding.

Two Approaches to Studying Human Behavior

The behavior of mankind can be studied from two points of view. The *first* focuses on the group processes of mankind. Broadly speaking, this is the *sociological* approach. It is used in Chapter 7 of this book in regard to people's attitudes toward authority in general and toward the police in particular.

The *second* means of approaching the study of the behavior of mankind is by *studying the individual*. The present chapter will concern itself with this.

Obviously, each of these methods cannot be completely independent of the other. Since man is a social being as well as an individual, both aspects must be considered independently. Considering the behavior of the individual must be done within a certain framework. The framework we will use views social behavior as being influenced by various factors. Suggested by S. Stansfeld Sargent,[2] it is set forth here.

---

[1] The President's Commission on Law Enforcement and Administration of Justice, *The Challenge of Crime in a Free Society* (Washington, D. C.: Government Printing Office, 1967), p. 100.

[2] S. S. Sargent, *Social Psychology: An Integrative Interpretation* (New York: The Ronald Press Company, 1950), pp. 242–71.

Influences on social behavior can be divided into five factors. The first is the *nature* of the social situation. An example of this is that an onlooker might cheer for a fighter in the boxing ring but not at a street fight. The two fights are generally considered different social situations.

The second factor is *norms*, or the prevailing way of behaving, of a certain social group. An example of this is the difference between how a delinquent gang member and a member of the middle-class react to the police. The norms of these two social groups are different; consequently their behavior will probably be different.

The third revolves around how an individual's behavior at any given time depends to a certain extent on his *personality*, and personality is the result of heredity and environment. Consider, for example, a person who has an authoritarian personality as opposed to a one not having such a personality. The individual with the authoritarian personality will act more rigidly in social situations. He may well be the policeman who handles any and all situations strictly "by the book."

A fourth factor centers around a person's more *transitory condition*, such as his emotional states, illness, drunkenness, etc. These are not enduring characteristics of an individual's personality, but their influence can be very significant at a particular time. An angry individual will probably react to a peace officer in a much different manner than one who is not angry.

Finally, how a *person perceives* and interprets a situation undoubtedly has a subtle effect on how that individual reacts to the situation. The other four factors have an effect on this factor; however, it is clearly distinguishable from these. If a person perceives the police as a Gestapo-like organization, that individual will react to them in a much different manner than if he perceived the police in a more benign role.

SOME REFLECTIONS ON ATTITUDES

When social scientists wish to describe how an individual perceives situations and objects, and his behavior regarding these, they do it in terms of attitudes. David Krech and Richard S. Crutchfield[3] define attitude *as a long lasting perceptual, motivational, emotional, and adaptive organizational process concerned with a person or object.* Attitudes may be either negative or positive. Basically, this means that an individual might be favorably or unfavorably predisposed toward a person or object.

It can be seen that by this definition that prejudice would be regarded as a kind of attitude. It is an attitude that categorizes persons or objects in a good or bad light—usually in a bad light—without regard to the facts. Furthermore, particularly in the United States, prejudice is thought of in connection with race. In this light, it is covered quite thoroughly in Chapter 5, and here our attention will be focused on the general concept of attitude.

[3] D. Krech and R. S. Crutchfield, *Elements of Psychology*, (New York: Alfred A. Knopf, Inc., 1960), p. 692.

Attitudes are regarded as having various dimensions and attributes. There are five dimensions which appear to be most descriptive to attitudes. These were modified from Krech and Crutchfield[4] and Klineberg.[5] They are briefly described and illustrated below:

1. *Direction*: What is the direction of the attitude? Is it for or against the person or object?

2. *Degree*: By degree is meant, How positive or negative is the attitude? In other words, is it extremely positive or just barely positive?

3. *Content*: Although various individuals may dislike the police in the same degree, this does not necessarily mean that the attitude is the same in each of these people. Investigation of the content of their attitudes may show that they perceive the police in markedly different way. One's may stem from unpleasant personal contacts, while another may feel antipathy to police officers because as a child he was taught to dislike them.

4. *Consistency*: Attitudes differ in how they are integrated and related to other attitudes that a person may hold. One person, for example, may show enmity toward police because he sees them as enforcers for the power structure, while another has a dislike for the police—a dislike that does not fit into his general framework of beliefs and attitudes. Consistency is important in that the amount of internal consistency may well relate to the dimension which is discussed next.

5. *Strength*: Some attitudes continue for a long time despite data that contradict them. These are known as strong attitudes. A weak attitude toward law enforcement officers might well be changed after a person has had one experience with a policeman. On the other hand, a strong attitude toward police, either positive or negative, probably would not be changed much by one experience with them.

With these dimensions of attitudes in mind, it can be seen that attitudes may serve many functions. Generally speaking, a man's ability to react consistently in situations is made possible by his attitudes. These combine his many feelings and experiences, creating a meaningful totality. How this comes about has been speculated upon by many social scientists.

Some Speculation on the Development of Attitudes

There have been a number of suggestions as to how attitudes are formed. Two theories which should be examined in this regard are the

---

[4] *Ibid.,* pp. 672–73.

[5] O. Klineberg, *Social Psychology* (New York: Holt Rinehart & Winston, Inc., 1954), pp. 489–90.

psychoanalytical theory and the *learning theory*. These theories will be looked at more closely because they have been used considerably more frequently than other theories to explain the development of attitudes by minority-group members and/or ghetto residents.

MINORITY GROUP ATTITUDES AND THE PSYCHOANALYTICAL THEORY

Psychoanalytical theory is concerned with the development of the individual from early childhood, as well as with motivational conflicts that might occur at any time. Basically, development is a kind of unfolding of the sexual impulses, certain transformations being the result. This theory emphasizes changes within a person, with a stronger emphasis on biological maturation than on social and environmental influences. The influence of the environment and of society is considered to be on the sexual impulses. Greatly simplifying the matter, we can say that culture and experience affect sexual impulses, these, in turn, affect behavior and attitudes. On the other hand, the *learning theories* when reduced to their most simple, explanation, suggest that culture and experience directly affect behavior and attitudes.

The psychoanalytical theory of how attitudes are acquired by minority-group members, is set forth in a book by William H. Grier and Price M. Cobbs,[6] which uses the Negro as an example. According to these authors, everyone in the United States grows up with the idea of white supremacy. Some Americans, furthermore, find that it is a basic part of their nationhood to despise black people. No one who lives in this country can avoid this hatred. Black men are no exception, and in essence, they are taught to hate themselves.

Grier and Cobbs believe that these attitudes have been rooted in American life since the days of slavery. So many times and in so many ways black people have been oppressed and treated as inferiors that often now they themselves are convinced that they are inferior. Their thinking has been so perverted that they now feel there is a connection between high status and fair skin. The book, *Black Rage*, concludes that the black woman's personality is undermined from girlhood. She is the antithesis of the American concept of beauty, for her blackness is the opposite of the creamy white skin that seems so desirable in the American culture.

Conversely, the black man occupies a very special sexual role in American society. He tends to be thought of as possessing great masculine vigor. However, at the same time, he is rendered socially, politically, and economically impotent. Almost universally, he lacks the power to fulfill the fundamental male role of providing a good living and protection for his family. Grier and Cobbs feel that consequently, the Negro

[6] W. H. Grier and P. M. Cobbs, *Black Rage* (New York: Basic Books Inc., Publishers, 1968).

male's attitudes toward American society and toward law enforcement, the guardian of that society, are greatly affected by his self-concept. A suggestion that can be made from this fact is that the black man's self-concept needs to be enhanced, particulary in the social, economical, and political areas. Furthermore, he must be made to feel that blackness is equivalent to handsomeness.

The second theory in regard to how attitudes are acquired by minority groups can broadly be termed *learning theory.*

MINORITY GROUP ATTITUDES
AND THEIR ACQUISITION
AS EXPLAINED BY
LEARNING THEORY

Learning theory, in its broadest sense, suggests that a person is born into a social environment, which generally speaking, is considered to be the culture or subculture in which he lives. An individual's personality is shaped as a result of his interaction with other human beings in his social environment.

The distinguishing characteristic of a culture is that it contains a body of behavioral patterns such as skills, habits, and activities. Also, certain types of thought patterns may be as much a part of the culture as are behavioral patterns. Thus, it can be seen that attitudes and opinions may well be determined by culture and, in turn, may reflect that culture and/or subculture.

Some insight into this can be gained when the subculture of the ghetto is examined. This subculture tends to be made up of persons from the low class, by virtue of their inability to succeed economically. As explained in Chapter 6, this inability does not appear to be the ghetto resident's fault in most cases. Nevertheless, a large body of persons living in the ghetto belong to the lower class and, according to Walter B. Miller,[7] lower-class culture has a set of attitudes that are passed on to each succeeding generation. He says it in a most succinct fashion:

> A large body of systematic interrelated attitudes, practices, behaviors, and value characteristics of lower class culture are designed to support and maintain the basis of the lower class structure.

The lower-class attitude toward the police tends to be hostile. A study by August B. Hollingshead and Frederick C. Redlick describes this hostility thus:

> A deep seated distrust of authority figures pervades ... [lower socio-economic class] persons from childhood to old age. Suspicion is directed towards police, clergymen, teachers [et cetera]....[8]

[7] W. B. Miller, "Lower Class Culture as a Generating Milieu of Gang Deliquency," *The Journal of Social Issues*, Vol. 14, No. 3 (1958), pp. 5–19.

[8] A. B. Hollingshead and F. C. Redlick, *Social Class and Mental Illness: A Community Study* (New York: John Wiley & Sons, Inc., 1958), p. 130.

In addition to frequently being a member of the lower class and being taught the values set forth by this class, the black man has had experiences which have acted to further alienate him from law enforcement. By and large, the black man's most important contact with white society has been through the white policeman. Therefore, the policeman has personified white authority. In the past, he not only enforced laws and regulations but also the whole set of social customs associated with the concept of "white supremacy." Historically, law enforcement was on the side of the slavemaster. In more recent times, the so-called Jim Crow laws (primarily found in the South) of separate facilities were stringently enforced by the police. Minor transgressions of caste etiquette were punished by the policeman on an extrajudicial basis.[9]

Figure 8.2 *Typical of the South before the mid 1950s. (See the Report of the National Advisory Commission on Civil Disorder, 1968, pp. 92, 112.) Separate facilities were the rule.*

It can be assumed that this kind of contact has had its telling effect upon the black man's subculture and attitudes in the United States. And studies concerning the attitudes of minority-group members toward the police usually show that they are antagonistic toward them.

A Review of Some Studies of Attitudes Toward the Police

Opinions are closely related to attitudes. The term *attitude* implies a preparation to act, while *opinion* refers to what we believe to be true. Since what we believe to be true affects our readiness to act in a certain way, it can be seen that opinions and attitudes are intertwined. The two

[9] A. Rose, *The Negro in America* (Boston: Beacon Press, 1948), pp. 170–88.

terms have often been used interchangeably and are sometimes referred to as studies of attitude. Because of this, we shall be concerned with both attitudes and opinions while reviewing studies of what their authors refer to as attitudes.

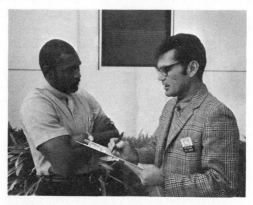

Figure 8.3 *An opinion pollster gathering information.*

Another thought to be considered when reviewing studies of attitudes is that, at this time, mankind cannot apply the scientific approach to human behavior with the same degree of certainty that he applies it to the physical sciences. We know, for example, that just amassing data does not necessarily lead to understanding human behavior. It may not, however, be necessary to make exacting evaluations of all the factors that operate in regard to human behavior. Rather, it may be possible, from a practical standpoint, to identify only the major trends of behavior to begin to understand human behavior and attitudes more fully.

INDICATIONS OF THE PUBLIC'S ATTITUDE TOWARD THE POLICE

Research has been conducted into the public's attitude and opinions regarding the police. Research of this nature has been extensively reported upon in the 1967 *Task Force Report: The Police.*[10] It drew upon a number of sources for its information, such as a 1966 Harris Poll, a 1965 Gallup Poll, and a survey conducted by the National Opinion Research Center.

The results of these three surveys showed substantially the same thing. The Harris Poll indicated that the public rated local law enforcement as good or excellent 65 percent of the time, state law enforcement as good or excellent 70 percent of the time, and federal law enforcement

[10] The President's Commission on Law Enforcement and Administration of Justice, *Task Force Report: The Police,* (Washington, D. C.: Government Printing Office, 1967), pp. 145–49.

good or excellent 76 percent of the time. The Gallup Poll found that 70 percent of the public had a great deal of respect for the police, 22 percent had some respect, and only 4 percent had hardly any respect for the police. The National Opinion Research Center, which is affiliated with the University of Chicago, conducted similar studies in 1947 and in 1963. In 1947, 41 percent of those polled indicated that they thought the police had an excellent or a good standing in the community. In 1963, 54 percent were of this opinion. No other occupational group achieved such a striking improvement in its image as did the police during that 16-year period.

The *Task Force Report* cites a number of other studies which suggest that there is no widespread police-community relations problem. However, the report goes on to point out that these surveys only show *part* of the community's reaction. When a comparison is made between the Caucasian and Negro community, an interesting difference of opinion and/or attitude becomes apparent.

The National Opinion Research Center surveys show that non-whites, particularly Negroes, are much more negative than Caucasians in evaluating police efficiency. Nonwhites indicated, only half as often as Caucasians, that police gave protection to citizens at a very good rate. Furthermore, nonwhites tended to give a not-so-good rating twice as often as whites. According to the report, these differences are not merely a result of greater poverty among nonwhites; rather, the differences exist at all income levels, and among both men and women.

The *Task Force Report* further indicates that a bare majority (51 percent) of nonwhites, as recorded on The Louis Harris Poll, believed that local law enforcement was doing a good or excellent job. This is 16 percent lower than the rating among Caucasians. Another survey by John F. Kraft cited in the *Task Force Report*[11] indicated that 47 percent of Negroes believed the police did an excellent job, while 41 percent thought they were doing a not-so-good or a poor job.

Generally, the information seems to show that approximately two-thirds to three-fourths of the Caucasian community believe that police deserve more respect and are doing a good job, while approximately half of the Negro community feel police deserve more respect and are doing a good job. Percentage differences between what the racial groups think about police performance range from 16 to 25 percent. Obviously, the Negro population has a much less favorable attitude toward police than does the Caucasian population. However, the surveys may not accurately reflect the extent of minority-group dissatisfaction with law enforcement. When in-depth interviews are held with minority-group members, frequently neutral or even favorable statements at the beginning of the interview give way to strong statements of hostility before it is over. A study by Paul A. Fine reported upon in the *Task Force*

---

11 For more complete information see, *Task Force Report: The Police*, p. 146.

Report[12] points up the fact that there is intense hostility towards police in the Negro community.

In an attempt to measure the attitudes of people in the cities where riots have taken place, a survey team interviewed 1,200 persons immediately after the disorders occurred. The results are reported in the *Report of the National Advisory Commission on Civil Disorders.*[13] This study identified the different types of grievances appearing to be of greatest significance to the Negro community in each city. Judgments with regard to the severity of a particular grievance were assigned a rank. These ranks were based on the frequency with which a particular grievance was mentioned, the relative intensity with which it was discussed, references to incidents that were examples of this grievance, and an estimate of the severity of the grievance obtained from the persons interviewed. The grievances were ranked from one to four—a weight of four points was assigned to the most severe, three points for severe, two points for the still less severe, and one point for the mildest grievance. The points were added together for each grievance for all of the cities to create an intercity ranking. Although grievances varied in importance from city

TABLE 8.1

First Level of Intensity
1. Police practices
2. Unemployment and underemployment
3. Inadequate housing

Second Level of Intensity
4. Inadequate education
5. Poor recreation facilities and programs
6. Ineffectiveness of the political structure and grievance mechanisms

Third Level of Intensity
7. Disrespectful white attitudes
8. Discriminatory administration of justice
9. Inadequacy of Federal programs
10. Inadequacy of municipal services
11. Discriminatory consumer and civil practices
12. Inadequate welfare programs

Source: *Report of the National Advisory Commission on Civil Disorders* (Washington, D. C.: Government Printing Office, 1968), p. 81.

---

[12] *Task Force Report: The Police*, p. 147.
[13] *Report of the National Advisory Commission on Civil Disorders*, (Washington, D. C.: Government Printing Office, 1968), pp. 80–83 & 344–45.

to city, the deepest grievances were ranked in three levels of intensity, which are shown in Table 8.1.

As can be seen, police practices were a significant grievance in the intercity average, they also were a significant grievance in virtually all of the cities—often being one of the most serious complaints. Included in this category were complaints about physical or verbal abuse of black citizens by police officers, lack of adequate channels for complaint against law enforcement personnel, discriminatory police employment and/or promotional practices with regard to black officers, a general lack of respect for black people by police officers, and the failure of police departments to provide adequate protection to black people.

A more complete picture of how these grievance categories were ranked in intensity can be seen from Figure 8.4, which was prepared for the National Advisory Commission on Civil Disorders.

RESULTS OF WEIGHTED COMPARISON OF GRIEVANCE CATEGORIES*

* See right hand column of Chart 1 (Part 1).

Figure 8.4 *(Source: Report of the National Advisory Commission on Civil Disorders, Washington, D.C.: U.S. Government Printing Office, 1968, p. 83.)*

This study, in which 1,200 persons participated, was made in 20 cities. Nineteen of the cities were found to have significant grievances against police practices. In fact, grievances concerning police practices were ranked first in eight cities, second in four, third in none, and fourth in two cities. It should be noted that such grievances were present in five other cities; however, they were not ranked in the first four orders of intensity.

This research seems to indicate that negative attitudes towards police practices are related to riotous behavior.

A study conducted in Los Angeles shows another facet of attitudes towards police which may be quite useful to law enforcement in general.

Attitudes and Attitude Change

Data from a study by Robert L. Derbyshire[14] conducted with third grade youngsters in the Los Angeles area shows that social class and ethnic background influence children's perception of the police. Following is the sample upon which the data were gathered; 30 Negro youngsters from an area of low social and economic stability; 30 Mexican American youngsters from a neighborhood having average to below average socioeconomic stability, and 30 Anglo American youngsters from an area of high socioeconomic stability.

The research consisted of asking the children to draw pictures of policemen at work. The results, were analyzed and assigned basically into two categories. These categories were scored: (1) aggressive police behavior, such as fighting, chasing fugitives, and shooting; or police assistance having negative overtones, such as searching a building, unloading a paddy wagon, driving in a car with prisoners, or giving a traffic ticket; or (2) neutral behavior, such as directing traffic, riding in a car, or walking; as well as assisting with positive overtones, such as talking with children or giving directions.

Negro and Mexican American youngsters differed significantly from the upper middle-class Caucasian/Anglo youngsters in that the minority-group children were much *more likely* to picture police as aggressive or with negative behavior connotations. On the other hand, Anglo American upper-middle class children tended *not* to see the policemen's tasks as aggressive, negative, or hostile, but rather as being neutral, nonaggressive, and assisting.

There is every reason to believe that these children accurately reflected the attitudes of their parents and/or other significant persons in their environment.

After the children had been tested, the Los Angeles Police Department in conjunction with the Los Angeles Public Schools exposed them to their Policeman Bill program. In essence, this program is one in which a police officer presents a 20-minute discussion to first, second, and third grade children. In it he describes the function of the police. After this 20-minute discussion, the youngsters are taken outside the school building and allowed to sit in the police car, blow the siren, etc.

When the 30 Negro children were retested two days after being exposed to the Policeman Bill program, their pictures revealed a somewhat different content. They showed significantly *less hostility* toward the police after this short contact.

This research seems to confirm the learning theorists' assumption that attitudes are learned from one's culture and/or subculture. *The most significant finding for the practicing policeman, however, is that*

[14] R. L. Derbyshire, "Children's Perceptions of the Police: A Comparative Study of Attitude Change," *The Journal of Criminal Law, Criminology and Police Science,* Vol. 59, No. 2 (June 1968), pp. 183–90.

*with a little effort, attitudes learned from one's culture and/or subculture
can be changed.*

Changes in attitudes are brought about in various ways. Some involve the change in an *individual situation*. An example of this is a young
man's having a new attitude toward police upon his being sworn in as
a policeman. Change in *group membership*, too, may cause a shift in
attitude. An example of this is a youngster's ceasing to be a gang member and consequently his changing (for the better) his attitude toward
police. Other changes in attitude are brought about through the impact
of *education*. Broadly speaking, *each policeman* can do something about
effecting attitude changes through this last means.

What Each Policeman Can Do to Improve the Public's Attitude Toward Police

Nelson A. Watson of the International Association of Chiefs of
Police put the problem quite succinctly in a *Guides for Police Practice*
article.[15] He indicated that every law enforcement officer should be aware
that he is a symbolic threat to many people. The policeman is regarded
as a disciplinarian and often as someone to fear.

That many people view a police officer as a threat, has some undesirable consequences. One is a tendency to avoid the officer. Another
consequence is a lack of cooperation by some citizens because they are
reluctant to contact the police. Still another is the belief by certain people that the police are their enemies. This is not to detract from the
fact that the policeman should be regarded as a threat to law violators.
However, if he is regarded as such and as a person to be avoided by
law-abiding citizens, this does not act in the best interests of either
law enforcement or citizens.

Observation and experience have shown that there are many police
officers who have the knack of dealing effectively with almost everyone.
Part of the key to this seems to be that they have found a way to present
themselves in a nonthreatening manner. They have found ways of
minimizing the threat that their identity as policemen seems to foster.

On many occasions, unfortunately, a situation develops into a police
matter even though the police have no intention of having it become
one. Oftentimes, this happens because people expect it to happen—and
because police officers do nothing to offset this expectation. As was
pointed out in the beginning of this chapter, acts of individual officers
can best offset these kinds of expectations. Nelson A. Watson gives

[15] N. A. Watson, "Issues in Human Relations, Threats and Challenges," *Guides for
Police Practices* (Washington, D. C.: International Association of Chiefs of Police
1969), pp. 1–22.

police officers the following guidelines to help them improve human relations skills and consequently to improve attitudes toward police.

1. Don't be trapped into *unprofessional conduct* by a threat or challenge.

2. Make sure everything you do is calculated to *enhance* your reputation as a good officer—one who is firm, but fair and just.

3. When you are faced with a threat and you can't tell how serious it is, try to "buy time" in which to *size up the situation* by engaging the person in conversation. Make a comment or ask a question to divert his attention, if possible.

4. *Don't show hostility* even if the other fellow does. Many times a quiet, calm and reasonable manner will cause his hostility to evaporate or at least to simmer down. And an important point is that the next time he will not be so hostile because he doesn't think you are.

5. *Reduce* your "threat" potential. Avoid a grim or expressionless countenance. Be an approachable human being. Too many officers habitually appear gruff and forbidding.

6. *Cultivate a pleasant, friendly manner* when making non-adversary contacts. Be ready with a smile, a pleasant word, a humorous comment when appropriate.

7. Let your general demeanor and especially your facial expression and tone of voice indicate that *you respect the other person* as a human being.

8. Let the other fellow know by your reception of him that *you don't expect trouble* from him and that you don't consider him a nuisance. (Maybe you do, but don't let it show.)

9. Show an *interest* in the other fellow's problem. Maybe you can't do anything about it, but often it is a great help just to be a good listener. Most people will respond in kind.

10. *Go out of your way to contact people* in the interest of improving police-community relations. Even though your department may have a unit which specializes in community relations, never forget that you are the real key to good police-community cooperation. No group of specialists can establish or build readily effective police-community relations without you. More important, however, is the fact that effective police-community relations means more to you than to anyone else. This means that you more than anyone else should be actively working towards the establishment of or the improvement of police-community relations. *The essence of good working relations between the people and the police is to be found in the way you handle yourself.* You and your fellow officers on the street can do more to improve (and to destroy) police-community relations in one day than your specialized unit and your command staff can ever do.

11. There is an old show business maxim which runs, "Always leave 'em laughing." Let us paraphrase that and say *"Always leave 'em feeling satisfied."* There are people who react to an arrest or a traffic ticket by feeling the officer was fair, was just doing his job, and

that they had it coming. They don't like it, but they have to admit the officer did his job properly. When you render a service or react to a request, *show some interest* and give some explanation. This will promote good feelings which if carried on consistently by the entire force will have a cumulative effect resulting in vastly improved human relations.

12. Try in every way you can to *encourage people* to work with the police for their own protection. Let the average citizen know that, far from being a threat, you are interested in being a help. Drive home the point that he is threatened by crime and disorder, not by the police.[16]

Summary

A brief study of the nature of attitudes, with particular emphasis upon the hostile attitude of citizens toward police, was the main concern of this chapter. Five influences on social behavior are: the nature of the social situation, the prevailing social norm, a person's personality, a person's transitory condition, and the way a person preceives and interprets a situation. Most social scientists regard the latter factor as being equivalent to *attitude*.

Attitudes have certain dimensions. The five most important were felt to be: direction, degree, content, consistency, and strength.

After defining the word *attitude* and listing some of the important dimensions of attitudes, concern was given to how people acquire attitudes. First, psychoanalytical and then learning theory was used to explain the acquisition of negative attitudes toward police. Psychoanalytical theory was explored because many militants feel this theory explains why minorities tend to acquire negative attitudes toward the police. On the other hand, learning theory, besides suggesting how attitudes are acquired, suggests some ways that each law enforcement officer can help to change attitudes.

From theory the focus shifted to concrete matters and some studies of attitudes toward the police were reviewed. The population of the United States as a whole was felt to have a positive attitude toward police. However, minority-group members were more likely to have a negative attitude.

Finally, some suggestions as to what each individual law enforcement officer can do to improve attitudes toward the police were enumerated. Twelve very practical suggestions were advanced for your thought and consideration.

---

[16] Watson, "Issues in Human Relations," pp. 21–22.
  [Italics supplied by authors.]

QUESTIONS

1. Of what concern to the police student is the study of attitudes?

2. What is the difference between attitude and prejudice?

3. Describe very briefly how attitudes may be acquired.

4. What do studies suggest about minority groups' attitudes toward the police?

5. List eight ways in which each police officer can attempt to improve community relations.

. ANNOTATED REFERENCES

Derbyshire, R. L., "Children's Perceptions of the Police: A Comparative Study of Attitude Change," *The Journal of Criminal Law, Criminology and Police Science*, Vol. 59, No. 2 (June 1968), 183–90. This report of a very interesting study certainly leads one to the conclusion that negative attitudes toward police can be changed.

Grier, W. H., and P. M. Cobbs, *Black Rage*. New York: Basic Books, Inc., Publishers, 1968, p. 231. This book sets forth the psychoanalytical theory of the acquisition of attitudes by minorities. Because many militants espouse this theory, it is felt that police officers should have a knowledge of it.

Hollingshead, A. B., and F. C. Redlick, *Social Class and Mental Illness: A Community Study*. New York: John Wiley & Sons, Inc., 1958, p. 442. Although this book is primarily concerned with mental illness, it certainly gives one a good picture of the attitudes and behavior of the different social classes in the United States.

Krech, D., and R. S. Crutchfield, *Elements of Psychology*. New York: Alfred A. Knopf, Inc., 1960, Chapter 25, pp. 666–94. This text has a good working definition of attitudes and also does a creditable job of discussing the dimensions of the concept of attitude.

Miller, W. B., "Lower Class Culture as a Generating Milieu of Gang Delinquency," *The Journal of Social Issues*, Vol. 14, No. 3 (1958), pp. 5–19. This article reveals the cultural heritage which the lower class pass on to their offspring.

Watson, N. A., "Issues in Human Relations, Threats and Challenges," *Guides for Police Practice*. Washington D.C.: International Association of Chiefs of Police, 1969, p. 22. This excellent article explains how police may inspire positive attitudes toward themselves. It goes on to enumerate twelve very practical ways of striving for a positive police image.

PART THREE

COMMUNITY RELATIONS:

Programs

for

Prevention

AFTER CHICAGO

The symbols of the Democratic Party are the billy club and the
Mace. Its face is a composite of Hubert Humphrey, Mayor Daley, and
Johnson. Its policies are an affirmation of the criminal Vietnam war,
bloody repression directed against Black people, students, and all
who would demonstrate their opposition to the course of American ...

New Politics? A change in American society? A meaningful
ending the Vietnam War? Whatever hopes some may have pinned on ...
of Eugene McCarthy—illusory hopes in our opinion—today it must ...
the Democratic Party at its very heart represents the Establish ...
in a different way does the Republican Party. Beatings, bloody ...
"Gestapo tactics", "racism", "police state atmosphere"—the v ...
respectable Democrats—these describe the Democratic Party. ...
erty, exploitation, injustice—to support Black liberation ...
Democratic Party. No one who wishes to rebuild American so ...
no one who wants these things can remain in the Democratic ...

After Chicago no one can doubt this.
Is it necessary to grind one's teeth in helpless r ...
(as McCarthy himself is doing), however reluctantly, to ...
out of fear for Richard Nixon? We already know the th ...
People gritted their teeth and supported Johnson in 19 ...

The lesson of Chicago, the lesson of the last fo ...
of vicious repression of Black rebellion, is that the ...
and cannot be the instrument of basic change which a ...
not be changed from within. What was necessary in 1968: not support for so-called
more necessary in 1968: not support for so-called
the hard and perilous task of building a movement ...
of such magnitude, drawing upon all of those comm ...
for support to the struggle of the Black people ...
White America—a movement of such unwavering op ...
ty and all of its tendencies that even the rot ...
now it but must attempt to appease and meet ...
movement must take place in the streets, outs ...
the political system (and with Nixon or Hump ...
anteed it will take place outside of the old ...
on an organized political form. A one-shot ...
no movement or organization behind is no ...

After four years of war can anyone ...
The Peace and Freedom Party is a st ...
political break with the Democratic Part ...
only a start. Without the supp ...
a new beginning ...
f ...

SYMPOSIUM
HOW TO STOP POLICE REPRESSION ON CAMPUS

PANELISTS:

GLUSMAN UNIV. OF CALIF, BERKELEY - ONE OF THREE
BERKELEY DEFENDANTS

MEYERS SAN FRANCISCO STATE COLLEGE STRIKE
COMMITTEE

...EMAN SAN FRANCISCO STATE COLLEGE STRIKE
COMMITTEE

ACTIVISTS FROM SAN FRANCISCO STATE COLLEGE

Protest Outlawing of French Student Movement !

FR...
JI...

sponsoring groups:
BLACK PANTHER PARTY
CAMPUS MOBILIZATION COMMITTEE
INDEPENDENT SOCIALIST CLUB
IRANIAN STUDENT ASSOCIATION
PEACE AND FREEDOM PARTY
SOCIALIST WORKERS LEAGUE
SPARTICIST LEAGUE
THE MOVEMENT (SNCC-SDS newspaper)
TRI-CONTINENTAL PROGRESSIVE STUDENTS
YOUNG SOCIALIST ALLIANCE

speakers:
DOMINIQUE BARBIER former National Staf...
PETER CAMEJO Socialist Workers Party
CHARLIE CAPPER Independent Socialist
HELENA HERMES Young Socialist, arr...
RAJ NAZAVI Iranian Student Associa...
DAVE KIRAN Peace and Freedom Party
OTHERS

PLUS: S.F. MIME TROUPE GUERRILLA ...

DEMONSTRATE SO...

FRENCH V...

"Law and Order"?

The police perform a very well defined role in society; the prevention
of crime and the maintenance of order. Only through an understanding of
what this means can the question of whether the police serve or oppress the
majority of Americans be answered. We believe that the established order in
this country is one of an enormously rich small group of people who profit
off the labors of the working people (industrial workers, white collar
workers, etc.) We call this small group the ruling class.

The prevention of crime is not a prime duty of the police. Crime prevention is what the people who run this country would have us believe the
police do. Any honest cop on the beat will tell you that it is up to the
people to prevent crime. Such crimes as murder, assault, mugging, etc.,
are preventable only by the people who are at the scene of these crimes.
Police can find out who did it, (they often don't), but this does not stop
these things from happening.

The price duty of the police is to maintain the established order. A
glance at our labor history, Black liberation movements, student protests,
etc., easily proves this. The police are always used when there is a
serious threat to the people who run this country.

What are some specific examples of how police are used in this country?
The role played by cops during the struggles of workers is again that of
maintaining the established order.

Black and white workers come up against the police every time they
organize to fight the boss (security police and company spies), and most
blatantly during strikes where cops are called out to "maintain law and
order", to escort scabs into the plant, and to break strikes by terrorizing
the workers with their guns and clubs.

Students should be clear that the police never protect the workers
from the company thugs or from the hired police. The police are watchdogs
of the corporation, against workers who must fight constantly to better their
standard of living (or barely stay even), their working conditions, and all
the dehumanization of factory work.

Since the large corporations own all the strength in terms of police,
education, courts, judges, local, state and federal governments, etc., the
workers'—both black and white— only recourse is to stand together and
refuse to work.

During the recent hospital workers strike and also during the oil
workers strike, the cops really exposed themselves. In each strike, they
shoved and pushed workers around, brought in laundry trucks and oil trucks
so that the big men wouldn't lose any of the thousands of dollars they make
daily. In the oil strike, one worker was run down by a truck escorted by
police and killed. That's cold blooded murder!

In Los Angeles, the cops brought in hundreds of scabs through the
picket lines at the L.A. Times. The workers faced not only losing the...

SDS Meeting -Today- CH 226 - 4:00
Rally - Demonstration -Friday

CHAPTER NINE

SIGNS

OF

THE

PROBLEM

Figure 9.1 *Signs of the problem: Written derogatory material distributed by militant organizations may serve as a catalyst for heightened tension in a community. Material courtesy of the San Francisco Police Department's Intelligence Section, San Francisco, California.*

IT HAS BECOME COMMONPLACE AMONG BEHAVIORAL SCIENTISTS to say that there are many signs of change in the social structure throughout the world. The evidence they point to is the great social unrest found in many geographic areas of the globe.[1]

The three main branches of the behavioral sciences, which are anthropology, sociology, and psychology, each check on changes in social structure in their own manner. The *anthropologist* is concerned with any significant alteration in cultural patterns. Changes in technology, architecture, food, clothing, or art forms, as well as in values, customs, and social relationships, are the concern of the cultural anthropologist, and they are the means through which he investigates social change. The *sociologist* studies cultural change primarily through the alterations of nonmaterialistic culture. Such things as values, mores, institutions, and social behavior are the means by which the sociologist examines social change. Sociologists usually find a pattern of social change's following technological advances.

People's attitudes following technological advancement are the concern of the *psychologist*, primarily the social psychologist. The psychologist feels that these attitudes affect social change, either by retarding it or allowing it to progress at a rapid pace.[2]

Speculation is that attitudes have begun to change more rapidly in the last twenty to thirty years than previously. This is probably due to the advanced technology of communications. Now more persons can and do express their dissatisfaction than in the past. Nevertheless, recorded history indicates that a certain portion of men in any particular place at any particular time were dissatisfied with their lot. To control the overt expression of this discontent has been one of the responsibilities of government. And because of their philosophical commitments, various forms of government tend to control or allow it in a different manner. Chapter 3 is more directly concerned with these matters. For our purposes here we are interested only in democracy which holds that one can verbalize his resentments if these verbalizations are true. If they are not true, they are libelous or slanderous.

To reiterate, it should be noted that built within each philosophy of government are certain concepts which bear on how dissatisfaction can be voiced. For example, in the philosophy of democracy are the cornerstone concepts of freedom of speech and the freedom of assembly. These freedoms create a different set of circumstances for the keepers of the peace in a democracy than are present in a nation governed in a different manner. The philosophical rationale for these differences is covered elsewhere in this book, but an examination of the practical implications of these freedoms as they affect law enforcement will be made here.

[1] W. A. Heaps, *Riots, U. S. A. 1765–1965* (New York: The Seabury Press, Inc., 1966), p. 1.

[2] S. S. Sargent, *Social Psychology: An Integrative Interpretation* (New York: The Ronald Press Company, 1950), pp. 409–19.

Demonstrations:
Implications for the Police

The practical implications for law enforcement regarding a citizenry that can assemble and peacefully demonstrate are quite significant. This is especially true when the demonstrators run the gamut from ghetto minorities to affluent college students.

UNRULY COLLEGE STUDENTS AS POLICE PROBLEMS

The sight of college students involved in politically motivated mass public disorder is a rather new phenomenon on the American scene. However, it should be noted that this type of behavior has been in evidence in many other countries for a considerable period. Because this is a recent problem in the United States, law enforcement agencies here do not have a backlog of experience for dealing with it. One glaring difference in handling unruly mobs of college students and in handling other unruly mobs is the emotional support the students often can muster because many people tend to view them as the flower of the nation's youth. For this reason there is a tendency to view police control of student violence as police brutality.

In 1968 a number of civil disorders occurred which involved college youths. Three of these disorders illustrate problems that law enforcement agencies might have in dealing with such demonstrations. These demonstrations were at *Columbia University*, at the *Democratic Convention in Chicago*, and at *San Francisco State College*.[3] All were under the scrutiny of television cameras, which relayed them to millions of living rooms across the country.

Columbia University has relatively high tuition; consequently many of its students are rather affluent. Here, law enforcement was truly faced with mass disorder among affluent college students.

The rough treatment of students and other demonstrators in Chicago was televised to the general population. Whether such action was necessary on the part of the police is not the issue here; the issue is that it did take place and was beamed to millions of living rooms.

Like the other disorders, the San Francisco State College student strike was televised and was composed of somewhat wealthy students. But in addition it had overtones of being concerned with minority-group grievances. Law enforcement's problems in trying to handle a minority-group demonstration in a peaceful manner need to be considered.

---

[3] For further information see "Freedom vs. Anarchy on Campus—Warning from Governor Reagan," *U. S. News and World Report*, Vol. LVX, No. 27 (December 30, 1968). In the same issue, see also: "Rights of Protesting Students—A New Issue in Courts," pp. 50–51; and "A Cure for Campus Strife—Interview with Educator Clark Kerr," pp. 52–56.

POLICE AND THE PEACEFUL PROTESTS OF MINORITIES

How effectively law enforcement agencies handle organized protests from the minorities of the ghetto may well make the difference between a peaceful demonstration or violence. As previously indicated, members of minorities often view police with a great deal of resentment and hostility, and any police act which might be construed as imprudent could well trigger these pent-up feelings to erupt into violent behavior.

Figure 9.2 *How an assembly is handled may well determine its behavior—eruption into violence or peaceful demonstration? Photo courtesy of the Elizabeth Police Department, Elizabeth, New Jersey.*

The many marches inspired and directed by the late Martin Luther King[4] are examples of peaceful protests by minority groups. It should be noted, however, that these protest marches remained nonviolent certainly as much through Dr. King's influence as through good handling by the police. The important point is that imprudent treatment of peaceful protests of minorities by law enforcement agencies might well cause a large segment of society to revolt against constituted authority or at least to lose confidence in it. *A loss of confidence in authority can also happen when misdirected youthful exberance is not controlled well by law enforcement agencies.*

[4] See the nonviolent philosophy set forth in M. L. King, Jr. *Why We Can't Wait* (New York: The New American Library, Inc., Signet Books, 1964), pp. 25–26.

The Police:
and the Handling of Youthful Exuberance

Handling youthful exuberance can pose problems for law enforcement agencies. The high spirits and enthusiasm found at teen-age dances and at high school athletic events, if misdirected and mismanaged by police can become a serious problem, perhaps turning into youthful rebellion.

When large crowds of young people assemble in one place, their vivacious, uninhibited behavior can easily transform itself into a minor rebellion. This has happened at Fort Lauderdale, Florida; Seaside, Oregon; and Hampton Beach, New Hampshire among other places.[5]

Bearing on the above are investigations made by the President's Commission on Law Enforcement and the Administration of Criminal Justice,[6] which indicated that one of the most frustrating tasks in police work today is controlling riotous situations. Staff members of the commission studied in some detail how law enforcement personnel dealt with riots. They consulted with local police and state and National Guard officials. The conclusions they reached were that most large-city police departments have developed plans and some expertise for handling such situations. However, smaller police departments have much to learn in this area. This is probably especially true in small communities such as those named in Oregon and New Hampshire where youthful rebellions have occurred.

When a situation gets out of hand and develops into a civil disturbance, it becomes a threat to the social order in a number of ways. An examination in a factual, concrete way of how it a does so is worthy of our attention at this point.

Public Demonstrations which
Become Liabilities

Certainly from a theoretical framework, it can be argued that a riot is a threat to the authority of government and consequently a threat to the government itself. From the practical standpoint, there are numerous examples of governments being toppled by riotous actions. The classic example took place from 1789 to 1792 in France. Gustave LeBon[7] described this in his account of the French Revolution. Violent civil disobedience resulted in the storming of the Bastille, an old fortress in

---

[5] Heaps, *Riots, U. S. A.*, p. 170.

[6] The President's Commission on Law Enforcement and Administration of Justice, *The Challenge of Crime in a Free Society* (Washington, D. C.: Government Printing Office, 1967), pp. 118–19.

[7] G. LeBon, *The Crowd: A Study of the Popular Mind* (New York: The Viking Press, Inc., 1960).

Paris, used as a prison. A mob marched on the Palace of Versailles and forcibly removed the royal family and the assembly to Paris. This was followed by the storming of the Tuileries Palace, resulting in the massacre of the Swiss Guards protecting Marie Antoinette. These are among the incidents that led to the toppling of the government of Louis XVI.

Most acts of rioting do not bring down governments; they may well, however, cause injury to persons and property.

CIVIL DISORDER AND INJURY TO PERSONS

The *Report of the National Advisory Commission on Civil Disorders*[8] tells of the injuries and deaths suffered in the violent civil disorders in the year 1967. The commission's investigation disclosed that about 10 percent of the persons killed were public servants, and these were primarily firemen and law enforcement officers. This indicates that about 90 percent of the fatalities were civilians, and a great majority of these were Negroes. Of the injured, approximately 38 percent were public servants and 62 percent were private citizens.

It should be remembered that deaths and injuries are not the sole measure, in human terms, of the cost of civil disorders. For example, the commission found that the dislocation of families and individuals clearly could not be quantified in terms of dollars and cents. Other human costs were fear, distrust, and alienation—these occur in every civil disorder. Finally, it should be noted that even a relatively low level of violence and damage in absolute terms can very seriously disrupt a small or medium-sized community. This is an important consideration particularly when the Commission on Civil Disorders reported that violence is not limited to large cities. (The commission defined a large city as one having a population of more than 250,000 people.) Besides personal injury, much property damage was incurred in the cities through acts of civil disorder.

CIVIL DISORDER AND PROPERTY DAMAGE

In twelve cities investigated by the National Advisory Commission on Civil Disorders, nine reported less than $100,000 of damage. The other three reported damage of approximately $45 million, $10 million, and $1 million.[9] Where extensive damage occurred, it was generally caused by fire. The other great losses during civil disorders were caused by looting and/or damage to stock inventories, buildings, or both. Suffering the greatest loss through looting were, in descending order, liquor stores, clothing stores, and furniture stores. Generally speaking, public institutions were not the targets of serious attack, although police and

---

[8] *Report of the National Advisory Commission on Civil Disorders* (Washington, D. C.: Government Printing Office, 1968), pp. 65–66.

[9] *Ibid.*, pp. 66–67.

fire equipment was damaged in approximately two-thirds of the riots and/or civil disorders investigated by the commission.

Not all the listed damage was intentional or caused by the rioters. Some of it seemed to be a by-product of police and fire department efforts to control the situation. But although this damage was largely accidental, it was still of great consequence to certain individual businesses in the area where the riot occurred.

None of the damage figures given above include an estimate in dollars of the extraordinary administrative expenses of municipal, state, and federal government caused by the disorders.

The foregoing implies that the cost of civil disorder which erupts into rioting is enormous in terms of the threat to peace, to persons, and property, that such disorder should be prevented. To do so, one must be able to reasonably predict when it will happen. This seems very difficult to do, but there are some suggestions that it is possible.

Identifying the Potentials for Violent Disorder

It is imperative that a police department prepare long before violence occurs or even before the tension which signals that disorder is about to break out. The competent and farsighted police executive will be assessing the possibility of outbreaks of violence or of the staging of nonviolent demonstrations long before they happen. He will be making plans for action to be taken and should be especially involved with creating and developing a sound community relations program.

The law enforcement administrator is very much interested in maintaining a vigil against the possibility of violence erupting in his jurisdiction. According to William P. Brown,[10] invariably there is ample warning of potential interracial violence long before any large-scale incident occurs. Brown indicates that government officials, whether they be local or state, who believe that events occurring elsewhere are strictly the work of outside agitators and are therefore impossible in their city may well be in for a rude awakening.

The *signs* of an approaching problem seem to follow a definite pattern. Tensions rise rapidly, and responsible leaders on both sides of a question realize that this tension is building up and that it may erupt into violent disorder. Law enforcement officers will sense it when they find more and more hatred directed toward them. Incidents affecting the group wherein discontent is rising—perhaps members of an ethnic group from a ghetto, such as Negroes, Puerto Ricans, or Mexican Americans are expanded out of all proportion to reality.

[10] W. P. Brown, "The Police and Community Conflict," in *Police and the Changing Community: Selected Readings*, N. A. Watson, ed. (Washington, D. C.: International Association of Chiefs of Police, 1965), pp. 3–12.

Figure 9.3 *A peaceful demonstration is an acceptable method of conveying displeasure with a situation or circumstance. Police must accept the responsibility of communicating with the leaders of the "scheduled" demonstration prior to the actual demonstration. Such communication may avert violence. Photo courtesy of the San Francisco Police Department, San Francisco, California.*

Nonviolent demonstrations, on the other hand, may be anticipated almost anytime. Obviously, this is because the nonviolent demonstration is felt to be—indeed has legally been found to be—a means of conveying a group's feelings regarding a circumstance or situation. If a sincere, courteous, and honest effort is made to communicate with the leaders of such a demonstration before it takes place, the probability of its turning into a violent disorder will be greatly diminished.

As far as possible, law enforcement should request the leaders of demonstrations to disclose their plans. In most instances, these plans will be given, in full. Law enforcement personnel should explain the pertinent laws and official policies which may govern the demonstration. Obviously, no law should be invoked against protestors that would not be directed against any other citizen in the community.

Law enforcement personnel in the jurisdiction where the demonstration takes place must assume responsibility for the protection of the participants. When arrests must be made, they should be made quickly. Care should be taken that no unnecessary force or commentary is made by the arresting agency. It goes without saying that the arrest should be legally justifiable.

Returning our attention to tension situations capable of exploding into full-scale violent disorders, it should again be emphasized that major disorders usually are the culmination of a building-up process which is quite observable; they are set off by a final precipitating incident. When the developing process is under way, law enforcement supervisory personnel need to make an earnest attempt to understand it. For, if they fail to make a reasonably correct interpretation, the outcome could be disastrous for the community.

According to Joseph D. Lohman,[11] mobilizing constructive community elements to deal with tensions of this sort is first of all an *informational task*. Gathering such information can be done in a number of ways. *Law enforcement must have knowledge about the tension, its relative state, and where violence is most likely to erupt.* Law enforcement is in the best position to observe rising tensions and to make their presence known to responsible persons. By using the vast network and coverage of law enforcement agencies, the mood and tempo of the community can be assessed. Each law enforcement officer should be required to report incidents which might be stress-producing—particularly those involving ghetto residents. These incidents should be reported in detail. Also, an effort should be made to obtain information from such persons as schoolteachers, social workers, ministers, and reporters as well as employees of the transportation industry. Persons in these fields often can offer important data regarding the buildup of pressures. Informally obtained information from members of the business community, particularly tavern owners and liquor store operators, can often be most useful because incidents reflecting tension often occur in public places.

All information should be *screened* by supervisory personnel. By evaluating the location and kinds of incidents that have occurred, they should be able to arrive at a conclusion as to the amount of tension present in a given area. As pressures rise, this should be reported to the head of the law enforcement agency and to other government agencies which would be interested in such information and in a position to act upon it.

George Edwards[12] feels that an important method of observing tensions and indeed of resolving or preventing conflict between police and members of the public is through *communication*. He feels that police administraters must open and maintain contact with all sections of the community they serve, particularly with ghetto citizens. Furthermore, law enforcement supervisory personnel such as police captains or inspectors, should know the local principals of high schools and junior

[11] J. D. Lohman, *The Police and Minority Groups*, (Chicago: Chicago Park District, 1947), pp. 104–105.
[12] G. Edwards, *The Police on the Urban Frontier: A Guide to Community Understanding*, Pamphlet Series No. 9 (New York: Institute of Human Relations Press, 1968), pp. 69–71.

high schools, the directors of social agencies, and the priests, rabbis, and ministers.

In each police precinct, open house should be held at least quarterly. Law enforcement officers should use these occasions to explain their work to the public. Also, an opportunity should be provided for people to air their complaints to the precinct commander or to a high-ranking officer the department has sent to the station house for just such an occasion. Making it possible for individuals to present their hostile feelings toward the police in this kind of a situation, although probably difficult for the officers involved, may be tremendously valuable in dealing with openly antagonistic groups.

Communication with the public is not only valuable in helping to prevent problems, it can also be quite useful in preparing for problems that may arise. Law enforcement officers should be encouraged to attend various functions in the districts they ordinarily patrol—PTA meetings, neighborhood association meetings, block clubs', and the like. At these meetings the officers might well discuss the problems of law enforcement.

According to George Edwards, in the city of Baltimore,[13] members of an integrated community relations unit of the police department work on a day-to-day basis with civil rights organizations. This unit also meets periodically with teen-age groups in an effort to ward off troubles before they start. Contacts like these may help weaken the picture of the police department as an "enemy occupation force."

Indications of the tensions mounting in a particular group may also be ascertained by appraising the written material that group produces.

WRITTEN MATERIAL OF
AN INFLAMMATORY NATURE

Often within the ghetto organizations, material written may set forth their position. On the college campus, organizations also do this. It should be noted that often this is the case with the most militant organizations. Therefore, the material produced often verges on the libelous and/or the seditious. From a law enforcement standpoint these writings should be examined carefully with the old cliche "the pen is mightier than the sword" clearly in mind. As a measure of heightening tension, written material, when it is used properly, can be an important informational asset to law enforcement. This is true because disorders don't just spontaneously occur; they go through a build-up process.

ROUTINE MINOR POLICE MATTERS
AS PRECIPITATING INCIDENTS

The Commission on Civil Disorders[14] found that civil disorders *do not* erupt as a result of a *single* precipitating incident. Instead, these

---

[13] *Ibid.*, p. 72.
[14] *Report of the National Advisory Commission on Civil Disorders*, p. 68.

Figure 9.4

disorders are generated out of an increasingly disturbed atmosphere. Typically, over a period of time a series of tension-heightening incidents become linked in the minds of the persons who become involved in the civil disorder. The commission's investigation was directed toward the disturbances that occurred in the Negro ghettos in 1967. The commission found that at some point in a potentially explosive situation a further incident—often a routine or trivial one—becomes the so-called "straw that broke the camel's back" and the tension spills over into civil disorder with the violence that this entails.

In approximately 50 percent of the disturbances, prior incidents which increased the tension as well the incidents immediately preceding the outbreak of violence were *actions taken by law enforcement agencies.* Two examples follow that illustrate this point.

The *first* example was the arrest of a black cab driver on July 12, 1967, in Newark, New Jersey. According to police reports, he was tailgating a Newark police car. The man appeared to be a hazard as a cab driver. Within a short period of time he had had a number of accidents, and his license had been revoked. When the police stopped him for tailgating, he was in violation of the revocation of his license. As a result, he was arrested and transported to the Fourth Precinct Station at about 9:30 P.M.

When the police arrived at the precinct with the cab driver, the cabbie either refused to or was not able to walk. Therefore he was dragged by the officers from the car to the door of the station. Within minutes, civil rights leaders received a call from a hysterical woman, saying that a cab driver had been beaten by the police.

Shortly thereafter, crowds began to form across the street from the precinct station. As the people gathered, descriptions of the purported beating grew more and more exaggerated. Three leaders of the Negro community—Thomas Still of the United Community Corporation, Robert Curvin of CORE, and Oliver Lofton, Administrative Director of the Newark Legal Services Project—tried to disperse the crowd. They attempted to channel their energies into a nonviolent protest but were unable to do so. Although these men tried gallantly to calm the situation, by the next evening it had erupted into a full-scale disorder.

A *second* disorder which began with a rather routine incident might well be examined because it points out an important principle regarding civil disorder.

JUVENILE ACTIVITIES AS POSSIBLE PRECIPITATING INCIDENTS IN RIOTS

On September 28, 1966, a white patrolman in San Francisco saw several Negro youths in an approaching automobile. When they jumped out of the car and began running away, the officer became suspicious. He claims that he fired three shots into the air before hitting one of the youths with a fourth shot. The youth—sixteen years of age—died just a few feet from his home. Four hours after his death, the automobile he and his companions had been riding in was reported stolen. When other young blacks living in this section of San Francisco, who were reportedly members of juvenile gangs, viewed the body, they began breaking windows, looting stores, and burning buildings.[15]

Youths, particularly those who belong to juvenile gangs, are often in the *forefront* of civil disorders. Therefore, it seems logical for law enforcement agencies to keep a close tab on the activities of juvenile gangs. Out of their activities many serious incidents occur which increase tension or which precipitate incidents of civil disobedience.

Once a demonstration or some form of civil disobedience begins, the police can deal with it in a number of different ways. Two extremes in methods of handling situations will be presented here. From the point of view of the police the first, was a rather unfortunate situation.

The Demonstrations during the Democratic Convention of 1968

During the week of the Democratic convention in Chicago, the police were targets of much provocation. Rocks, bathroom tiles, sticks, epithets, and even human fecal matter, were hurled at the officers by demonstrators. Some officers responded to the extreme provocation in an unrestrained and indiscriminating manner. Considering that it often inflicted violence upon persons who had broken no laws, disobeyed no orders, and made no threats, the response was even more inappropriate. Peaceful demonstrators, onlookers, and residents passing through the area where the confrontations between police and demonstrators occurred were among the victims.

A report entitled Rights in Conflict[16] indicates that a significant number of Chicago Police units faced with this situation which called for a great deal of discipline and restraint, simply dissolved into violent gangs and attacked protestors, press, and bystanders rather indiscriminately. The report went on to say that the situation was one which could be called a "police riot."

It should be remembered that this report exemplifies a conflict between rights in which law enforcement is more or less in the middle—rights such as free assembly for some citizens as opposed to the rights of other citizens to access to the streets for travel. The right of news

---

[15] C. Werthman and I. Pelavin, "Gang Members and the Police," in *The Police*, D. J. Bordua, ed. (New York: John Wiley & Sons, Inc., 1967), pp. 56–98.

[16] D. Walker, *Rights in Conflict*. The Walker Report to the National Commission on the Causes and Prevention of Violence (New York: Bantam Books, 1970).

media to cover the action as opposed to law enforcement agencies' responsibility to control the movement of people in circumstances of public danger. As can be freely seen, these rights were in conflict, and the result was violence.

Non-Violent Handling of a Demonstration

There are a number of examples of the non-violent handling of demonstrations. The handling of the Viet Nam War Moratorium demonstrations in New York, Washington, D.C., and San Francisco in November of 1969 are some of these. The demonstrations took place without any reported violence or mishandling. They were all demonstrations involving a great number of people and consequently, the potential for mishandling the situation was therefore great. Due to the lack of complaints, it can be concluded that the police of these cities handled these demonstrations in a manner that exemplifies the best in professional police work.

Another example is also regarding a demonstration against the Viet Nam War. It occurred in London when a large crowd of people demonstrated in front of the United States Embassy. *Containing* the demonstration rather than *breaking it up* was the law enforcement tactic which resulted in a confrontation without a violent outcome.

A platoon system was worked out whereby squads of police relieved one another at intervals to avoid frayed nerves and short tempers resulting from being too long on the line. In general, police strategy for handling the crowd was by linking arms to form a human wall capable of splitting a menacing crowd into harmless fragments. As the spearhead of the demonstration group plunged through, they were isolated and propelled away from the line. This tussle continued, and the report indicates that it was viewed as a contact sport, rather a than bloody one.

At the end of the day a large group of tired demonstrators were singing "Auld Lang Syne." The bobbies joined in the singing, which somehow seemed to be a quite fitting tribute to a job well done by the police.

Summary

Anthropologists, sociologists, and psychologists have noted signs of change in the social structure. These changes tend to highlight people's dissatisfactions. This is not to say that some people have not been dissatisfied with the social structure from the beginning of recorded history. It does indicate that now more and more people are becoming aware of its inadequacies.

In a democracy individuals are able to express these dissatisfactions in approved manners. Law enforcement officers must allow people the prerogative to express dissatisfaction as long as it is done in a lawful manner. From a practical standpoint, this is a very difficult job with many implications. For the person who demonstrates his dissatisfaction may be any citizen from any social station. And when any of the demonstrations are not handled well by the police, the result is a loss of confidence in constituted authority, or worse—civil disorder.

When a situation of this sort gets out of hand, it becomes a threat to the social order. It may become a threat to government itself, a threat to person or property. Identifying these situations and their potential for violent disorder is a must for the well-functioning police department. The signs of an approaching situation seem to follow a certain pattern. Tensions rise rapidly, and responsible leaders on both sides of a particular question view this tension buildup as potentially erupting into violent disorder. Generally speaking, at such a time law enforcement personnel become the object of more and more hatred.

Nonviolent demonstrations, on the other hand, may be anticipated almost anytime. To diminish their chance of erupting into violence, a sincere effort should be made by law enforcement personnel to communicate with the demonstration's leaders. Pertinent laws and policies should be explained to them. Demonstrators should be protected, and when and if arrests are made, they should be quickly made, with as little force as possible.

Because once tensions are aroused, precipitating incidents easily set off violent disorders, a check of the buildup of tension is important. Gathering information regarding its rise should be done by patrol officers, as well as by supervisory personnel. Law enforcement is in the best position to do so, but other persons and agencies also are in a position to observe the rise of tension. Law enforcement personnel should make a great effort to get information from such persons and agencies.

Written material, especially that produced by militant organizations, is another measure of heightening tensions. When such material is screened, it can give law enforcement agencies important clues regarding the buildup of stress conditions.

Tension followed by a precipitating incident triggers civil disorders. Sometimes a youthful gang reacts to an incident in such a manner that violence erupts. This occurs because gangs of youth seem to have a reservoir of tensions. With this in mind, a check of juvenile gangs should be a part of every law enforcement agency's effort to check and control pressure which leads to civil disorder.

Communication between police and public is of great help in resolving or preventing the rise of tension and, consequently, of open conflict. Especially helpful is giving minorities and ghetto residents the chance to express their grievances. Particular efforts should be made to do this.

Police must handle with care a demonstration that is a lawful expression of discontent or else the protest may degenerate into a civil disorder. When tensions are high, poor police handling of an arrest can become the precipitating incident of a civil disorder.

The most significant sign of impending civil disorder seems to be rising tensions. Once they are aroused, any rather insignificant precipitating incident can cause a ghetto to flare up in violence or, for that matter, can spark a nonviolent demonstration to violence.

QUESTIONS

1. Name several ways behavioral scientists measure social change.

2. In what way does social change tend to cause civil disorder?

3. Explain what a precipitating incident has to do with civil disorders.

4. Explain what tension has to do with civil disorders.

5. In what ways can the police evaluate tension within the community?

ANNOTATED REFERENCES

Bordua, D. J., ed., *The Police: Six Sociological Essays*. New York: John Wiley & Sons, Inc., 1967. This book has six essays by sociologists about the problems of police work in a society in which freedom of the individual is of great concern.

Edwards, G., *The Police on the Urban Frontier: A Guide to Community Understanding*, Pamphlet Series No. 9. New York: Institute of Human Relations Press, 1968. This pamphlet outlines relations between the police and the public. It suggests some ways to modernize and improve law enforcement, particularly in the ghettos of large cities.

Heaps, W. A., *Riots, U.S.A. 1765–1965*. New York: The Seabury Press, Inc., 1966. This book covers the history of some of the riots and civil disorders during the 200 years of this nation's history.

King, M. L., Jr., *Why We Can't Wait*. New York: The New American Library, Inc., Signet Books, 1964. The late black leader tells about frustrations caused by the lack of Negro participation in the American society.

Walker, W., *Rights in Conflict*. The Walker Report to the National Commission on the Causes and Prevention of Violence, New York: Bantam Books, Inc., 1970. The investigation of the civil disorders and the police reaction surrounding the Democratic National Convention of 1968.

CHAPTER TEN

IMPLICATIONS OF GROUP BEHAVIOR FOR POLICE

Figure 10.1 *Police must have some understanding of group behavior. Knowledge of theories relating to group behavior may suggest some alternatives to violent confrontations in the control of pugnacious demonstrators. Photo courtesy of the San Francisco Police Department, San Francisco, California.*

IN 1968, THE CONGRESS OF THE UNITED STATES passed the Omnibus Crime Control and Safe Street Act. Under the terms of this act, almost four million dollars were allocated for programs to prevent, detect, and control riots and other disorders. Specifically, the funds are earmarked for small arms and ammunition, photography and video equipment, chemical agents, protective equipment, communications, training programs, and police-community relations programs.[1]

Investigation into the last two items on the above list and giving thought as to how the knowledge and theories of the behavioral sciences can be applied to training programs and community relations programs can be quite helpful. With the knowledge that methods of handling civil unrest are now of great concern to many people throughout the nation, a brief look at some of group behavior might suggest alternatives to physical force in controlling unrest.

Group Behavior

Traditionally, mob behavior has been interpreted in two widely different ways. One has emphasized the group itself. This interpretation suggests that groups are more or less independent of the individuals of which they are composed. The other emphasizes the behavior of the individuals who make up the crowd. The *first* type of interpretation of crowds is associated with Gustav LeBon,[2] who illustrated his point with the behavior of the aggressive mobs of the French Revolution. LeBon felt that a crowd might have a "group mind," which supersedes the minds of the individual participants. He believed that the individuals in such crowds are "swept up" and thereupon lose individuality. The crowd is considered uncivilized and irrational. The participant, no matter how rational or civilized a person he might be, is reduced to a bestial level.

The opposing concept stresses that members of a crowd act as individuals, while recognizing that individual behavior changes in certain respects in the presence of other people. In most instances, their presence tends to have a restricting effect on behavior. However, under certain conditions there is a permissiveness about a crowd situation that induces individuals to act in a less restrained way. An individual may normally never think of looting a store, but when other are doing so, he may join them. The thought that "everybody is doing it" and the feeling that as an individual he cannot be singled out and punished for his act may be responsible for this change in behavior.

Because police sometimes need to intervene in the activities of various groups, a systematic study of the social, psychological, and cultural factors related to the behavior of people en masse should help prepare a police officer to discharge his duty more intelligently and effectively.

---

[1] Public Law 90–351 (1968).
[2] G. LeBon, *The Crowd : A Study of the Popular Mind* (New York : The Viking Press, Inc., 1960).

However, at the beginning of this study, we must first note the different names and definitions used for people as a group. Behavioral scientists generally refer to people en masse as a *collectivity*. They use this term to denote crowds, groups, classes, and the public. Practically all group activity can be thought of as collective behavior. Group activities are individuals acting together in some form; in the action there is some fitting together of the different lines of individual conduct.

Because the collectivity police are most concerned with is the crowd, concentration here will be on that kind of collectivity. Therefore, the structure and function of crowds will be examined. This will be followed somewhat later by an examination of the individuals who make up the crowd.

TYPES OF CROWDS

For our purposes, four types of crowds will be discussed. Herbert Blumer has described these groups quite well.[3] The first type can be identified as a *casual crowd*. A group of people observing a display in a store window is an example. Characteristically, the casual crowd has a momentary existence. However, more important, it is loosely organized and has very little unity. The members of this crowd come and go, giving temporary attention to the object which has captured their interest. They have little association with the other members of the crowd. These individuals are classed a crowd because the chief mechanisms of crowd formation are present in the casual crowd. These are described in the next section of this chapter.

A second type of crowd can be designated the *conventionalized crowd*. An example is the spectators at a football game. The spectators' behavior is essentially like that of the members of the casual crowd, except that it is expressed in established ways. For instance, the crowd at the game probably stands for each kickoff. This established way of being involved in an activity is what sets off the conventionalized crowd from other types.

The *expressive* crowd is the third type. Its distinguishing characteristic is that excitement is expressed in physical movement, and the excitement, instead of being directed toward an objective, is a form of release. This type of crowd is commonly found in certain religious sects.

The last type of crowd that will be considered is the so-called *acting* or *aggressive crowd*. Its outstanding feature is that there is an objective toward which *activity* is directed. An aggressive crowd could easily be classified as a mob. This type of crowd is an object of concern to most law enforcement students.

Based on Neil Smelser's *Theory of Collective Behavior*,[4] the so-called acting crowd should be divided into two subtypes. The first could

[3] H. Blumer, "Collective Behavior," in *Principles of Sociology*, ed. A. M. Lee (New York: Barnes & Noble, Inc., 1951), pp. 165–222.

[4] N. J. Smelser, *Theory of Collective Behavior* (New York: The Free Press, 1963).

be called "the crowd acting because of panic." The reaction of the audience to a fire in a theater provides an example. The second subtype could be called "the crowd acting because of a hostile outburst." This crowd is also known as a riot mob. It should be noted that panic and hostile outbursts frequently occur in sequence. There are many examples in which panic behavior by a crowd is followed by hostility and attacks on persons and agencies held to be responsible for the panic in the first place.

Because the appearance of a hated individual or symbol can transfer a reckless crowd into a mob, some consideration will be given to how a crowd is formed, at this time.

THE FORMATION OF CROWDS

Most social scientists are in general agreement regarding the phases in the formation of a crowd. An exciting event which catches the attention of people and arouses their interest seems to be the *first* occurrence. In the process of being occupied with the event and the excitement generated by it, a person is likely to lose some of his self-control. Characteristically, impulses and feelings are aroused which tend to press one on to some type of action. A number of people stimulated by some exciting event, therefore, are inclined to behave like a crowd.

The second phase in the formation of a crowd involves a milling process. Characteristically, individuals who are aroused by some stimulating event are inclined to talk to one another and/or to move about, if this is possible. This tends to cause the excitement to become greater. Each person's excitement is conveyed to other people. Furthermore, excitement is reflected back to each individual, thereby, intensifying the whole condition. The milling process seems to generate a common mood among members of the crowd and also to increase the intensity of that mood. Individuals are inclined to take on a common identity and are therefore much more likely to act as a unit than in other circumstances.

Phases of crowd formation beyond the two just described apply only to the *acting* or *expressive crowd*. They will be examined after a discussion of some of the primary dimensions of a crowd.

CHARACTERISTICS OF A CROWD

Certain general characteristics apply to all crowds. Others apply only to certain types of crowds. Let us examine the general characteristics one after the other in turn:

Size: It is obvious that, under certain circumstances, the very size of a crowd may cause problems for police. The thousands of people at an athletic contest necessitates careful planning and organization, particularly regarding orderly movement. Police will also probably be quite concerned with plans for protecting people in case of an emergency caused by a disaster. However, with the possible exception of traffic control, generally speaking, the size of a crowd gives little indication as to the nature and seriousness of problems law enforcement officers will face. Problems regarding a crowd are usually related to other characteristics of the crowd. However, because ineffective handling owing to a lack of adequate police personnel may prove troublesome, it can be seen that the size of a crowd is an important dimension.

But a knowledge of size alone is not very satisfactory from the police operational point of view. It is too indefinite and does not provide a sufficient basis for deciding how many police may be needed. This leads to the conclusion that other dimensions must be taken into account. One of these is duration.

Duration: By duration is meant how long a group has been in existence. For example, a gang of boys may have existed a number of months before it congregates as a crowd on a street corner. Merely to chase the boys off the corner may disperse the crowd, but, in actuality, it brings more solidarity to the gang. Rather than dispersing a group, social agencies, such as police and juvenile probation department, may be more interested in steering it into constructive channels, making it healthy and useful.

The foregoing example suggests that the actual formation of a crowd may be the culminating or precipitating event in police problems with a group. Because the police objective is to avoid precipitating events, it becomes important for officers to handle a crowd situation with good judgment. Good judgment is much more likely if all the pertinent facts are known. Therefore, it is of prime importance that police obtain as much intelligence or information about a group and its composition as possible.

In bygone days when patrolmen walked beats, a good officer knew the people who lived on his beat. He could predict where trouble was likely to occur and who would be involved in it. Often as not, he could prevent an act of violence and avoid the necessity of picking up the pieces afterwards or of making an arrest.

No one would suggest that we give up modern police organization and go back to the officer on the beat per se. However, as we continue to expand and refine our law enforcement techniques and police use of intelligence, we do so with the knowledge that efficiency may be impersonal. And while people appreciate efficiency, they resent impersonalization; this in itself may cause problems.

Besides ascertaining the duration of a crowd or group, other factors regarding the crowd should be considered if better understanding is to be reached. One of these factors is identification.

Identification: Whether or not a person considers himself a member of a group and/or identifies with it is a dimension of groups. Identification is a process that occurs within an individual. Nevertheless, groups can be distinguished on the basis of the degree of identification of the members. Other members of a group are frequently aware of one's membership in that group, especially if there is some kind of formal organization, congregation, or interpersonal communication. Strangers are often able to identify members of a group. An example is police, who are readily identified by their uniforms. When a person is easily identified as a member of a given group on the basis of his appearance or behavior, he is said to be highly visible.

Figure 10.2 *"Free Huey Newton" Black Panther Rally in May, 1969 in San Francisco. Photo courtesy of the San Francisco Police Department, San Francisco, California.*

The tendency of people to identify with various groups plays an important part in determining their values and their behavior. As previously stated, their behavior in turn may help to identify them as belonging to a particular group. Knowledge that a person identifies with the Black Muslims, the Black Panther Party, or the Ku Klux Klan may be an important piece of information. These groups are based on racial prejudice, social avoidance, active discrimination, and hostility; and persons who identify with them may be expected to behave in accordance with the group's beliefs.

The authors believe that the above example does much to clarify why the dimension identity should be remembered when a group is being analyzed.

Polarization: Another dimension of the crowd is polarization. This occurs when members of a group focus their attention toward some object or event. A crowd may be polarized toward a speaker, a movie, or an athletic event, for example.

A group may or may not be polarized. A group of passengers on a commuter train would probably not be; they would be involved in individual pursuits such as reading or talking. But suppose someone fired a gunshot into their commuter train car. At this point, in all probability, every passenger in the car would immediately be polarized toward that event.

Polarization is one of the dimensions characterizing the relationship between a leader and his followers. In controlling the behavior of masses of people, police may use the tactic of removing the leader from the group. Removing the leader of a mob will change the pattern of polarization.

N. A. Watson has described the dimensions of crowds—polarization, identification, duration, and size—more thoroughly than we have done here. You may wish to consult his writing on the subject.[5]

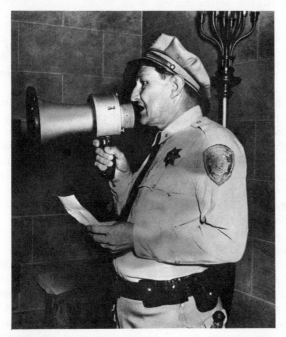

Figure 10.3 *Berkeley police officer is attempting to communicate with demonstrators. Prior to any "unlawful assembly arrest," the group must be advised of possible violations. Photo courtesy of the Berkeley Police Department, Berkeley, California.*

[5] N. A. Watson, "Police and Group Behavior, in *Police and the Changing Community: Selected Readings*, ed. N. A. Watson (Washington, D. C.: International Association of Chiefs of Police, 1965) pp. 179–212.

Many times police manipulate these dimensions in crowd control. The following are examples of this:

1. The use of *bull horns* for giving orders in an attempt to command the attention of a crowd is essentially an attempt to change the polarization of that crowd.
2. Taking *photographs* of participants in a mob action often makes persons forcibly aware that they are members of a group that is regarded with disapproval. Protective anonymity is lost, and identity with the crowd produces anxiety, causing individuals to withdraw from the group.
3. *Dispersing* a crowd may well physically terminate its duration.
4. Often police *divide* a mob in two, thereby changing its size and converting it into two smaller groups, which can be dealt with more easily and effectively.

Besides our examining the dimension of crowds in general, a close examination of the acting crowd is in order.

The Acting Crowd, or the Hostile Outburst: a Sociological View

Often, hostile outbursts or mob action follows a panic situation. Apparently the important aspect of the panic situation is that people feel there are a limited number of escape routes and these are closing; escape must be made quickly. An audience rushing to the exits when it believes a theater is on fire is an example of a panic situation.

According to Neil J. Smelser[6] a hostile outburst usually takes place in the presence of three conditions. These are a *situation of strain*, a *structurally conducive setting, and a means of communication among the persons undergoing the strain.*

In the panic situation cited above, the situation of strain was physical danger. However, many situations of strain are socially instutionalized, such as strains resulting from differences in class, religion, political outlook, or race.

If hostilities are to arise from conditions of strain, these conditions must exist in a *structurally conducive setting.* This is a setting in which (a) hostility is permitted or (b) other responses to strain are prohibited or (c) both. An example would be in strained racial relations wherein hostility to members of another race is accepted by each race, and there are no means to alleviate the strain, such as by discussion between the two racial groups. This absence of a means of expressing one's grievances (the grievances caused by strain), followed by the group's receiving

---

[6] Smelser, *Theory of Collective Behavior,* pp. 222–69.

rumors which intensify its hostile beliefs, is the next phase of the process.

Adequate communication must be available for spreading a hostile belief and for mobilizing for an attack. Individuals who do not understand one another and whose background of experiences differ greatly are not easily molded into a mob. An audience, because it permits rapid communication, common definition of a situation and face-to-face interreaction, has many of the attributes for becoming a mob. These aspects in combination are referred to as *structural conduciveness*. The aforementioned aspects simply restated are: (*a*) *strain*, (*b*) *the presence of a structurally conducive setting*, and (*c*) *the means of communicating among the persons who are undergoing strain*.

With the spreading of truths, half-truths, and rumors through a group, the possibility of this information becoming a generalized belief increases. If the group begins to believe the rumors and half-truths, then, given a reason, it may be ready for a hostile outburst. The term for such a reason is a *precipitating cause*. A precipitating cause may justify or confirm existing generalized fears or hatreds. In a racial outburst, for example, the precipitating cause might be a report—true or false—that a person from the other racial group has committed some unwholesome and/or unsavory act.

With this precipitating cause comes the final stage of the outburst which is a *mobilization for action*. This does not occur unless the other determinants are present. Those determinants are *structural conduciveness and strain, generalized beliefs*, and a *precipitating cause*.

Considering mobilization for action calls for an examination of leadership and the organization of the hostile outburst. Leadership may take many forms. It may range from the simple model who may only be the first one to throw a stone in a riot to someone who is highly motivated and who deliberately agitates a group into action through organizations associated with a social or some other type movement. An example of an extreme lack of organization and leadership is the so-called brawl, in which there is no evidence of division of labor or cooperation between individuals involved in the situation. At the other extreme we find the paramilitary units whose members have specialized roles. These units have acted in certain incidents of civil disobedience.

Once a hostile outburst begins and people become aware that there is a crack in the social order that is conducive for expressing hostility, an interesting phenomenon takes place. A rash of hostile actions appear, many of them motivated by hostilities which are not related to the conditions or strain that gave rise to the initial outburst of hostility. This buildup effect, in which individuals capitalize on the fact that an outburst has occurred, is then generally followed by a complaint regarding inappropriate use of force by the police. It also suggests that these complaints should never intimidate police in their rightful use of authority.

It may very well be because the forces of social control have been brought into play against the expression of hostility. It is often found that a mob will have a number of people who become involved because of the initial strain and/or grievance, but a mob will also have persons who have grievances that are independent of the condition that caused the mob to form. This probably explains why participants in a riot situation may shift their attack from one object to another.

Once behavior has erupted into a hostile outburst such as a riot, social control must be exerted. By reexamining some of the phases in such outbursts, it is possible to see how and at what point a social agency can intercede to try to avoid the riot.

IDEAS FOR CONTROLLING HOSTILE OUTBURSTS

At the beginning of a buildup of a hostile outburst there is *strain.* This strain may be economic, caused by poverty; interracial, caused by prejudice; or of various natures, caused by any number of situations. It is quite obvious that social agencies can and should intercede in an attempt to alleviate some of this strain.

A *second factor* is a setting which is either *permissive of hostility, prohibits other responses,* or *both.* For this reason persons in the ghetto must be able to make complaints about police brutality to a responsible group that will investigate the complaints. Adequate means for registering discontent with police practices should be built into the police system. But this should never intimidate police in their rightful use of authority. This is most important, for it has been found that inadequate enforcement of law and order also tends to encourage hostile outbursts.

Social agencies can take action to correct *false beliefs* caused by rumors and half-truths. Constant efforts should be made to sustain a dialogue between the parties in discord and the police. By means of such two-way communication, police have the opportunity of showing up half-truths and rumors for what they actually are and preventing them from crystallizing into generalized beliefs.

In the event that a crowd begins *mobilizing* for action, it may be possible to forestall a hostile outburst by disrupting the organizational process. When there are designated leaders, either personal or of an organizational nature, removing them or rendering their leadership ineffective may result in quelling the outburst.

In the last analysis, when a hostile outbreak occurs, the *behavior of social agencies* in the face of the outburst determines how quickly the situation will be resolved. The manner in which force is exercised encourages or discourages further hostility. It has been shown that when authorities issue firm, unyielding, and unbiased decisions in short order, the hostile outburst tends to be dampened.

To this point in the chapter, groups have been viewed in regard to their structure and function. Now it will be of value to view groups as a number of individuals.

The Individual in the Group Situation:
Psychological Views

While Gustav LeBon[7] insisted that a crowd had a unique nature distinct from the individuals of which it was composed, Floyd Allport took the other extreme and insisted that there is no real difference in the behavior of individuals in a crowd or when they are isolated. According to Allport, "The individual in the crowd behaves just as he would behave alone, only more so."[8]

It is felt that the actions of a crowd express the emotional needs, prejudices, and resentments of the members of that crowd. In a crowd individuals may do things they ordinarily would not do, but a crowd does only those things which most of its members would like to do. It is felt that the stimulation of the crowd, coupled with its protection, allows individuals to express hostility they might not be inclined to express in normal circumstances. For example, people often have an impulse to break something; in a riot situation the individual can do this without feeling guilty. To support further the theory that individuals in a crowd act as they ordinarily would, it has been noted that records show that a high proportion of persons arrested during riots have previous arrest and criminal records. Many of these persons were looters, who were taking advantage of the situation.[9]

Crowds constitute a danger to orderly social life since they tend to suppress the selection of rational alternatives in making a decision regarding possible intelligent social policy. How they tend to do this will be examined here.

The circumstances that excite a crowd or increase its excitement are common referred to as *stimuli* by psychologists.[10] If a stimulus is to affect the crowd, most individuals in the crowd must respond to it. The word *fire* shouted in a crowded public place would be a stimulus. It would tend to arouse a common mass action in the people there. Besides the original stimulus, another may be present. A person observing the responses made by other individuals in a crowd may find these have become an additional stimulus to him. This accounts for people acting "more so" in a crowd.

There is speculation that most people have not been punished but have more or less been rewarded for acting with a large group. Supposedly, this begins when children in school are disciplined for stepping

[7] LeBon, The Crowd.
[8] F. H. Allport, Social Psychology (Boston: Houghton Mifflin Company, 1924), 295.
[9] M. E. Wolfgang, "Violence, U. S. A.—Riots and Crime," Crime and Delinquency (October 1968), pp. 289–305.
[10] N. E. Miller and J. Dollard, Social Learning and Imitation (New Haven, Conn.: Yale University Press, 1941), pp. 218–34.

out of line while the children who remain in line are not. From childhood on, most people learn to conform to the group and are rewarded for doing so by feeling relaxed because they have no fear of punishment.

Some psychologists, particularly M. Sherif,[11] believe that when people are in a crowd their past experiences and subsequent behavior are changed by the special social conditions around them. For example, when life becomes difficult and is full of stress and strain, such as widespread hunger and unbearable living conditions, individuals in a group may view certain social norms differently. Certainly persons who are starving may view the taking of a loaf of bread as something other than theft.

It is probable that most behavioral scientists see a blending of the theory that an individual reacts directly to a stimulus and the theory that an individual sees a situation differently because of past experience. It is generally felt that an individual learns attitudes, prejudices, and biases, and these affect how a situation is seen by that individual—and thus, how the individual reacts to the situation. This does not mean that behavioral scientists will not continue to talk about individual's reacting to stimuli. It does mean that they are aware that this reaction is very complex.

HOW LEADERS MANIPULATE CROWDS

Some psychologists, such as Neil Miller and John Dollard[12] feel that men act in crowds the same as they do alone but, under some circumstances, more so. They feel that crowd behavior is often surprising because people really have such a poor idea as to how individuals act when they are alone. Often persons conform on the surface, in social circumstances, but they have within them the potential to act antisocially when the right type of stimulus unleashes an antisocial response. Many times leaders are able to release such antisocial responses.

Most people have been trained to follow a leader in certain circumstances. Even the rules of a childhood game are based on this concept. However, people have also been taught to follow the crowd under a different set of circumstances. The example of children made to stay in line in school is an appropriate one.

A leader is able to use these two factors of having people follow him and also following the crowd. He generally tends to center attention on himself by standing alone and speaking. Some leaders use repetition and rhythm to stir crowd to a frenzy. Good examples of this can be found in old newsreels of World War II; there thousands of Nazis are shown responding to Adolf Hitler at party rallies.

Crowd leaders use such kinds of tactics to get an "emotional build-up" rising in a crowd. They may use verbal symbols such as "rape," "defense," or any one of a number of racial and/or religious names of

---

[11] M. Sherif, *The Psychology of Social Norms* (New York: Harper & Row Publishers, Harper Torchbooks, 1966), pp. 67–88.

[12] Miller and Dollard, *Social Learning and Imitation.*

a derogatory nature. These words are "emotionally laden," and they tend to stir up rage in a person, causing him to act in a violent manner.

It has been said that individuals in a crowd tend to respond uncritically to the stimulation of others. They do not critically evaluate the leader's use of rhythm and repetition. To be critical one must wait and evaluate a number of alternates in regard to how a situation should be dealt with. Incidentally, a means of introducing debate between a crowd leader and someone trying to control the crowd can often stem a violent outburst. This is because debate checks impulsive activity which may take place under the stimulation of repetition and rhythm within the shelter of the crowd.

In summary, psychological theory, identifies some of the variables which contribute to a crowd's reactions. It suggests that the initial stimulus in a situation is magnified by stimulation from the crowd, and this, in turn, strengthens the response to both. The importance of a leader in a crowd and his use of repetition and rhythm was examined. Finally, the uncritical response of persons in a crowd situation was mentioned. Having provided this sketch of how a crowd might theoretically react, how a crowd can be managed will now be examined.

Some Thoughts on Crowd Control Based on How Individuals Act

When a group of people gets together in a crowd they can be stimulated by the crowd itself to act in a manner beyond the limit of any actions they would take in other circumstances. If this is true, then preventing crowds from gathering may be in order. This is just what is often done in riotous situations. It is done by declaring martial law and/or by imposing curfew and restrictions against assembly.

In ghetto areas, riotous situations have been touched off when police have made what originally appeared to be routine arrests. Joseph Lohman, Dean of the Criminology School at the University of California, until his untimely death, set forth some ideas regarding how to deal with this kind of situation. They are as follows:[13]

1. The police officer must refrain from impulsive actions; therefore, he must ascertain the facts first.
2. Once the police officer has the facts, he should act quickly. A quick decision can anticipate and cut short the gathering of a crowd. A quick disposition of a matter tends to neutralize the consequences of much inter-racial hostilities when such emotions are present.
3. A police officer should constantly try to emanate a "fair" and professional attitude. This type of behavior commands the confidence and cooperation of the best elements in a gathering crowd.

[13] J. D. Lohman, *The Police and Minority Groups* (Chicago: Chicago Park District, 1947), pp. 102–7.

4. If the persons involved in the original incident that the officer was called to investigate are excited and emotionally upset, efforts should be made to separate them from the crowd situation as soon as possible. Such a practice helps prevent the communication of emotions and excitement to the more excitable spectators in the gathering crowd.

5. Generally speaking, indiscriminate mass arrests have a most undesirable effect on public attitudes toward the police. Mass arrests of this type invariably involve great numbers of innocent people. This magnifies the difficulty since the arrest of innocent bystanders creates the impression of excessive and unbridled use of authority, as well as incompetence.

6. When unruly crowds gather, it should be possible to mobilize an adequate number of police quickly. A show of force is preferable to a belated use of force. Once an incident gets beyond the control of the police, it can only be brought into control again with a great deal of difficulty, and the possibility is then quite high of damage to property taking place, coupled with the possibility of the loss of life. A situation should never be permitted to develop wherein control passes from the hands of the police authority to the crowd.[14]

Figure 10.4 *When necessary, an immediate removal of the law violator with a sufficient show of force may neutralize the consequences of much interracial hostilities—particular when such emotions are high. Photo courtesy of the Atlanta Police Department, Atlanta, Georgia.*

[14] *Ibid.*

The foregoing fit in quite well with our theory of crowd behavior. Ways of keeping a crowd from gathering are suggested. Regarding the handling of potential crowd leaders, whether real or symbolic, Item 4 recommends removing such persons from the crowd situation as soon as possible when this is feasible. The show of force hopefully will remind individuals in the crowd that the possibility of punishment for wrong-doing is near at hand.

Besides knowing how to handle direct confrontation situations, police should keep other community relations practices in constant operation.

Community Relations and Group Behavior

The police are only one of several resources that may be used in problems of human relations and in relieving the consequences of crowd tension. Many times police are accused of aggravating and inciting tension. These accusations are often untrue; however, they probably arise because the police are necessarily constantly involved in incidents involving public order. They will be blamed by a certain segment of the society for what they have done, and they will be blamed by another segment for what they have not done. Police however, can do a great deal toward enlisting the cooperation of responsible elements in the community, thereby bringing about adequate public support in crisis situations.

To get the cooperation of responsible persons the police must make known to them latent problem situations. A police department is in an unusual position to know when tension may lead to an outcropping of crowd behavior. By making each patrolman report on all incidents which might cause a crowd to gather, a picture of potential reaction can be obtained. Certainly interracial group incidents should be reported.

Incidents nearly always occur in public places. Therefore, school-teachers, community workers, ministers, transportation employees, housing directors, and social workers will be able to add more information about these situations. Information of this sort can also be obtained from local businessmen, particularly poolroom operators and tavern owners. Because crowd situations are sometimes set in motion by the activities of juveniles, it is well to keep close tabs on juvenile gangs. From the predatory activities of such groups, many serious incidents of friction have begun.

The reporting of incidents by patrolmen, however, will be of no value unless the information is assimilated and proper steps are taken to alleviate the tension revealed by the reports. It would appear that one of the proper steps for doing this would be to enlist the cooperation of neighborhood leaders, particularly in ghetto areas. Such individuals might serve as an advisory group. They should participate at the planning level well before their direct appeals to the people are needed during critical periods.

If, after attempts to resolve the situation have failed, a confrontation does take place between police and a hostile crowd, then it should be remembered that excessive use of force is to be avoided. This means that just enough force should be used to restrain an individual who needs restraining. It does not mean that adequate numbers of officers should not be called in to try to help quell the disturbance. A large group of police represents a show of force which is usually quite different from an excessive use of force. Generally speaking, there is no substitute for judicious and impartial action by all police officers, but at the time of an incident, tact may well be the ingredient which prevents the incident from getting out of hand.

Our concern with incidents that are potentially riotous in nature should not be taken as to suggesting that the role of the police agency in human relations is basically one of riot control. Rather it is essentially one of preventing such occurrences, for the very foundations of government are involved in the police's success in minimizing internal strife. This means that the competence and integrity of the police in their ability to guarantee public order is a cornerstone of government. Riots cannot be tolerated by any nation, for once lawful procedures for the solution of conflicts and redress of wrongs are violated or abandoned, the collapse of society is inevitable.[15]

Summary

In 1968 the U.S. government allocated monies to study ways and means of controlling civil disorders and riots. Recognition of these problems by the United States does not imply that they are peculiar to the United States. At this stage in history, these problems appear to be common to mankind in general.

These occurrences of civil disobedience, when examined by the behavioral scientists, seem to have many things in common. This suggests that they can be studied with an eye toward learning certain generalized facts about them—facts that can be utilized by police in managing or quelling these occurrences.

Behavioral scientists begin their study of group behavior, by separating people en masse into different groupings. Because the main concern of the police is with the grouping called the crowd, types of crowds were examined. The casual crowd, the conventionalized crowd, the expressive crowd, and the acting or aggressive crowd were examined with emphasis on the study of the latter.

How crowds are formed and the characteristics of crowds were viewed. By examining such characteristics as size, duration, identification, and polarization, certain strategies for handling a crowd were formulated for police use.

The acting or aggressive crowd was also viewed from a sociological

---

[15] W. T. Gosselt, "Mobbism and Due Process," *Case & Comment, The Lawyers Magazine Since 1894*, Vol. 74 (July-August 1968), pp. 3-6.

frame of reference. By examining the structure and function of the hostile outburst of an acting crowd, certain other police strategies for handling crowds could be examined and formulated.

Finally, the behavior of the individual in the crowd situation was examined. Essentially, this was to view the crowd from the psychological standpoint. From this examination, certain practical suggestions for the handling crowds were made.

The government's responsibility in the just, speedy, and effective handling of potential situations of civil unrest is a problem which the police are genuinely concerned.

QUESTIONS

1. Discuss the idea that different acts of civil disorder have many things in common.

2. List the types of crowds named in this chapter.

3. Explain how the characteristics of a crowd may be used by the police in handling a crowd.

4. Based on sociological theory, what are some suggestions for dealing with civil disobedience?

5. Based on psychological theory, what are some suggestions for handling of civil disobedience?

ANNOTATED REFERENCES

LeBon, G., *The Crowd: A Study of the Popular Mind.* New York: The Viking Press, Inc., 1960. One of the first serious treatises on crowd behavior; therefore, the work is of considerable historical significance. (It was originally published as *La Psychologie des foules* in 1895 in France. One year later it was translated into English as *The Crowd.*)

Lohman, J. D., *The Police and Minority Groups.* Chicago: Chicago Park District, 1947. Although this book is over twenty years old, it brings much to bear on the subject of civil disorder.

Miller, N. E., and J. Dollard, *Social Learning and Imitation*, New Haven, Conn.: Yale University Press, 1941, pp. 218–34. The application of the learning theory to crowd behavior.

Smelser, N. J., *Theory of Collective Behavior.* New York: The Free Press, 1963, pp. 131–69 and 222–69. A discussion of the panic situation and of the hostile outburst as they relate to human behavior.

Watson, N. A., ed., *Police and the Changing Community: Selected Readings.* Washington, D. C.: International Association of Chiefs of Police, 1965; and New York: New World Foundation, 1965. This is a good reference for the whole subject of police-community relations.

CHAPTER ELEVEN

INTERGROUP AND INTERRACIAL HUMAN RELATIONS

Figure 11.1 *A lack of adequate communication between urban American minority groups and the police generated certain frictions which aided in igniting the summer riots. Intensity of the conflict was related to the lack of contact and openness between the disputants. Photo courtesy of the San Francisco Police Department, San Francisco, California.*

THROUGHOUT HISTORY THOSE FINDING THEMSELVES IN THE ROLE OF police have tended to conceive of their work in terms of either apprehending criminals or in dealing with them in some other way. The comprexity of modern law has increased the proportion of individuals who may technically be defined as "criminal"; the police, nevertheless, tend to continue the historical conception of their role in terms of law violation— particularly, police who identify their occupation as law *enforcement*. Certainly no valid criticism can be leveled at such a tendency. But in view of the material presented in the preceding ten chapters, certainly there should be substantial broadening of the police role to include not only control of crime but control of disruptive influences in the changing community as well. The manner in which the police role might be broadened might well profit from a modern theoretical explanation of the traditional role (even though "classical" law violation is by no means the main concern of this chapter, nor of any chapter in this book).

In recent years a Freudian-trained psychiatrist, Eric Berne, developed what he considered a new theory of human relations, which he called transactional analysis.[1] In describing the reasons why people behave as they do, Dr. Berne provides a great deal of insight into many of the problems of law enforcement. He identifies the *rewards* that motivate people and calls these rewards *payoffs*—a notion that he elaborates in terms of a reward not necessarily appearing to be such except to the person being rewarded. From this point of view, the individual law violator may seem to have no motive, but he may, nevertheless, be receiving a payoff by "proving" earlier beliefs—perhaps beliefs about how unfair policemen are —*unfairness* being defined as arrest, etc. The rioter, in burning down the house in which he or his associates live, may well be proving a belief about *fairness*.[2] In other words, if humans find a reward in proving their beliefs to be correct, perhaps this is sufficient motivation for them to *provoke* situations that "create proof." An example of this could be the individual seeking to prove his long-standing belief that police are brutal—with "proof" made available simply by his behaving in a manner requiring police to use force. Perhaps a more cogent example might be proving the racial prejudice of police either by provoking situations with racial overtones or by constantly isolating racial issues and situations that require police action. In both cases, the proof is rewarding in terms of the confidence gained in one's beliefs—beliefs that may or may not be valid. Of course police officers may also find reward in such proof, in terms of their beliefs that certain individuals are "naturally criminals or troublemakers."

These examples are mere conjecture, and yet it may well be that influences of that kind determine the degree of respect certain groups

[1] E. Berne, *Games People Play* (New York: Grove Press, 1964).

[2] W. Grier, *Black Rage* (New York: Basic Books, Inc., Publishers, 1967), p. 212; see also E. Cleaver, *Soul on Ice* (New York: McGraw-Hill Book Company, 1968), p. 210; J. Cohen, *Burn, Baby, Burn!* (New York: E. P. Dutton & Co., Inc., 1967); and R. Conot, *Rivers of Blood* (New York: Bantam Books, Inc., 1964), p. 93.

in the community hold for police. Indeed, of influences that kind may well determine the respect held by virtually any group in the community for any other. And it is to this intergroup aspect of the changing community that this chapter is addressed.

Intergroup Attitudes Versus Behavior

In discussing various problems relating to psychiatric treatment, Maxwell Jones wrote, "community attitude studies do not necessarily tell us what people actually do."[3] If this is true in psychiatry, then it is certainly true in law enforcement. Rare is the criminal who does not respect at least some of the laws that he does not break. His attitude toward *those laws* is possibly just as "law abiding" as the attitudes of noncriminal groups. Embezzlers, for exemple, may identify with groups that are appalled by violent crimes, perhaps many burglars maintain a similar group identity. Conversely, many assaulters and perhaps rioters may identify with groups that consider the embezzler or the burglar an unwholesome person. The income-tax cheat may well consider himself a member of a group that maintains a generally law-abiding attitude. The reward or payoff that presumably motivates violation of one law may, for any number of reasons, not be rewarding in the violation of other laws. Violation of law, therefore, may not be motivated by "criminal attitude"—particularly, if one's *general* attitude tends to correspond with that of a noncriminal group.

Attitude in this context then, is certainly less significant than specific *behavior*—at least to law enforcement personnel. This raises a question regarding the relationship of attitude and intergroup behavior. And if attitudes in a community are not efficiently correlated with the kinds of behavior which concern law enforcement, a method is necessary to anticipate at least some of the problems between groups before disruptive behavior occurs—a method not dependent on attitude or speculation about attitude.

Perhaps a brief discussion of what the community groups actually are might prove valuable before considering a prediction of behavior from these groups. And some consideration of what the community *is* may be a good starting point.

THE COMMUNITY

One of the accepted sociological definitions of *community* is "a human population living within a geographic area and carrying on a common, inter-dependent life."[4] But the depth and breadth of social problems dis-

---

[3] M. Jones, *Social Psychiatry* (Springfield, Ill.: Charles C. Thomas, Publisher, 1962), p. 32.
[4] G. Lundberg, C. Schrag, and O. Larsen, *Sociology*, (New York: Harper & Row, Publishers, 1958), p. 128.

cussed in the first three chapters and elsewhere in this volume could scarcely support the notion of the "human population" enjoying a "common, inter-dependent life." As a matter of fact, the notion that humans "living within a limited geographical area" are necessarily just one population group fails to gain support from discussion of the social problems to which this volume is addressed. But if the community has more than one population, and the law enforcement goal is a method of anticipating behavior that does not correspond to law-abiding attitudes, then the first step in achieving this goal must be to identify each population.

Before methods are devised that identify population groups or anticipate their behavior, it should be stated that the ultimate goal of law enforcement is the reduction of potential stress between one population group and another. When no stress exists between populations, law enforcement can deal with other tensions that we have discussed, or it can simply perform traditional police functions. However, when stress between populations does exist, law enforcement, in its effort to anticipate disruptive behavior, becomes committed to reducing that stress (if for no other reason than its primary responsibility for maintaining an orderly environment). And the type of stress to be reduced, unlike the tension stemming from social change discussed in Chapter 7, is stress generated through intergroup and interracial friction. Of course, all sources of tension are inextricably related to all law enforcement interest in social problems. But friction between different populations in the community will be the focus of this chapter. Further consideration of what a population group *is*, therefore, may be of value.

THE MULTIPLE-POPULATION COMMUNITY

A population is a group that might be called any number of things, such as the public, a crowd, mob, gang, etc. What the population is called or the kind of group it is becomes important because this influences both the behavior of the population, and the response to the population by other groups including law enforcement. A population that "gathers" and calls itself (or is called) a gang or a mob may well behave in a different manner than a population labeled the public, or more simply a crowd. Care then is needed in defining each population, particularly since the label changes (or should change) when behavior changes.

A particular population may never become a crowd or a mob, simply because the members of this population never gather. But gathering alone does not create a mob or a crowd. Sociologists commonly refer to gatherings of people as plurals, or aggregates (also known as aggregations).[5] A plural is simply more than one person, and so an aggregate is a plural. *Gathering* simply means being in physical proximity, and so a crowd that gathers is an aggregate or plural, temporarily in physical proximity and, of course, without organization. So when members of a population group gather, the *behavior* exhibited is the most significant considera-

[5] Lundberg, *Sociology*, pp. 382–85.

tion in determining the label for the population, inasmuch as behavior is frequently the only significant difference in any gathering. For instance, *crowds* have been defined throughout this book in terms of their *behavior*. But *crowds* can also be defined in terms of gathering, and in this sense perhaps even a mob might be equated with a crowd.[6] For that matter, even a demonstration might be viewed simply in terms of gathering. Because, after all, a *crowd* is simply an unspecified number of persons gathered temporarily in proximity—just as is a demonstration, except for its purposes and *behavior*.

Figure 11.2 *Black Panther Party demonstrating in front of the Federal Building in San Francisco, California, May, 1968. Photo courtesy of the San Francisco Police Department, San Francisco, California.*

But in order to move toward the kind of population to be considered in this chapter, let us consider the gang. For the gang may provide some clarity inasmuch as it does more than gather, regardless of it *behavior* after gathering. And unlike other groups, the gang is usually the same population each time it gathers. It is this sameness that permits law enforcement to examine not only the *behavior* of the gang but predictable and controllable influences on this *behavior* as well. The gang, like a crowd or a mob, is a *group*, but it is a group that is distinguished from other groups in terms of sameness. This sameness is the focus of this chapter because of its relevance to law enforcement on a *continuing basis*.[7]

[6] K. Davis, *Human Society* (New York: The Macmillan Company, 1949), pp. 303–56.
[7] J. Toro-Calder, C. Cedeno, and W. Reckless, "A Comparative Study of Puerto Rican Attitudes Toward the Legal System Dealing with Crime," *Journal of Crimiminal Law, Criminology and Police Science*, Vol. 59, No. 4 (December, 1968), pp. 536–41.

Sameness in a group on a continuing basis suggests still another sociological label—in this case, the *category*. The gang group is a category because each member of the group is a gang member, whereas each member of a crowd may or may not be a crowd member. The category of gang member suggests a sameness in the group—having a characteristic in common—just as does the category of Anglo-Saxon, Negro, Puerto Rican, etc. But unlike the category of gang member, there is no requisite that the categories of Anglo-Saxons, Negroes, or Puerto Ricans "gather" in order to be a category. Categories, are the community population groups between which stress may occur—stress that forewarns of violence between community groups. Some consideration of the sizes of categories may be helpful here.

THE SIZE OF COMMUNITY POPULATIONS

The size of a community population group or category refers, of course, to the number of persons in the group. But if the concept of multiple populations in the community is accepted, then size also refers to *proportion*—the relative size of a population as compared with other population groups in the community. Moreover, consideration of the size of a population group implies enough of the sameness just discussed to classify the group a category. Categories of people in the community that outnumber other categories of people are *majority groups*. Categories that are outnumbered by others then are *minority groups* and are referred to as such throughout this volume. Stress and tension between these different-sized groups remains a focus of this chapter.

Group Goals and Intergroup Relations

While the *relationship* between majority and minority groups is of vital concern, specific consideration of the minority group is necessary before examining the intergroup relationship in terms of potential stress.

With the obvious exception of the ruling class, the position of minority groups down through history has been far less favorable than that of majority groups. Still in more recent times there have been varying degrees of interest in human rights, pertaining to both the majority and minority categories. In various treaties following World War II, this interest really became evident. The ruthless, wholesale slaughter of millions of members of certain minority groups by the Nazis no doubt motivated many of the demands for human rights voiced at the first meeting of the United Nations in San Francisco in 1945. On December 10, 1948, at the meeting of the UN General Assembly in Paris, a declaration was unanimously adopted that proclaimed to be "a common standard of achievement for all peoples." This standard would "strive to promote respect for rights and freedoms." Although the declaration was geared to the international scene, it is noteworthy that it nevertheless implied universal endorsement of the constitutionally guaranteed "rights and freedoms" in America. Many envisioned this declaration as the threshold of an enlightened era of increasing tolerance. But far from ushering in such an era, this historic declaration was made during the early stages of perhaps the greatest unrest America has ever witnessed between majority and minority groups.

INTERGROUP HUMAN RELATIONS

Certainly there is little reason to believe that the United Nations declaration caused unrest between groups. But it may well be that the same worldwide concern with individual dignity was the basis for both the initiative of the UN and the increasing militancy of various minority groups. Whether they are related or not, however, at least some American minority-group members have done more to "promote . . . rights and freedoms" than has the UN, which declared this intent in 1948. But in the process, some of the behavior of certain members of the minorities may have slowed development of "respect," thereby increasing the stress between groups. Nevertheless, there can be little doubt that the period since World War II has been marked by a definite movement toward greater individual freedom and, it is hoped, toward dignity as well—with or without intergroup stress. In fact, the primary motive for seeking the political and economic power needed to influence one's own destiny (as discussed in Chapter 3) is probably to gain the dignity proclaimed by the United Nations as a human right.

The question then becomes, Why cannot achievement of such a laudable goal serve as a positive payoff or reward in the context of discussion at the beginning of this chapter? Why, indeed, it might be asked, should tension arise between groups in the community when all seek merely to control or influence their own destiny? Law enforcement must first understand tension between groups as a source of disruptive behavior (even when such behavior fails to correspond with the law-abiding attitude of the group). Law enforcement must then conceive of such understanding as the source of a remedy for stresses and tensions emerging from many groups pursuing a goal—even a laudable goal.

GOALS AND CONFLICT

Individual freedom, it has been said, "ends at the end of the other fellow's nose." In terms of various community groups having the mutual goal of individual freedom, the end might instead be "the other group's dignity." That is, the individual cannot be "free" to strike the other fellow's nose, nor can one group be "free" to deprive the other group of dignity. It follows then that there must be restrictions on the goal of individual freedom—at least if *dignity* is to be part of the goal of freedom. The freedom to strike the other fellow's nose (or to deprive the other group of dignity) is not, and cannot be dignified. Freedom to seek control over one's destiny in such diversified areas as education, economics, and personal respect, must by necessity be *restricted freedom* —perhaps, the most freedom possible. When intergroup tension, or conflict, occurs between the majority and minority, with both proclaiming the mutual goal of freedom, it is most often traceable to the failure of either or both groups to recognize the restrictions on their own freedom —necessary restrictions if dignity is to accompany freedom. The first step in bringing these restrictions into focus is *meaningful dialogue* between the groups.[8]

Two-Way Communication

Two-way communication, or meaningful dialogue, implies a great deal more than two points of view. Two-way communication, particularly when geared to clarifying certain restrictions on the freedoms of the majority and minority, must first consider limitations existing on the freedoms of minorities—particularly, since frustrations resulting from them have so often exploded into violent outbursts in recent times. Most of these already existing restrictions have been discussed elsewhere in this text in terms of bias and prejudice; but a more subtle, yet nevertheless equally significant, restriction needs clarification, perhaps under the title of *motivation*.[9]

Motivation is restrictive through its absence. Chapter 3 referred to the Puritan ethic which holds work of any kind to be sacred. So ingrained in the American cultural pattern is this concept of work for work's sake that the Industrial Revolution failed to dislodge it, in spite of virtually removing the farm as a source of almost guaranteed work.

Dialogue between the majority and the minority must conceive of motivation as being equally restrictive as bias and prejudice because motivation or, more properly, the lack of it is the basis of much existing bias and prejudice.

The majority group is from what sociologists are prone to call the middle class. This group values steady employment if for no other reason than that most of the "material prizes" that are culturally valued are thought to be accessibly only through work. Far more important, however, is the virtual certainty that when a middle-class child reaches work age, he will be in the position of being limited only by his own talent and initiative. Of course, such an expectation does not apply to the children in certain minority groups.[10] The very educational process may

---

[8] S. Coppersmith, *The Antecedents of Self-Esteem* (San Francisco, Calif.: W. H. Freeman and Co., Publishers, 1967), p. 264.

[9] B. Berelson and G. Steiner, *Human Beavior* (New York: Harcourt, Brace & World, Inc., 1964) p. 668.

[10] M. Drimmer, ed., *Black History* (Garden City, N. Y.: Doubleday & Company, Inc., 1967), p. 530. See also S. Bronz, *Roots of Negro Racial Consciousness* (New York: Libra Publications, 1964), p. 93.

indeed support the implication that the expectation of work is inapppropriate to many minority-group members, although in a far more subtle manner in some areas than in others.[11]

Whenever motivation is examined, the significance of expectations emerges. Two-way communication, dependent as it is on each group's *expecting* to hear and be heard, also isolates the significance of expectations. Put another way, a group that does not *expect* to be heard or to hear is not likely to feel motivated to attempt meaningful dialogue, thereby preventing two-way communication. But more than the motive to attempt communication is lost when a *minority* group fails to develop the *expectation* that cultural rewards are as available for it as for the majority. Lost along with the motives to *try* is confidence in government, as discussed in Chapter 3.

Some consideration might be given at this point to the possible manner in which *expectations* are developed, or not developed, and the alternative expectations that may occur.

Interracial Human Relations

MINORITY TO MAJORITY—EASIER FOR SOME

As noted elsewhere in this volume, membership in a minority group is sometimes difficult to determine—at least by persons outside the group. Intergroup relations often function without knowledge or concern about the racial background of the members.

Earlier in American history, any number of European immigrant groups were minorities and, as such, suffered many of the disadvantages referred to in Chapter 5. But unlike racial minority groups, minorities from Europe have traditionally been encouraged to *expect* that a single generation's "turnover" would remove the language barrier that clearly set them apart from the majority. These minorities were also encouraged to expect even more; in a single generation the typical European minority group could reasonably expect that they would acquire the majority group's clothing styles, living habits, and social skills along with its language.

Being able to *expect* such a dramatic loss of minority identity may well have *motivated* the incredible speed with which many immigrant groups undertook, on their own, the loss of their minority identity—and did, in fact, lose it. Frequently enriched with occupational skills from the old country, most Europeans have taken a comparatively short time to "join" the majority. And once joined, there are methods of identifying the minority background of the European immigrant. But the *race* of these immigrant minorities is Caucasian, the race of the *majority*.

---

[11] L. Harlan, *Separate and Unequal* (Chapel Hill: Universty of North Carolina Press, 1968), p. 275; and J. Conant, *Slums and Suburbs* (New York: McGraw-Hill Book Company, 1961), p. 147.

Many American minorities, however, are forever identifiable by racial characteristics. These minorities often do not *expect* to joint the majority to the same level or degree as minorities identifiable only by language and dress. Indeed, in many respects, acquiring the social behavior, the dress, and the language habits of the majority often tends to draw attention to the "minority stereotype"—more often than not, a degrading and undignified stereotype.

Interracial human relations, then, acknowledges a great deal more than the inherent frustration of membership in a "relegated minority." They go far beyond acknowledging the racial minority despair that accompanies generation after generation witnessing the elevation of *nearly* all relegated minorities but theirs and a system that includes severe socioeconomic penalties for those already penalized in terms of dignity. *To be meaningful*, then, interracial human relations must avow the *right* of every human being to be respected as a human being. Moreover, this respect must flow from the belief that *all* humans are of the highest form of life, and that only the *behavior* of people can be called good or bad; bad behavior is always subject to modification in proportion to the degree of human dignity accorded.

In this sense, interracial human relations differ very little from intergroup relations. After all, both are intergroup human relations. But a sensitivity to all the problems affecting intergroup relations is only the beginning of interracial human relations. With interracial groups comes a sense of urgency, following the recognition that time alone did not— and cannot—resolve problems that it has resolved for other intergroup relations. Time, on the contrary, has amplified racial problems, and as has been expressed throughout this text, time appears to be running out —at least when it is filled with apathy.

Summary

Chapter 11 began with an assertion that down through history the police function has been conceived of in terms of either apprehending criminals or in some other way directly responding to crime. A further observation was made that complexities in modern law have done little to modify this conception of enforcement, in spite of an ever-increasing proportion of persons formerly not considered "criminal" who may now be so defined. This chapter noted the need for a vast broadening of the police role beyond crime—beyond crime to the point that crime *itself* is controlled while disruptive community influences are also controlled (or at least anticipated). Broadening the police role in this manner was proposed in terms of reviewing one of the theoretical explanations of the behavior with which the traditional police role is involved. The theory chosen was *transactional analysis*, the modern ego-state psychology flowing in part from early Freudian models.

The concept of motivational *reward* was presented as crucial in terms of whether the reward is rewarding to the person being rewarded. This was contrasted with the popular notion that rewards must *seem rewarding*. Behavior designed to "prove" one's beliefs (beliefs are always significant to the believer, whether they are valid or not) was presented as rewarding sufficiently to motivate certain kinds of behavior. Motives to violate law might then be thought of in terms that appear subtle and subjective, yet very powerful—regardless of how senseless such motivation may seem to those not experiencing the reward of "proving" beliefs.

Groups of individuals in a community were discussed as susceptible to beliefs that also tend to "motivate proof" of their beliefs. Attitudes of a group may be to some degree law-abiding, even when certain laws are collectively violated by the group membership. Examples of aversion to violence by "property" criminals and disdain of embezzlers by assaulters were cited as hypothetical evidence that even "defined" criminals retain a quasi-respectful attitude toward *certain* laws. Having a law-abiding attitude was thus shown to be weakened as a predictor of general law-abiding behavior.

The concept of a community was discussed in terms of geographical area but, more important in terms of the community's various populations. The social problems discussed throughout the text were cited as evidence of more than one population in the community and were further cited as the rationale for law enforcement to actively seek the reduction of stress between varying populations when such stress is in evidence.

In discussing law enforcement's interest in friction between population groups, this chapter distinguished between, crowds, mobs, gangs, plurals, aggregates, and demonstrations. Group activity on a *continuing basis* with a category of membership, such as race, was presented as helpful for identifying population groups between which stress may occur.

Stress between population groups was also discussed as relating to rights, freedoms, and dignity; their absence in any group militates against community cohesion. Achieving freedom was presented as *conflict*, when freedom was either gained or maintained at the expense of another's freedom or dignity. This, in turn, implies certain *restrictions* on the freedom of many to insure the freedom and dignity of all.

Meaningful dialogue resulting from two-way communication was presented as the prime ingredient of all human relations. Human motivation was related to dialogue and the lack of dialogue—motivation developing only when dialogue permits certain expectations to be realized.

The racial identity of minority-group members was further discussed in terms of permanence of minority-group status. This permanence was contrasted with the relative ease with which various Caucasian minority groups have lost such status by "joining" the population majority within a few generations.

QUESTIONS

1. Discuss the expansion of the police role beyond that of direct response to law violation.

2. Discuss the relationship between law violation, beliefs, and motivation. Between beliefs and the "proving" of beliefs.

3. How can social problems divide the community's population?

4. How do racially identifiable minority groups differ significantly from minority groups in general?

5. Discuss the community in terms of "joining" the majority population group. In terms of criteria for distinguishing between the community's population groups. In terms of stress between population groups.

6. Discuss two-way communication, stress, and population groups in terms of restrictions on freedom. In terms of dignity.

ANNOTATED REFERENCES

Berne, E., *Games People Play.* New York: Grove Press, 1964. A candid, easy-to-read translation into laymen's language of modern psychiatric beliefs that even complicated human behavior is both meaningful and understandable.

Drimmer, M., ed., *Black History.* Garden City, N.Y.: Doubleday & Company, Inc., 1967; and Bronz, S., *Roots of Negro Racial Consciousness.* New York: Libra Publications, 1964. Both are valuable as contrasts to the typical stereotyped Negro background of American culture.

Grier, W., *Black Rage.* New York: Basic Books, Inc., Publishers, 1967; along with Cleaver, E., *Soul on Ice.* New York: McGraw-Hill Book Company, 1968; Cohen, J., *Burn, Baby, Burn!* New York: E. P. Dutton & Co., Inc., 1967; Conot, R., *Rivers of Blood.* New York: Bantam Books, Inc., 1964. Each of these books contributes a new dimension to the magnitude of social unrest.

Harlan, L., *Separate and Unequal.* Chapel Hill: University of North Carolina Press, 1968; along with Conant, J., *Slums and Suburbs.* New York: McGraw-Hill Book Company, 1961. Both provide an excellent perception of the depth of cultural institutions impinging on minority groups.

CHAPTER TWELVE

COMMUNITY

RELATIONS

PROGRAMS:

Nature

And

Purpose

Figure 12.1 *As a practical matter, the* validity *of police brutality may matter less than the* strength *of the belief that such does occur. Individuals usually function on the basis of what is believed regardless of the validity of the belief. Therefore, before programs geared to alleviate combinations of community problems can prove effective, establishment of a community's attitude toward police (or the police image) is of crucial importance. Photo courtesy of the San Francisco Police Department.*

IN DISCUSSING THE IMPACT OF CONSTITUTIONAL GOVERNMENT and of social problems on law enforcement, Chapter 3 set forth the requirement that law be enforced if society is to survive—at least survive in a civilized manner. The theme of Chapter 3, and indeed one of the themes of the entire text, is the position that enforcement of law prevents society from depending completely on persuasion to induce law observance. The term *enforcement* and the very nature of man implies a potential use of force. This potential to wield force, then, is necessarily a part of the police image. And the public's opinion of how police use this potential largely determines whether its image of the police is good or bad. As explored in considerable depth in Chapter 4, the ramifications of a bad image in itself provide considerable motivation for acquiring a good image. Additionally, a good police image and similar influences tend to promote in individuals a willingness to observe the law voluntarily; this is a singularly practical consideration in the understaffed police organizations charged with the responsibility for nonvoluntary law observance. So the question becomes: What can be done to promote the understanding and use of social influences to encourage voluntary law observance?

It has been noted in the literature of criminology that certain influences either encourage or discourage crime. These influences are necessarily of concern to police and the police effort to insure conformity to society's rules and regulations.

One such influence is the manner in which enforcing rules, or law enforcement, is perceived by the public. Another related influence is the manner in which the children in a society are raised. Resentment of law enforcement learned as a child impinges on adult behavior. The conditions and tensions discussed throughout this text contribute to an absence of childhood respect for law enforcement. But of even greater significance is unfortunate childhood experiences with law enforcement. The pressing need to deal with the lasting detriments of unfortunate childhood experience is an integral part of community relations programming—a part that might be called *human relations* in order to stress the fundamental nature of this segment of the program.

HUMAN RELATIONS

As noted earlier in this volume, human relations has been defined in terms of the goal: "police participation in any activity that seeks law observance through respect rather than enforcement."

Police interest in human relations of course relates to behavior that requires police action. These "behaviors," whether or not the "causes" are known (i.e. childhood experience; poverty; neglect; etc.), seem to dictate that police examine the relationship betwen the behaviors and those *influences* on which police can have impact. For it is these influences that relate most often to the problems most susceptible to *prevention*, rather than "cure." Successful community relations programs deal with these influences as they relate to behavior and the *human relations* segment of the program seeks to facilitate a community attitude of accepting this police role (the police image). For the citizen who is convinced that police are brutal is reluctant to participate in the broader community relations program. And the *validity* of the belief matters less than the *strength* of the belief.

Personnel selection, training, and supervision that adhere strictly to an ethical code usually insure public respect of law enforcement officers. Strict adherence will help eliminate corrupt practices and cut down on those in the marginal, gray area as well. And, of more importance, men striving to follow the ideals should become better human beings and, therefore, better officers.

But in spite of high ethical standards and conscientious performance of duty by police, certain members of the community often require further persuasion, or "selling," to change the bad police image they have. The news media can frequently have a significant impact on this segment of the community.

Unhappy is the department that functions in a community in which the typical citizen expects law enforcement to *completely* eliminate crime and safety problems. Equally detrimental is a community that expects absolutely nothing from law enforcement insofar as crime and safety are concerned.[1] Fortunately, *public opinion* usually falls somewhere between these two extremes, and the news media is frequently instrumental in determining where it settles.

One of the more difficult tasks of a community relations program is to evaluate public opinion precisely enough to determine with accuracy the degree of public *support* police enjoy at a given time. In recent years considerable evidence has emerged that public support of law enforcement changes as rapidly with respect to "classical" crime as with community unrest and civil disobedience. A tragedy such as one that occurred in the Queens section of New York City in March 1965 is but one example. During dark early morning hours, a twenty-eight-year-old woman named Kitty Genovese was attacked three times over a span of 40 minutes by a knife-wielding assailant. No fewer than 38 persons heard her scream for help or actually witnessed the attacks. Yet not one of them telephoned the police or went to the aid of the victim. Finally, after nearly 40 minutes, a seventy-year-old woman living in the neighborhood called the police. A squad was at the scene two minutes later, but by that time Miss Genovese was dead.

Rather than producing answers, attempting to judge public opinion raises the further question of whether the news media *reflects* opinion or *creates* it. This question is of particular concern in cities where the news media consistently headline crime, giving the impression of a higher crime rate than is actually the case. The news media, of course,

---

[1] O. H. Ibele, "Law Enforcement and the Permissive Society," *Police* (September-October 1965), p. 15.

argues that the public is entitled to all possible infòrmation on crime and other social problems. The ensuing compromises are traditionally resolved in favor of the news media's poiñt of view. Assigning priority to the types of problems that are of most concern to the public, nevertheless, the task of the community relations program.[2] Of course, any such program must take into account the long-range consequence of removing line officers from "nearly-jelled" stakeouts, from patrols in "recently quieted" areas, from "barely adequate" traffic programs, and so on. The policy of "stripping" all services to satisfy a single, and possibly, temporáry need in no way serves the community's long-range interest. And yet a crucial variable in any community relations program is evidence that the police are responsive to public opinion.

REWARDING FALSE BELIEFS

Community relations programs that seek to promote or sell respect for police goals must take into consideration the apparent reasons for disrespect of law enforcement. It seems reasonable to assume that a person brutally mishandled by one policeman may have difficulty in conceding how helpful most policemen really are. This possibility alone

Figure 12.2 *Carnival-like atmosphere of the Stanford Research Institute Protest (May 17, 1969) subsequently ended abruptly as police were forced to use tear gas to control demonstrators. Photo courtesy of the San Jose* Mercury, *Staff photographer, Al Magazu.*

[2] O. W. Wilson, "Police Authority in a Free Society," *Criminal Law, Criminology and Police Science*, Vol. 54, No. 2 (June 1963), 175.

should afford a most convincing argument for eliminating force wherever possible. Behavioral scientists believe that a kind of "selective perception" sets in which causes an unjustly abused individual to look for and "see" only those incidents that prove that the police are brutal. Years and years of looking for and seeing such incidents, combined with reassurances from others doing the same thing, of course, creates such an individual's undesirable image of police.

Community relations programs attempt to prevent the incidents that are being looked for, which "give police a blackeye." This is to suggest that officers' efficiency should be reduced. Indeed, to achieve the ultimate respect that accrues to a good police image demands vigorous and conscientious performance of all duties. But such respect further demands sensitivity to anything that could give police a bad name.

Recall that in the preceding chapter transactional analysis was offered as one explanation of people's conduct. Devised by psychiatrist Eric Berne,[3] it describes the reasons people behave as they do in terms of rewards or payoffs. Recall that, from this point of view, the individual law violator might be able to "prove" a belief that police are brutal simply by behaving in. a manner that requires police to use force. People could use techniques similar to this to "prove" police to be racially prejudiced, etc. In these incidents the "proof" is rewarding in terms of confidence gained in one's judgment and one's beliefs, whether these beliefs are valid or not. Of course, a policeman who believes that someone is criminally inclined may also be rewarded if this judgment is "proved" correct. However, most crime and behavior requiring police attention may not be motivated in this manner. And yet influence of this variety may determine how much respect for police is held by community groups. (This is discussed in Chapters 3 and 11).

To whatever degree respect for law enforcement goals affects voluntary law observance, community relations programs are completely justified. Understanding this justification is one thing, nevertheless, whereas implementing effective programs may prove quite another matter.

Community Relations Programs

The community itself traditionally approaches problems, particularly social problems, through some kind of council. Councils usually function to coordinate the activities of groups or social agencies which would otherwise operate on the philosophy that "agencies exist to provide distinct services to groups able to accept them...."[4] A variety of opinions exist regarding how involved the coordinating of broad community prob-

---

[3] E. Berne, *Games People Play* (New York: Grove Press, 1964).

[4] H. H. Stroup, *Community Welfare Organization* (New York: Harper & Row Publishers 1952), p. 305.

lems outside specific neighborhoods should become. But the central idea, nevertheless, of bringing the combined forces of various agencies to bear on defined problems remains.[5] During an era in which a bad police image increasingly stimulates consideration of *civilian* police review panels,[6] law enforcement can scarely ignore the implementing of community relations programs. And yet there appears to be something less than a conspicuous national trend toward police-community relations programs.

> To date, the police have rarely sought civilian assistance—least of all in those areas where the forces of the law have been hardest pressed. Yet the great majority of residents in these areas, just as in others, are law-abiding. Thus, chances of obtaining citizen support for genuine efforts to curb crime are much better in such neighborhoods than people generally realize. Roy Wilkins, Executive Director of the National Association for the Advancement of Colored People, recently emphasized the Negro community's increasing willingness to support vigorous law enforcement:

> "Negro law violators enjoyed a sort of racial brotherhood status, not because all other Negroes were criminally inclined, but because black men have had such a hard way to go that other black men nearly always give him a break against law officers. The real news is that a part of the Negro community is now ready to blow the whistle on the robbers, muggers and knife men. It still works in many places but apparently the days of the black-skinned distress signals are numbered. Crime control becomes a real possibility as soon as law-abiding Negro citizens, always in the vast majority, take an active rather than passive role against crime and criminals."[7]

The urgency of this statement is delineated by the harshness of the following observation:

> Loss of faith in the law enforcement establishment is increasingly manifested among the citizenry, especially minority group members, by increases in crime rates and riots; community indifference; charges of police prejudice, brutality, and disrespect for citizens; and complaints of lack of police protection.

> On the other side, police officers frequently appear to have lost faith in the country's leaders and the public. They charge that they are subjected to strong political pressures and undue restraints, are held accountable for most social ills, are accorded low status and respect by the community, have little opportunity for redress of grievances, and must perform a tremendously complex job under conditions which, at best, are frustrating.

> The escalation of antagonisms between police and citizens in certain sections of society has tended to induce the formation of two separate and

[5] A. Dunham, *Community Welfare Organization* (New York: Thomas Y. Crowell Company, 1962), p. 31.

[6] A. Germann, F. Day, and R. Gallati, *Introduction to Law Enforcement* (Springfield, Ill.: Charles C. Thomas, Publisher, 1962), pp. 187, 188.

[7] G. Edwards, *The Police on the Urban Frontier*, Bulletin No. 9 (New York: Institute of Human Relations, 1968), pp. 77–8.

distinct groups who communicate with and understand each other minimally, if at all.

These are harsh statements. To be sure, it must be recognized that the problem is complicated by inadequacies in housing, welfare, education, and employment. Yet, the magnification of these "opposing forces" is, in considerable part, a cause of the problems described. It threatens to undermine the basis of support from more temperate, sensitive, and rational people who constitute the essential communication links through which we can reclaim the middle ground necessary for the de-escalation of antagonisms and the resolution of differences.[8]

Regardless of their discomfort while reading such harsh observations about the law enforcement scene, few, if any, professional policemen would deny that they contain at least a degree of validity. Indeed, some professionals interpret the mounting difficulties facing urban police organizations as clear evidence that such indictments are not only true but that they leave the police no choice but to embark on corrective programs in anticipation of an "escalation of antagonisms between police and citizens."[9] One facet of such programming is reflected in a publication by Nelson A. Watson entitled "The Fringes of Police-Community Relations" (Police Administrators Conference, Indiana University Medical Center, June 29, 1966). Another example is shown in the following handout:

The basic purpose of these talks is to develop a more positive relationship between the young people of the community and the police, and to foster a greater degree of social consciousness on the part of these young people. Rather than dealing simply in what the law is and how it affects young people, which tends very often to be somewhat sterile, we draw more on motivating good behavior in general. We attempt to define a role for the vast majority of young people who do not get into trouble but at the same time exert little influence, if any, on those that do. This represents the first phase of the presentation.

The second phase of the presentation is devoted to a colored slide program showing Juvenile Hall, the ranches and a Youth Authority institution. What we are striving to do is to take the glamour away from young people who go to these facilities. Very often they come back to school and become leaders because the rest of the young people think that this is some sort of achievement after listening to the stories fabricated by these individuals. Also, we found that most of the questions by students previously were directed to the nature of these facilities, and the slides provide the closest thing to a guided tour.

The third phase of the program is devoted to answering any questions that the students might have. This interaction hopefully develops the positive nature of the contact between the students and someone who represents the police department. It is with this in mind that we desire

[8] T. Eisenberg, A. Glickman, and R. Fosen, "Action for Change in Police-Community Behaviors," *Crime and Delinquency*, Vol. 15, No. 3 (July 1969), p. 394.

[9] M. E. Leary "The Trouble with Troubleshooting," *The Atlantic Monthly Special Police Supplement*, Vol. 223, No. 3 (March 1969), pp. 94–99.

to keep presentations at the classroom level to develop the highest degree of communication and interaction.

This handout is presented to teachers prior to addresses at schools by officers assigned to the community relations unit of the San Jose (California) Police Department. Although it deals primarily with improving youths' image of the police, it seems reasonable to assume that this activity might gain the respect of the community at large. Even citizens completely satisfied with conventional police services are likely to respond favorably to programs of this type.

Still more relevant to programs aimed at improving the police image, specifically among groups ordinarily resentful of law enforcement, is the message of the following letter:

Mr. Nat Shaffer, Council of Community Services
431 Sixth Street
Richmond, California

Subject: Relation of Police-Community Relation Aids to Police-Youth
Discussion Group Program

Dear Sir:
There has been exhibited throughout the nation a dislike, distrust, and in some cases, hatred of police by a large segment of our Negro citizens. The City of Richmond with one-fourth of the population Negro falls into the national pattern. I shall not attempt to go into the "whys" of this situation at this time. I would rather accept this situation as a fact and seek solutions.

It is my strong conviction that in today's society we must attempt to reach the youth with a concentrated effort to establish more meaningful lines of communication between them and the police, in particular, with Negro youth. We must try to bring about a better understanding, a deeper appreciation for one another and our problems.

We have in the City of Richmond taken steps to reach the Negro youth through a series of police-youth discussion groups. Our method of setting up such groups is quite simple. Take a small geographical area of the city, seek out the youth who have exhibited antisocial behavior, get them to a meeting with selected police officers. At such meetings the youth are encouraged to speak their minds regardless of how hard it is on police. On the other hand, the police are to answer all questions, avoiding none. They explain their responsibility, the law and the policy with which the police must govern themselves. I hasten to add that such a meeting is not attempted on the basis that all ills or misunderstandings will be cleared away at a single meeting or a dozen meetings. However, we have, through discussion groups, brought about far more understanding between these two forces. This is demonstrated by lessening of crimes committed by those youth who have participated and by many, having been school dropouts, having return to school.

Much of the success of the police-youth discussion groups can be attributed to the work and dedication of the five police-community relations aids. It is they who go out into the community and invite the youth to the group meeting. They pick them up at their homes (or wherever they can be located), bring them to the meetings and take them home at the

close. Further, the personal contacts with the youth in their homes oftentimes bridges the gaps of communication, counsels both the youth and
their parents.

At the present time, the Richmond police have conducted two 12-week
police-youth discussion groups within the Negro community. Just during
the past two weeks, three new discussion groups have been formed. We
cannot at this time even offer a guess as to the number of groups that
might form within the next six months. Regardless of the number now
or in the future, we can see the police-community relations aids as a very
important part of a program that shall have a present and lasting value
to those in the various groups, their families and the community.

Very truly yours,

C. E. Brown
Chief of Police

It might be noted that although youth is the primary subject of this
community relations project, the entire community stands to gain by it.

Still another facet, but again only a single facet of community relations programming, is in projects such as the Watts Rumor Control
Center, described most graphically by a United Press International Syn-
dicated Release of February 23, 1969. Published under the byline of Paul
Lowenberg, it acquainted the public with the twofold problem of escalating antagonism through unfounded rumor, and escalating antagonism by
action and reaction to unfounded rumor.

When the July, 1969, issue of *Crime and Delinquency* carried the
Eisenberg-Glickman-Fosen article "Action for Change in Police-Community Behaviors," police organizations in effect were provided with a number of useful instruments for formulating community relations programs.
Perhaps, one of the most significant of these is the suggestion of criteria
for evaluating effectiveness:

1. Changes in police and citizen attitudes
2. Changes in behavioral information, including crime statistics, police
   agency or precinct effectiveness, and citizen and community behavior
3. Nature of responses and opinions of policemen and citizens who have
   participated in the training program
4. Mass media indicators, including radio and television news reports,
   press clippings, etc.

The overwhelming need for the assessment of community relations
programming is customarily justified in terms of either research designs
or of the often-cited ramifications of civilian review boards for police.
An occasionally overlooked but equally compelling justification for
methods of estimating the effectiveness of such programming rests in the
sociological concept of *power*. To whatever degree power breeds discontent, to that same degree must police seek to establish *trust* from those

perceiving police *power*.[10] In the *Police and Community Relations Newsletter* of November, 1966, (a publication of the National Center on Police and Community Relations, Michigan State University) the problem of citizen trust and confidence was isolated in terms of the Flint, Michigan police finding "that the fear of becoming involved is a major factor in the reluctance of citizens to communicate with police." The fear of police power to excessively involve citizens in the reporting of crime became a target for community relations programming. The program serves as an example of a systematic effort toward establishing at least some degree of the *trust* needed to bridge the often tremendous gap between police power and ensuing discontent—discontent among a public whose support is vitally needed.

PUBLIC SUPPORT

Being unable to take citizen respect and contentment for granted,[11] and facing the need to persuade at least part of the community that a bad police image is inappropriate, community relations has indeed a tremendous task and yet a *seemingly* rather uncomplicated one. Regrettably, in actuality, the task is as complicated as it is tremendous.

Among the many police agencies currently involved in or undertaking community relations programs few, if any, could honestly claim success without at least some help from community leader. Leaders—whether the mayor, the president of a P.T.A., a neighborhood organization director, the head of a service club, a clergyman, or some combination of these—either directly assist or influence others to assist in most successful police-sponsored programs. In many instances gaining this type of support is relatively easy—merely a matter of showing a need. The difficulty then is often not whether community programs can be undertaken by police but rather *who* the programs influences and *how*.

SUCCESS

If the term *public support* simply involved a majority of citizens, most police-sponsored community programs would enjoy the success of public support. If, however, it includes the support of all minority groups and neighborhoods that pose the greatest problems, then many so-called successful programs fall short of the police goal of gaining public support.

This indictment must be examined in the light of payoffs or rewards discussed earlier in this chapter. If the law violator finds a reward in "proving" that police hate because they arrest (even if the arrest has to be provoked), then further rewards might be possible by "proving" that policemen sponsor programs only for those they do not hate and do not

---

[10] W. A. Gamson, *Power and Discontent* (Homewood, Ill. : Dorsey Press, 1968).

[11] *Crime and Law Enforcement, A Special Analysis*, College Debate Series No. 16 (Washington, D. C. : The American Institute of Public Policy Research, 1965), p. 81.

want to arrest. And in the case of misbehaving until confirming the belief that police hate enough to arrest, the "proof" that police-sponsored programs are meant for someone else may merely be a matter of not showing interest or of actually disrupting the program until police patience and tolerance are exhausted—thereby supplying the desired "proof."

SUCCESS DILEMMA

Here, then, is frequently overlooked dilemma in community relations programming. If, as recommended earlier in this chapter, police seek to understand what efforts are needed to remedy a bad image, they are likely to recruit the aid of community leaders in whatever human relations programming they undertake. Such aid is a virtual requisite to successful program promotion. But if the groups for whom the image change is designed prefer to view community leaders as police collaborators rather than real leaders, then much reward accrues to "proving" the program is for someone else (simply by forcing police rejection).

The solution to this problem varies greatly depending on the unique characteristics and social resources of the community. But in communities in which respect for law enforcement has deteriorated for a segment of the population, efforts are almost invariably needed to insure these people that program planning and operation involves leaders from both their segment and the community at large. However, even in a police agency sensitive to how a bad image is reinforced, it is anything but easy to combine the often divergent views of leadership from both areas of the community. This difficulty is singularly hard to overcome when years of resentment between the segments have fostered a belief that "the other guy cannot be trusted"—which again points up the need for establishing *trust* as a prime goal in all community relations programming.

But easy or not, a systematic effort invariably proves justified in its strengthening of respect for law enforcement. And because this respect can contribute to law enforcement goals even beyond preventing crime, using the principles of human relations to promote it is not only appropriate, but imperative.

A brief comment on various randomly selected community relations efforts might be useful.

PROGRAMMING

Writing in the Sunday supplement of the *San Francisco Examiner and Chronicle* (July 15, 1969), Robert deRoos delineated a number of crucial issues in community relations programming. Among other relevant comments, in deRoos's "Required Reading for Police Officers" was "the idea of police as we know them is relatively new, I was surprised to learn. In the 1820's in England there had been no police at all for many years. And when the Metropolitan Police came into being in 1829, almost everyone was against the idea. . . ." The article went on to tell of early policemen "being assaulted and sometimes kicked to death on the pavements. . . ." and in court facing "shameful hostility from counsels, juries and judges."

After reading deRoos's piece, one can scarcely conceive of the need for improved police-community relations as being a twentieth-century phenomenon. And yet, as pointed out throughout this text, systematic efforts to establish community relations programming is indeed relatively new. On October 14, 1966, the New York City Police Department issued Standard Operating Procedure No. 8 as "a guide for commanding officers in developing and operating precinct community councils." Although this was scarcely the first effort by New York City police to initiate community relations programs, Section 1.0 nevertheless launches its instructions to commanding officers in this manner: "The primary objective of the department's community relations program is to emphasize the mutual interdependence of the police department and the community-at-large in the maintenance of law and order and in the prevention of crime; to develop mutual respect and understanding between police and the people they serve; to promote an atmosphere conducive to the greater public cooperation and, as a consequence, greater police effectiveness." On the other side of the country, the San Francisco Police Department, issued a circular entitled "Community Relations Unit," which begins with the statement: "The San Francisco Police Department's community relations unit was established by a directive from the police commission. The directive was in the form of a permanent order. The police-community relations unit began with a lieutenant and a patrolman. At the present time there are a total of 13 officers in the unit, one lieutenant, two sergeants and ten patrolmen." The San Jose Police Department's training bulletin (Volume 7, Bulletin 13), entitled "Police-Community Relations" begins, in a similar vein, begins with the statement: "Over 20 years ago the International Association of Chiefs of Police held its 52nd annual conference in Miami, Florida. Joseph T. Kluchensky delivered an address at that conference entitled 'Minority Group Problems.' In his talk he pointed out 'in times of group tensions, the ability of the police to prevent or curb disorders will depend upon their own attitudes toward the minorities involved and upon the attitudes of minority groups toward the police.'" Also in the 1960s the Los Angeles County Sheriff's Department issued a policy statement entitled "Police-Community Relations."

In the face of evidence that the community somewhat less than enthusiastically supported nineteenth-century police organizations, waiting till past the middle of the twentieth century to establish community relations programs might be considered inordinate delay—myriad new sociological-psychological factors reviewed throughout this text notwithstanding. But whether or not such efforts were late in getting underway, there is considerable evidence that they are meeting with considerable success. At the 76th Annual Convention of the American Psychological

Association, held in San Francisco from August 30 through September 3, 1968, a paper was read at a symposium entitled "Innovations in Police Techniques: Community Service and Community Relations." A program involving the citizenry and police department of Houston, Texas, was reviewed in the paper, which closed with this summary:

> One of the sources of conflict in our urban centers today is the distrust that exists between the community and the police. In an effort to improve relations between the community members and police so that both groups might work together more effectively in solving community problems, the Houston Cooperative Crime Prevention Program was organized. The program consists of six three-hour sessions during which community members and police meet together in face-to-face confrontations to examine the damaging stereotypes they have of each other, to explore how their own behaviors reinforce these stereotypes, to consider cooperatively the sources of frictions or key issues that keep them divided and to plan steps to resolve these issues. The groups are assisted by group leaders who facilitate the interactions. The program design is described and design problems discussed. To date, over 800 policemen and an equal number of community members have completed the course. The sessions will continue until the entire police force has completed the program.

The Peace Officers Standard Training (POST) issued a 39-page "Check List for Police Administrators to Establish Effective Means of Dealing with Community Tensions on Civil Disturbances," which outlines virtually every facet of good community relations programming. On page 38 of this document the following inconspicuous yet singularly significant instructions are given on "Repairing Rifts—Restoring Community Relations":

1. Meet with all community groups
   a. Get their reaction to the disturbance in terms of:
      1) causes
      2) response by the city government
      3) appropriateness of police action
      4) police conduct
      5) community conduct
      6) *did the disturbance have a purpose?*
      7) was it accomplished? corrective measures needed?
      8) transmit information to appropriate city agency or community group
      9) *keep press informed of findings*

These instructions, although intended as guidelines for action following a disturbance, might well serve as a reference point for all community relations planning *before* disturbances occur. For if it is what people do rather than what people are that cause problems, then some misery is optional and can indeed be prevented.

Summary

As the final chapter of this text, Chapter 12 examined the concept of police organization programming to anticipate and to deal with community problems discussed in preceding chapters. This text began with two chapters which described the nature and scope of community problems relating to police. In the chapters that followed, the implications of social problems were considered in terms of constitutional government, police image, and racial prejudice. Increasingly concerned with the concrete and the specific, the text moved toward the concept of community relations programming as social change and its accompanying problems were discussed. Finally, in the two chapters immediately preceding this, the implications of group behavior were examined in the context of behavior per se, and then in terms of racial considerations.

This chapter concludes the text by considering both the nature of community relations programs and the purpose of such programming. In this context, influences on behavior were presented as *forces*, and forces were related to the power to encourage voluntary conformity to law. *Human relations* was cast as the instrument through which respect for police might be sought, and respect for police was cast as a prime requisite of voluntary (rather than enforced) observance of law. The attitudes, ethics, and conduct of police were presented as the essential ingredients of human relations efforts to gain needed public support.

The basis for both founded and unfounded *beliefs* about police were reviewed in terms of ways in which an unfavorable police image is perpetuated, and in ways in which community support for police is lost. Programming for community support of police goals was discussed first as a pressing need. The value and potential of such support were presented. This was followed by a review of various facets of community relations programs, presented through examples reflecting the universal necessity for public support and the variations in specific local needs.

It was noted that success in community relations programming often depends on general community support, but establishing majority support in some instances poses a great dilemma by producing minority rejection—rejection among the very persons to whom community relations programming is essentially addressed. Examples of concrete efforts to systematically meet this dilemma were cited. It was pointed out that the need for such efforts is not new to police, being evidenced in the last century. Sources of relevant guideline material were sampled, and this text concluded with: *For, if it is what people do rather than what people are that cause problems, then some misery is optional and can indeed be prevented.*

QUESTIONS

1. Discuss societal influences on the causes of human behavior. On police activities.

2. Relate human relations to police programs for community relations.

3. Discuss police ethics and the police image.

4. Discuss the police image and public support.

5. Relate the concept of rewarding false belief, as discussed in this chapter, to community relations.

6. What do the various existing community relations programs cited have in common? How do they differ?

7. What is the dilemma in seeking successful public support for community relations programs?

ANNOTATED REFERENCES

Earle, H., *Police-Community Relations: Crisis in our Time.* Springfield, Ill.: Charles C. Thomas, Publisher, 1967. This text attempts to examine the complexity of problems confronting modern police in terms of the future role of community relations programming.

Marx, J., *Officer, Tell Your Story: A Guide to Police Public Relations.* Springfield, Ill.: Charles C. Thomas, Publisher, 1969. In reviewing the need for public support of police goals, this book deals with the attitudes and procedures of police agencies in the context of community relations programming.

Momboisse, R., *Community Relations and Riot Prevention.* Springfield Ill.: Charles C. Thomas, Publisher, 1969. The theme of this text is: *the only effective way to control a riot is to prevent it*, and this theme is reviewed in the context of community relations programming.

———, *Riots, Revolts and Insurrections.* This text examines the subject of the title in terms of standards and guidelines for police organizations.

Van Den Berghe, P., *Race and Racism: A Comparative Study.* New York: John Wiley & Sons, Inc., 1969. This book provides an excellent background for examining the cross-cultural ramifications of race relations and affords the scientifically minded the peripheral advantage of analytical objectivity with concomitant concern for political ideology.

The footnotes of this chapter are also recommended to the reader as in-depth embellishment of the concept reviewed.

INDEX